Praise for the *New York Times* bestselling novels
of The *Oregon* Files written by
Clive Cussler and Craig Dirgo

# SACRED STONE

"[An] action-packed page-turner."　　　　*—Publishers Weekly*

"Ablaze with action."　　　　*—Kirkus Reviews*

# GOLDEN BUDDHA

"Readers will burn up the pages following the blazing action and daring exploits of these men and women and their amazing machines."　　　　*—Publishers Weekly*

"Fans of Cussler will not be disappointed."　　　　*—Library Journal*

"Honestly fabulous."　　　　*—Kirkus Reviews*

Praise for Craig Dirgo's first John Taft novel

# THE EINSTEIN PAPERS

"Intriguing . . . Fast-paced . . . offers a shipload of fantasy escapism . . . Cussler fans will be glad to know he has a clone to carry on the macho adventure tradition."
　　　　*—The Colorado Springs Gazette*

"An entertaining debut that should definitely appeal to Cussler fans."　　　　*—Publishers Weekly*

"Well done and much fun with ironic dialogue." *—Kirkus Reviews*

*Titles by Craig Dirgo*

TREMOR
THE EINSTEIN PAPERS


*Fiction by Craig Dirgo and Clive Cussler*

SACRED STONE
GOLDEN BUDDHA


*Nonfiction by Craig Dirgo and Clive Cussler*

THE SEA HUNTERS II
THE SEA HUNTERS
CLIVE CUSSLER AND DIRK PITT REVEALED

# TREMOR

## CRAIG DIRGO

BERKLEY BOOKS, NEW YORK

**THE BERKLEY PUBLISHING GROUP**
**Published by the Penguin Group**
**Penguin Group (USA) Inc.**
**375 Hudson Street, New York, New York 10014, USA**
Penguin Group (Canada), 90 Eglinton Avenue East, Suite 700, Toronto, Ontario M4P 2Y3, Canada
(a division of Pearson Penguin Canada Inc.)
Penguin Books Ltd., 80 Strand, London WC2R 0RL, England
Penguin Group Ireland, 25 St. Stephen's Green, Dublin 2, Ireland (a division of Penguin Books Ltd.)
Penguin Group (Australia), 250 Camberwell Road, Camberwell, Victoria 3124, Australia
(a division of Pearson Australia Group Pty. Ltd.)
Penguin Books India Pvt. Ltd., 11 Community Centre, Panchsheel Park, New Delhi—110 017, India
Penguin Group (NZ), Cnr. Airborne and Rosedale Roads, Albany, Auckland 1310, New Zealand
(a division of Pearson New Zealand Ltd.)
Penguin Books (South Africa) (Pty.) Ltd., 24 Sturdee Avenue, Rosebank, Johannesburg 2196,
South Africa

Penguin Books Ltd., Registered Offices: 80 Strand, London WC2R 0RL, England

This book is an original publication of The Berkley Publishing Group.

This is a work of fiction. Names, characters, places, and incidents either are the product of the author's imagination or are used fictitiously, and any resemblance to actual persons, living or dead, business establishments, events, or locales is entirely coincidental.

PRINTING HISTORY
Berkley trade paperback edition / January 2006

Library of Congress Cataloging-in-Publication Data

Dirgo, Craig.
    Tremor / Craig Dirgo.— Berkley trade pbk. ed.
        p. cm.
    ISBN 0-425-20750-1 (trade pbk.)
    1. Government investigators—Fiction. 2. Terrorism—Prevention—Fiction—Fiction. 3. Earthquakes—Fiction. 4. Serbs—Fiction. I. Title.

PS3554.I74T74 2006
813'.54—dc22
                                                                          2005054559

PRINTED IN THE UNITED STATES OF AMERICA

10   9   8   7   6   5   4   3   2   1

# PROLOGUE

NIKOLA TESLA STOOD framed by a yellow circle of light coming from inside his laboratory outside Colorado Springs, Colorado. He watched as a mosquito landed on the back of his hand, then stared as the bug inserted its thin stinger and began to draw off blood. Once the bug had its fill, it withdrew the stinger, then slowly buzzed into the twilight.

Just another bloodsucker, he thought, as if there were not enough around me already.

Tesla looked west as the setting sun disappeared behind Pikes Peak. There was one last flicker of light, then the sky filled with a waning glow. Swiveling around, Tesla turned east and glanced across the plains leading toward Kansas. There, above the vast expanse of grasslands, the light was a purplish blue fading to black. Within the hour a blanket of stars would stretch overhead, joining the thin crescent moon, which was already barely visible on the horizon.

Tesla glanced down the hill toward the city. As if ordained by his thoughts, a streetlight flickered to life and began lighting the growing darkness. He smiled a thin smile, for he knew it was he who was responsible for the streetlight. Tesla's discovery had made this and thousands of other lights now being fitted on street corners, in homes and businesses, on ships and in railcars across planet Earth possible. But there was more. The electrical buggies being developed in shops in the United States, the many machines being built and installed that promised to rid man of physical toil, the heating units, the electric trains, the endless flowing power.

They all owed a debt to Nikola Tesla and his discovery of alternating current.

Scratching the mosquito bite, he brushed at a wrinkle on his black trousers. Tesla was age forty-three, a fastidious man bordering on compulsive, some six and a half feet tall, thin as a signpost, with a growing ego. Tesla was a genius, and he knew that well. He only wished more people would recognize the fact.

Since Tesla's discovery and the subsequent construction of the electrical generating station at Niagara Falls in New York State, the electrification of his adopted country had begun in earnest. The construction of the transformers and the stringing of electrical wires was first completed in the eastern United States, where the population was denser and the costs more easily absorbed. But now, like a cloud of locusts, the electric lines were spreading to the north, south, and west, with the thin tendrils transporting the magic juice being draped across the land as fast as they could be laid.

The vast spiderwebs of wire were bringing with them the promise of a new age.

Millions had already been invested in the infrastructure, with thousands of companies already formed. Entire forests had been leveled for the poles to string the wires, giant mountains in Arizona dug up for the copper. Factories in the East had been formed to turn out fittings, transformers, sockets, and lamps. New inventions and uses for electricity were being discovered almost daily. Bankers on Wall Street were throwing caution to the wind and betting big, pouring money into the new technology.

It was like a gold rush—and Tesla had held the mother lode.

When his discovery had first been made, Tesla's patent had originally called for a payment to him for each horsepower of alternating current generated. This arrangement, had it been honored, would have easily made him the richest man alive. But that had not happened.

Instead, Tesla's patent claims were being ignored in the pell-mell race to bring power to the masses. The engineer had exhausted all his friends on lawyers, but to no avail. His discovery was rapidly becoming part of the public domain, and he was certain he would never reap the financial benefit if things continued as they were. The millions he felt he was already owed went unpaid and the contract providing him a royalty ignored. There were too many people now trampling on his discovery to sue them all. If he didn't figure something out, the world would simply ignore his rights to the process and stampede over the top of him like one of the few remaining herds of buffalo.

His dreams of fame and riches would be gone, the worth of his patent just paper.

But Tesla was not planning to give up quite so easily. He had a plan—and it was both brilliant and ambitious. Tesla was planning to pull the rug out from under the cheaters. If the invention he had constructed in his Colorado Springs laboratory worked, the power plants, wires, and poles that had sprung from his discovery, and had been wrested from his control without compensation, would all become as obsolete as a whale oil lamp.

Tesla's plan was to shift the game—and this time he would make sure he would benefit.

Lighting his pipe, Tesla drew the smoke into his mouth, then exhaled. A light gray cloud blew on the cooling wind. Then he smiled. This time would be different. This time his invention would remain a secret until it was properly patented and protected. This time he would make sure his invention was not stolen like a piece of penny candy. Used properly, this would be Tesla's grandest invention yet—a safe and simple process that would benefit all mankind and change the entire face of a growing industry.

Done wrong, the results could prove catastrophic.

Tesla walked back into the laboratory to begin his tests. The date was July 21, 1899.

AT THE SAME instant Tesla walked through the door into his laboratory, Iver Esbenson was on the roof of the New Collins Hotel in the bustling mining town of Cripple Creek, Colorado, some twenty miles due west of Colorado Springs. The brick wall forming the upper edge of the building stretched waist high from the roof, hiding all but Esbenson's upper body and head. He was hidden from those walking on the street below. The twinkling notes from the piano in the bar on the lower level of the hotel drifted skyward, and he caught enough of the notes to realize the song was "My Wild Irish Rose." Esbenson started to hum along with the tune to pass the time.

A light wind was increasing from the west, and it blew the dust on the street. Esbenson stared at his pocket watch as he waited. Farther down Third Street, the sound of an approaching horse-drawn stagecoach grew louder. Esbenson watched as the stage raced up the street and slowed to a stop in front of the hotel. Several men wearing derby hats climbed from the coach and walked inside. Another, who was wearing a cowboy hat, remained to reach inside to help a woman dressed in a long black cotton dress, hat, and gloves climb down. Straightening her clothes, the woman scanned the street, gradually raising her gaze higher, toward the upper windows of the New Collins Hotel.

Esbenson ducked back into the shadows, out of sight.

Esbenson had told no one of the crazy Croatian inventor's plan. He had decided it was just best that he sink the pole in the dirt alongside the building, lightly attaching it to a drainpipe. Once the test was completed, he was planning to quietly dismantle the pole in the darkness, then spend the night in the room he had rented and return to Colorado Springs in the morning.

Truth be told, Esbenson considered the mad inventor something of a crackpot, and he usually kept his involvement with Tesla a secret. Adjusting his bowler hat slightly to the rear, Esbenson checked the electrical leads on the string of lights laying on the roof of the hotel, then stared at his watch again.

Esbenson reached in the pocket of his long canvas coat and removed a thin cigar. Taking out a box of wooden matches, he struck one and puffed the stogie to life. Then he stared overhead at the blackness as the first few stars became visible. Night in the Colorado mountains can be cold, even in July, and Esbenson could feel the temperature dropping as he waited patiently. He pulled his coat tighter.

Holding the glowing cigar close to the face of his pocket watch, he stared at the dial. One hour and eleven minutes until 9:33 P.M. Esbenson had no idea why the crazy inventor had picked that exact time. Another mystery from a strange and unusual man.

NIKOLA TESLA WAS scribbling notes and formulas on a pane of glass with a wax crayon. When he needed to erase a passage and rewrite he would take a small glass vial of alcohol and tilt it over to wet a clean, white handkerchief. Then he would meticulously clean the glass. He liked numbers divisible by three and favored the number seven. Once he had completed the writing and series of formulas to his satisfaction, he stared at them intently. Then he flipped the glass around and stared at the numbers in reverse.

Excellent. Now all he had to do was make sure he had fuel to fire the beast.

Walking outside, he approached his mechanic, Kolman Czito, who was working on a power line at the base of a pole near the laboratory. "Mr. Czito," Tesla said, "are we properly linked?"

Earlier this afternoon, Czito had started at the power station for El Paso Power Company, some six miles distant. With a lineman's belt and a pair of hobnailed shoes he had climbed each pole and checked each connection carefully while working his way back toward the laboratory. He was weary, but this feeling was offset by his growing anticipation. Czito finished tightening the last connection with a wrench, then slid the tool in his pocket and wiped his hands on a rag.

"Checked and double-checked, sir," Czito said quietly.

Tesla nodded and stared back at the building housing his laboratory. The wood-framed structure was 66 feet by 33 with a roof that rolled back to prevent fires. The second level was nearly 80 feet off the ground, with a walkway that allowed access to the transmitter. The transmitter itself was a metal mast 144 feet in height, which was topped by a large copper orb 3 feet in diameter. Tonight, lit by the light from inside the laboratory, the entire apparatus looked like a giant caramel-covered apple on a round stick. It seemed harmless enough—almost comical to see.

"The lines will need to take a heavy load," Tesla said easily.

"My end will handle it," Czito said confidently.

"Good," Tesla said. "I'll head inside and check out the coils and resonator."

Entering the laboratory, Tesla stopped and stepped atop one-foot-tall thick blocks of cork shaped like shoes and lashed them down with leather straps. Once attached to the safety shoes, Tesla walked over to the coils and checked the distance between each set. He made a few minor adjustments. The third coil, the resonator, was the most important. It was the critical link between man and earth.

Tesla fine-tuned it carefully—he needed it to match the vibrations in the earth exactly for his experiment to work. Even a slight deviation would bring failure. On a pad of paper, Tesla made notes of the settings then walked over to the pane of glass and read his formulas again, checking them against the settings. Perfect!


ESBENSON SHIVERED FROM the cold night air blowing down the canyon, then stared down at the street from his perch atop the hotel. A man stumbled from the bar below, reached out, and steadied himself on the hitching post. He seemed liquored up, and as if to verify this, the man began talking to the Appaloosa that was tied to the post. Continuing to mumble to the horse, the man suddenly remembered something. Removing his felt cowboy hat from his head, he reached inside and removed a five-dollar bill tucked in the lining. Pleased with his newfound wealth, he stumbled back inside for another few rounds.

The cigar was long gone, and Esbenson struck a match to illuminate his pocket watch. Six minutes to go. Making sure the string of lights was properly placed, he checked the connections leading over to the pole, then took up position inside the circle made by the wires and lightbulbs.

Only a few more minutes.

"ONE-QUARTER FOR a check!" Tesla shouted across the laboratory to Fritz Lowenstein, the engineer who was working with Tesla on the project. Lowenstein was also perched atop a pair of cork safety shoes. He took a few slow steps over to a wall and flipped a large metal switch to the first slot.

The first and largest coil began to glow. Then it spit small balls of plasma toward the second. The second coil sent thin tendrils of lightning toward the third. The stream sputtered and broke as it attempted to form the connection, but with insufficient power it failed.

"Okay, now one-half, please, Mr. Lowenstein!" Tesla shouted.

Lowenstein flipped the switch to the midpoint.

IVER ESBENSON FELT a tingle in his legs. The sensation was strange, as if the muscles in his legs had fallen asleep. His feet felt warm and tingly, and he watched as dust began to vibrate from the roof of the New Collins Hotel into the air.

THE BALLS OF plasma flowing from coil one formed into a stream that twitched up and down like a sidewinder racing across desert sand. Coil two received the electricity and sent it in hundreds of thin streams of lightning to the third.

Looking out from the open roof of the laboratory, Tesla could see that the copper orb high overhead was glowing like a beacon in the night. The wooden floor of the laboratory began to vibrate, and puffs of dust began to creep up through the cracks in the board. A few long strands of dried glass levitated from the floor and hung in midair.

The earth was coming alive.

Tesla's black hair began to lift from his scalp, as if a vacuum high above were sucking it upward. His eyes were alive, and a maniacal smile crept across his face.

"Ignore three-quarters to full!" he shouted to Lowenstein.

Lowenstein flipped the switch down against the wood wall.

The electricity was sucked from the main El Paso Power Company through the lines to the laboratory and into the first coil. There the power was processed and pulled toward the second coil, which altered it slightly before it moved on to the third. There, the resonance was altered, and it was sent to the metal pole with the copper orb atop.

High above the laboratory, the copper orb glowed like a miniature sun as the pole itself hummed like a distant wind. The end of the pole was buried thirty-three feet deep into the earth, and it began to electrify the earth itself. A stream of electricity traveled down a natural highway inside the earth and toward Cripple Creek, where a receiver sat waiting.


ONE MINUTE THE night was black as crude oil with a blanket of stars overhead. The next instant the string of lightbulbs lit up all at once. Esbenson blinked from the sudden burst of light and placed the back of his hand across his eyes. The intensity of the light increased. Esbenson felt the skin on the back of his arm and the lower part of his face grow warm. His skin grew hot until the elements inside the lightbulbs melted all at once. The ground around Cripple Creek rumbled.

Then it was dark again, leaving Esbenson a sunburnlike glow on his exposed skin.

He waited until his eyes had adjusted to the darkness; then he quickly began to remove all traces of the experiment from the rooftop. He heard footsteps from the street below.

"Blasting at the mine," a voice said.

"Big one," a second voice said.

Esbenson peered over the edge of the wall. The two men stared toward the mountains in the distance for a moment, then walked back inside the bar.

Esbenson still had work to do. First, he needed to take down the pole in sections. The actual receiver, basically a metal platform on stubby legs, was sitting on the ground in the alley. He would need to drag that up a ramp into the back of his wagon. Those duties would need to wait, however, he thought, lighting a match and staring at the pocket watch again. He had less than fifteen minutes until the Western Union office closed—and he had promised Tesla he would send a telegraph if the experiment was successful. Taking the canvas bag stuffed with the wires and burned-out bulbs down the ladder, he slid the bag into his wagon parked alongside the hotel and covered the bag with a blanket.

Then he quickly walked down the street to the telegraph office.


KOLMAN CZITO STARED down the power line leading the six miles from El Paso Power Company to the laboratory. The city of Colorado Springs was dark. The wires had turned red-hot during the test before melting and dropping to the ground. Several small fires were burning closer to the city, and Czito turned to race toward his horse tied up outside the laboratory. He was planning to ride down the power line with a shovel, throwing dirt on the flames. But before he mounted the horse, a bank of clouds suddenly blew in from west to east. In seconds a blanket of rain began to fall with drops the size of silver dollars. Soaked by the water, the fires quickly burned out.

Czito ran back to the laboratory and stepped inside. The air was dusty and smelled of ozone and hot copper.

"We blew the transformer in Colorado Springs!" he shouted. "The lights of the city are all dark!"

Tesla came out from behind the primary coil. His hair was still sticking in the air in spite of the rain pouring inside from the open panel on the roof. As Tesla waved his hand toward Czito, a thin trickle of sparks flowed from Tesla's fingers like pixie dust. Lowenstein was sitting on the floor next to the main power switch, twitching like a puppet controlled by a maniacal puppeteer.

"Don't worry about that now," Tesla said, his voice vibrating like he was rapidly manipulating his voice box, "jjj-usttt, ridddde innnn anddd checkkkk forrr theeee telegrammm."

Czito nodded. The rain was stopping, and he walked over to his horse.

It would be midmorning the next day until power was restored and the telegraph office reopened, but Czito would wait as ordered. By the time Czito retrieved the telegraph, Esbenson had already returned to laboratory to report that the test was successful.


## MARCH 6, 1906

Nikola Tesla was on the verge of financial ruin. After the success of the Cripple Creek experiment he had plunged headlong into the large-scale implementation of his plan for the wireless transmission of electricity. The problem with his finances was really quite simple. Because of the past debacle with his patent on AC power, he was unwilling to inform the investors he needed about the exact nature of his work. Instead he was financing his experiments himself—wanting to be absolutely sure his patents were recorded and protected before disclosing to anyone the truth of what he was doing.

All of Tesla's savings went into construction of a massive facility near Shoreham, Long Island, in New York State. The compound, which he named Wardenclyffe, was started in 1901 and had proved to be an expensive undertaking. A giant tower was constructed, 187 feet tall, capped by a massive dome built of steel pipes that sat atop a flat plate. Below the base of the tower was a shaft with a primary rod reaching more than 100 feet into the earth. This was augmented with over a dozen additional iron pipes that reached down 300 feet farther into the soil.

The powerhouse was situated 100 yards from the tower to protect it from lightning strikes on the dome. Large and rectangular in shape, the brick building had a tall chimney that punched skyward from the center. The inside of the powerhouse was filled with steam boilers and large AC engines that could supply prodigious amount of electricity to the tower through underground channels.

Wardenclyffe was an ambitious and magnificent undertaking. Tesla, who always thought big and was never one to count pennies, started to run short on funds by 1902. Turning to the banker J. P. Morgan for additional capital, he told the millionaire that the purpose of Wardenclyffe was wireless communications. Since 1901, when Guglielmo Marconi and his London-based Marconi Company sent the first wireless message across the Atlantic Ocean, everyone was interested in communications. Morgan invested some money, but he wanted to see immediate results, and that angered Tesla.

Marconi's growing fame and success only added to Tesla's paranoia; it would later be proved that Marconi had infringed on several of Tesla's patents to create his device. This caused Tesla to reaffirm his vow to tell no one the true nature of his experiments until he was certain he could control and benefit from their applications.

Tesla had an idea he was sure was worth trillions, but now he had no way to prove it.

Tesla had managed to do some spectacular tests in 1903 and 1904, and he was convinced he was within days of reaching the proper tuning on his coils. Once he reached the proper tune, he was convinced he'd be able to send electricity to anywhere on planet Earth. It would become a well of power, needing only to be tapped into.

His plan was simple. Customers would lease a simple receiver and meter from Tesla's company. Then cheap, abundant power would be available anywhere on the globe, from the highest mountain to the lowest valley. No lines would need to be run, no clusters of population required to make it financially feasible. Tesla's company would receive royalty payments that would make him the richest man alive.

But right now that was all just a dream. Wardenclyffe had been closed for nearly a year because of Tesla's inability to pay his workers or even purchase coal for the massive boilers. Tesla was becoming desperate. His credit was exhausted, and no more seemed forthcoming. But he was not giving up.

Tesla now knew he would need to come out in the open if he was to succeed. He figured his only hope now was a big splash that could attract millions of small investors to his idea. A million minnows he felt he could control; it was the robber barons of Wall Street—the corporate giants—and the trusts that he feared.

To do that he'd need to use his proven Colorado equipment, which until now he thought was safe in storage. Two days ago, Tesla had learned otherwise. Now Colorado would again hold the key to his work. He would do a large public test of his device, showing the possibilities. Then the money would pour into Wardenclyffe.


IVER ESBENSON STARED at the telegram that had arrived day before yesterday. When finished, he folded it in half and slid it into his shirt pocket along with the advertisement from the *Colorado Springs Gazette*. Since working with Tesla some six years prior, Esbenson had become successful in his own right. His Colorado Springs–based I. Esbenson & Company Machine Tools had become a respected producer of specialized equipment. Heavy and light implements, machined devices, boilers and fittings and tools used by mining concerns, railroads, and factories. His shop had two dozen employees, and he lived on a nice home on a hill overlooking the city.

Why he would want to again deal with the crazy Croatian inventor seemed a mystery.

Truth be told, Esbenson liked the man; he was strange, to be sure, paranoid about blueprints and demanding when Esbenson had worked for him, but also appreciative of Iver's skills and respectful of his ideas. He'd also paid Esbenson well at a time when he needed the money. The third thing was simpler: Tesla was a certifiable genius. If Tesla was involved in something, chances for making history were not far away.

The fact that Tesla had fallen on hard times meant nothing to Esbenson.

Wiping his hands on a rag, he walked into his office and turned to his office manager. "Mr. Goode," he said, "I'll be in town taking care of business for the rest of the afternoon. I'm leaving you in charge."

Goode, who was wearing a green felt visor, was staring down at the bookkeeping records. Making a notation with a pencil, he looked up. "Yes, sir," was all he said.

Esbenson glanced out the window. The sky was growing dark, and a spring snowstorm was predicted. Walking over to the coatrack, he removed his heavy sheepskin coat and pulled it on, then took his tin lunch pail. Wrapping a wool scarf around his neck, he walked out, hooked the bit into the mouth of his horse, then climbed atop his red buckboard wagon for the trip to the courthouse. As he drove along, he ate from the pail.

A venison roast sandwich, a block of cheddar cheese, and a slice of molasses pie.

TESLA SAT IN the compartment of the Union Pacific train, counting the power poles along the tracks. The train was passing atop the bridge over Kiowa Creek in eastern Colorado. Tesla was still some two hours out of Denver. There he would transfer to another train, which would take him south to Colorado Springs, arriving after the scheduled auction. If Esbenson did not come through, there was nothing he could do.

His writer friend Samuel Clemens, better known as Mark Twain, had advanced him enough money for his trip. Had Twain not pointed out the article in the New York paper mentioning that Tesla's equipment in Colorado Springs was being auctioned off by the sheriff for nonpayment of storage fees, Tesla would have missed his last opportunity.

Leaving New York as soon as Twain had loaned him the funds, Tesla had reached St. Louis before he realized he would not make it to Colorado in time. Quickly sending a telegram to Esbenson, he'd not had time to await a reply. As the train carrying Tesla raced west, the inventor stared at the blackening sky and prayed his Colorado friend would help him.

• • •

ESBENSON REINED HIS horse to a stop on the street near his bank, then unhooked the bit from his mare's mouth and slid a feed bag full of oats over her head. Once that was done, he walked inside and withdrew $1,000 in gold coins from his account. Placing the coins in a deerskin bag, he attached the bag to his belt and buttoned his coat.

Walking down the street to a café near the courthouse, he had a cup of hot coffee.

Forty-six minutes later, the auctioneer on the steps of the courthouse called Tesla's lot. Two junk dealers bid the lot up over $900, surprising Esbenson, who wondered if he should not have withdrawn more money. But the bidding stalled at $920, with only one junk dealer still interested. Esbenson bid $925 and won. With the sheriff's fees the total came to a little over $928.

Not knowing Tesla's plans, Esbenson paid to leave the equipment in storage for one more week. Then he returned to the wagon and rode over to the Alta Vista Hotel to make sure the staff had reserved Tesla's favorite room.

Once there, Esbenson left word for Tesla that he was successful at the auction and that he would meet him for breakfast tomorrow at the hotel. Then he rode back to his shop.


## APRIL 18, 1906

Nikola Tesla attached the last fitting on the power cable and glanced at his watch.

"That's that," he said, "to glory or failure—whatever the case."

Moving the equipment bought at the auction, arranging free electricity, and coordinating with Esbenson to travel west with the light wall had required nearly six weeks. Calling in a favor with his friend Mark Twain had gone easier.

Twain had needed less than a week to arrange that.

• • •

AT THIS INSTANT there was no more famous writer in the United States than Jack London. His novel *The Call of the Wild*, published three years earlier, had been an instant bestseller and had vaulted the California scribe to the top of the publishing heap.

His novels had also earned London enough funds to buy a beautiful farm near Glen Ellen, California, forty miles north of San Francisco, where he continued to write. Still, as successful as London had become, he was not one to turn down the request for a favor from Twain, the grand master of American fiction.

Twain had asked if London would cover what he claimed would be a major event in San Francisco just before sunrise this morning. The invitation had been vague and secretive, containing only a date, which had changed three times already, a time just before sunrise, and a location, next to the Dewey Monument in Union Square. The problem was that London, who yesterday had been working late on a new novel, had missed the last Sausalito to San Francisco ferryboat.

Now it was nearly three o'clock in the morning, and London had been as yet unable to arrange passage on a private boat. If something didn't happen soon, he'd miss the entire event. London was of medium height, hardened by a childhood of hard work and toil, and about as far from the stereotypical idea of a pipe-smoking bookworm as ice from fire. London had worked in a cannery, been a merchant seaman, and gone north for the Klondike gold rush before hitting it big. He was comfortable around workingmen—he *was* one. Roaming the docks in Sausalito, he sipped from a glass bottle of whiskey.

"Fifty dollars," London said to the captain of a fishing boat preparing for an early-morning run, "if you take me to the terminal in San Francisco."

The captain finished cutting a triangle from a hard plug of tobacco and popped it into his mouth. Before he had even spit, he answered.

"Sorry, friend," the captain said, "we're going north, to the Point Reyes area."

London continued down the dock, making his offer to the earliest rising of the fishermen, oystermen, and cargo haulers. No one was taking the bait. More and more London was getting that nagging feeling in the back of his mind that something big was about to happen. And he did not want to miss whatever it was.


IVER ESBENSON RUBBED his hands, which were stinging from the cold, damp air, then strung another line. The display was taking shape. The lines ran from the Dewey Monument to a metal pole with a strange rectangle at the base that Esbenson had sunk in the ground about a hundred feet away. Esbenson was staying just across the square at the St. Francis Hotel and it was there, at teatime yesterday afternoon, that Tesla's telegram had reached him. Esbenson had been at the St. Francis awaiting Tesla's word for nearly ten days.

I AM FINALLY READY STOP I WILL SEND JUST BEFORE THE SUN STOP

Esbenson stared at the string of bulbs he had just hung; then he tightened up the line to take out the slack. The top of the message was taking shape, and Esbenson smiled.

"Nik may be down," Esbenson said softly, "but you wouldn't know it by this."

He scanned Union Square for Jack London, but the area around the square was empty and strangely quiet. A pigeon landed nearby. He cocked his head and stared up at the strange spiderweb of electrical lines and lights that was being constructed.


IT WAS GOOD the generators were putting out heat, because outside, the temperature was below freezing. Tesla stared out the window and up at the mountain that was behind the power station. The full moon made 13,319-foot-tall Palmyra Peak glow eerily.

Suddenly Tesla felt very alone.

Ames, Colorado, a few miles above the town of Telluride, was a small, rough-and-tumble hamlet that existed primarily to benefit the miners who worked the gold and silver lodes nearby. In the middle of the night it was safe to assume that Tesla was the only man nearby who was awake and moving.

The Ames Hydroelectric Plant had been the first AC power station in the world. Constructed in 1890 and coming online in 1891 to supply power to the mines nearby, Ames as much as anything else had proved the feasibility of AC power. Because of the success of Ames, Niagara Falls and all the other plants had followed.

The power station, high in the Colorado Rockies and remote in location, had always been a special spot for Tesla. At a time when no one seemed to believe in his vision, a local banker in Telluride had seen Tesla's genius and bet against conventional wisdom to build the plant to supply his mines.

Ames was the first, so it seemed fitting that the plant should supply the electricity for Tesla's crowning achievement. That, and the fact that no one else in Colorado would offer Tesla free electricity.

The owner of Ames had been good to Tesla, offering men to help him move the equipment through the snow to the site, a cabin for him to stay in as he erected the coils and tested his apparatus, a small charge account at a hotel in Telluride so Tesla might visit town occasionally and enjoy a fine meal.

The only thing the owner asked was that Tesla not tap into the electricity during the day, when it was needed by the mines. That necessitated Tesla's plan to strike early in the morning. The early-morning hour was perhaps a godsend, giving London time to file his story and place it with the San Francisco newspaper for the morning edition. From there the big news could travel east on the telegraph lines. The timing was such that the story would then make the evening editions in New York City, Boston, and Washington, D.C. Only one more day and Tesla would be basking in celebrity once again.

And then the investors would flock to Tesla and his company.

It was just after 4:00 A.M. Colorado time when Tesla made the last adjustment, strapped on his thick cork shoes, and prepared to flip the switch.

• • •

ESBENSON FINISHED HIS labors and stared at the strings of lights.

**This Power Is from Colorado
Supplied Direct to You from
Nikola Tesla in Colorado or
Anywhere Else Worldwide**

Then he leaned against the Dewey Monument and waited for Tesla to light the string. London had yet to arrive, but a policeman and several early birds out for walks milled about. The policeman asked Esbenson his purpose.

"This will be a very special experiment," Esbenson told the man. "Wait and see."

THE TIME WAS twelve minutes after 4:00 A.M. Colorado time when Tesla finally flipped the power switch all the way down and full open. The electricity raced through the series of coils and down the shaft buried in the rock far below the Ames plant. Tesla stood near the tertiary coil, just out of range of the cloud of lightning bolts.

Tesla twitched like a popcorn kernel in hot oil as images flashed through his mind. Momentarily losing control of his extremities, he was unable to flip the switch off.

Outside, the mountain suddenly seemed alive. A low-pitched hum was heard that seemed to come from deep inside the Earth. High above the power station a series of avalanches swept down the slopes. A ptarmigan took to the air, and a herd of elk sleeping nearby jumped to their hooves and began to run down the slope. Billowing clouds formed in the darkness over Palmyra Peak.

At that instant, a few miles away in Telluride, the streetlights flickered and dimmed.

In San Francisco the situation was a little more serious.

• • •

THE LIGHTS IN Union Square burst on, illuminating Tesla's message to the world. The crowd, now nearly two dozen in number, burst into applause. Esbenson grinned a broad grin. He had been almost sure Tesla would fail this time—the distance between Ames and the western coast of California was simply too great.

Yet the crazy inventor had pulled it off.

For a second Esbenson forgot the financial benefit—the shares in Tesla's company he had been given in pay for his work. This was history in the making, and Esbenson was right at the center. Years from now he was sure people would still be asking him how it had felt when the lights had come on. Years from now he was certain both he and the world would remember this instant in time. History was being formed, and Esbenson had helped to make it happen.

And then the ground started to shake and sway.

The Great San Francisco Earthquake had started.

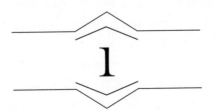

1

JOHN TAFT PUT his feet up on his desk and flipped open the morning intelligence intercepts.

Taft was tall—six feet, two inches in height—and a solid two hundred pounds in weight. Thick, sandy blond hair combed straight back covered his head. His eyes were a deep blue in color. If a member of the opposite sex was to see him walking down the street, her first thoughts were usually safety and solidness. Taft's chin was strong but not overpowering, his smile straight but not overly large, and his body was muscular but lacking the exaggerated bulges from hours in the gym.

Hockey forward, not bicycle racer; snow skier, not gymnast.

Taft was not a man who was easy to know well. Upon first meeting him—and in any subsequent interactions that did not lend themselves to closeness—the average person was usually struck with a sense of Taft's competence and control. Taft was someone you could trust, the type of man who returned borrowed books. The type of man who could fix a dripping faucet.

The truth was a little more involved than that.

Taft actually had a wicked sense of humor that relished in the ab-surdities of life—he just kept it hidden with those he did not know. He hated forced formality, unwarranted ceremony, and falseness, and he could detect them all from a long distance.

These mental twists, combined with the fact that as each year passed, Taft was becoming more and more cynical, were leading him lately to question both the wisdom of the elected leaders as well as his place as a cog in the wheel.

John Taft was a senior special agent with the National Intelligence Agency, but most people would refer to his job by the slang terms—secret agent, spook, spy. Taft reached down to the desk, lifted his coffee cup, and took a swig. Then he resumed reading.

Twelve minutes later his intercom buzzed.

"Egg and potato burrito is the special," his partner Lorenzo "Larry" Martinez said without preamble, "with refried beans and a choice of bacon or sausage."

"You been doing any work?" Taft asked, "or just patrolling the cafeteria for the latest menu ideas?"

"Actually," Martinez said, "I got here early and spent a few hours catching up on my reading. Then Benson called with an assignment. I think we should meet in the cafeteria and discuss it."

"Well," Taft said easily, "they say that breakfast is the most impor-tant meal of the day. How about I meet you down there in ten."

"I'll get us a table," Martinez said. "Would you like classified or nonclassified?"

"Something with a few security barriers would be nice," Taft jested, "near the bulletproof windows."

Hanging up the telephone, he continued to read.


IN GENEVA, SWITZERLAND, private banker Marcus Bernal logged onto the account to verify that the required funds were available and then prepared to place the order. Yesterday a wire had arrived with an additional U.S. $10 million. At the rate this client was buying, the $10 million would barely last out the week.

Watching the fluctuation in price, Bernal timed his entry point. Then he pushed the button on the keyboard, and the order began to fill. It was $1 million, then $2.2 million before the price moved out of range. Bernal scratched his ear with the cap from a cheap disposable pen and stared at the screen. The price would come back into range soon—maybe not today again—but soon. That was the beauty of a free market.

There were always buyers and sellers; one just needed to wait for the right time.

"SALSA ON THE beans or on the side, Mr. Taft?" the cafeteria line cook asked.

Taft was standing in front of a steam table with a brown plastic tray on the rails. There were silverware, napkins, and a large bottle of green tea already on the tray.

"Both, Jerry," Taft said. "I'll need some for the burrito."

The cook took a metal spoon and spread some across the beans, then filled a plastic cup and set it on the plate as well. Then he lifted the steaming plate up onto the top rail under a heat lamp. The plate was there only a second before Taft reached over, lifted it up, and then down to his tray.

He started to push the tray down the rail.

"The specialty coffee is that caramel pecan you like," Jerry noted as Taft moved away.

"Sounds good, Jerry," Taft said.

After stopping and filling a white ceramic mug with the coffee, Taft carried his tray over to the cashier and paid. Then he glanced across the cafeteria until he located Martinez at a table along the wall. Taft lifted the tray and walked over.

"I thought I said a window table," Taft said as he sat the tray down and began to offload the contents onto the table.

"They were all taken," Martinez said as he doused his burrito with green Tabasco sauce then reached down to lift the burrito in the air.

"But we're superspies," Taft said as he slid into a seat. "Most of these people are only support staff."

"Complain to management," Martinez said, finishing a bite.

"So," Taft said, biting the end off his burrito and spooning salso inside, "what have you got for me?"

"Drains on the European electrical system," Martinez said.


AT THE SAME instant Martinez and Taft were talking, in an office four floors above the cafeteria, the head of the National Intelligence Agency, General Earl Benson, was meeting with his second-in-command.

"It was a mutated flu virus," Richard "Dick" Allbright said. "We recovered the tanks and burned it off at Fort Meade."

"Did they test it?" Benson asked.

"Yep," Allbright said, "and it was a bad one."

"How far did the terrorist make it in implementing the plan?"

"The canisters were not yet mounted on the trains, but the racks to hold the tanks had been installed."

"So they were planning to spread the virus from the West to the East Coast right through middle America."

"A slow train right through the center of the country," Allbright agreed, "then secondary exposure through human contact transfer."

"It's like a whack-a-mole game nowadays," Benson said. "Every time we stop a terrorist cell another one pops up with a new threat."

"Well, anyway, boss," Allbright said, "these guys are done, the virus was destroyed, and the participants are at Gitmo in the prison camp. What else is happening?"

Benson reached for a file, then slid it across the desk to Allbright. "Surges on the European power grid," he said. "I gave it to Taft and Martinez to research."

Allbright opened the file and flipped through the pages.

"Probably just some glitch," Benson noted, "but it bears investigation."

"Do you want me to coordinate with them?" Allbright asked.

"Yep," Benson said. "You men seem to work good together."

"I'll do it," Allbright said. "What else?"

Benson reached for another file from the stack and slid it over. "Potassium cyanide," he said, "missing from a warehouse in Poland."

"SO," TAFT SAID as he finished his burrito and washed it down with the last of the coffee, "we could have crude particle beam weapon or death ray research. Is that the general idea?"

"Possibly," Martinez said, "or some secret factory that needs vast amounts of electricity to processes weapons-grade metals. Maybe an aluminum plant."

"An evil aluminum plant?" Taft said, making his voice sound like Mike Myers as Dr. Evil in the Austin Powers movies.

"Powdered aluminum could be used to make a fast-burning bomb," Martinez said.

"An evil bomb?" Taft said, smiling.

"Cut it out," Martinez said, grinning. "This could be serious."

Taft stood up with his coffee mug in hand. "I'll get serious, all right. As soon as I have some more coffee."

"Fill mine up," Martinez said, handing his mug to Taft.

"Sumatra or caramel pecan?" Taft asked.

"Surprise me."

TWELVE MILES SOUTH of Prizren, in the Serbian province of Kosovo, Vojislav Pestic read from a notebook he'd removed from a tattered leather steamer trunk. At first the early notebooks at the bottom of the trunk had made sense to Pestic. As an electrical engineer, the Serbian found the diagrams fairly straightforward.

Now as Pestic flipped through those on the top of the trunk, from later in the owner's life, he was finding his countryman's writings quite a bit more esoteric. It was as if the man who had written these notebooks had suffered a loss that had caused him to lose his grip on reality.

More and more the notes were about the habits of pigeons and the chance of afterlife.

Pestic was becoming concerned that he'd never find the exact information he needed, and failure carried too high a price. They had his family, and if Pestic did not figure out how to operate the devices soon, it would not be him, but them, who suffered the consequences.

He lit a cigarette and inhaled deeply.

BERNAL COULD SEE the weakness coming, and he prepared. As the waves trended downward, he bought on all the dips. By just after 2:00 P.M. Swiss time, Bernal had exhausted the $10 million most recently wired.

Staring at the screen, Bernal looked at the totals for the numbered account. As of this instant the holder had the equivalent of $83 million in stocks, options, and physical positions. The rising prices were adding millions daily in profit to the account.

Bernal was just about to take a break and go to the bathroom when his telephone rang.

"There is twenty-seven more coming across to you," the voice said. "Continue to follow the same strategy."

"Yes, sir," Bernal said quietly.

"Till next time," the voice said in closing.

"YOU SEEM TO forget something," Martinez said.

The two men had left the cafeteria twenty minutes ago and settled in Martinez's office. While they talked, Taft was playing solitaire on a small, handheld game of Larry's.

"I've got to get one of these," Taft noted as he cleared the screen and sat it down.

Martinez smiled and nodded.

"So what is it I'm forgetting?" Taft asked.

"Remember the Einstein Papers?" Martinez said. "The little riddle on the star chart?"

"Sure. It took us all of two minutes to figure out what Albert had written," Taft said. "'Tesla was right.'"

"Exactly," Martinez said. "What if the power surges are related to some advanced Teslanian weapons system?"

"Teslanian," Taft said. "You just made that word up."

"So," Martinez said, "it's a good word."

"True," Taft said.

He paused, sat back in the chair, and stared at the ceiling. Martinez relaxed in his chair and thought. The minutes passed in silence until finally Taft spoke.

"Man, that's some far-fetched stuff," he said, smiling. "What's the chance of you and me finding the Einstein notation, then later working on a case pertaining to the very person in the riddle? The odds are mind-boggling."

Martinez had played Taft like a finely tuned fiddle. It was time to sound the last note.

"Got you," Martinez said, sliding the file across the desk. "That's one of the possibilities the analysts came up with."

"I thought the NIA looked into that at the time of the Einstein affair," Taft noted. "The scientists reexamined all of Tesla's papers and were unable to make any sort of working weapon. Tesla's death beam ramblings were just that—ramblings."

"It's true the scientists could never produce a weapon," Martinez said, "but what if it was something else that someone has in mind? Or what if the papers that the government has are not complete—and there are more documents out there?"

Taft was flipping through the folder. He stopped at a map.

"When were you going to tell me this?" he asked as he flipped the folder around with the map facing Martinez.

"Oh, yeah," Martinez said. "That *is* important."

"I'd say so," Taft said. "The power drains seem to be originating somewhere in the former Yugoslavia. Wasn't Tesla born in what now is Serbia? And that his personal effects and papers are housed in a museum in Belgrade?"

"Sorry, old buddy," Martinez said, smiling, "but I thought considering your current state of mind it would be better if you figured it out

yourself. You know, to heighten your sense of intrigue and build inter-
est in the case."

Taft rose from his seat and smiled across the desk at Martinez. "Just
because I keep threatening to quit," he said easily, "doesn't mean I'm
not committed to my job."

"I'd sit back down," Martinez said easily. "They still haven't called
me back with your travel arrangements."

"I take it I'm going overseas?"

"Better you than me," Martinez said.

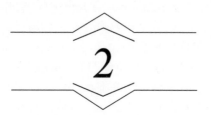

2

TAFT WAS SITTING in business class on a commercial jet flying over the North Atlantic. The route called for him to fly from Washington, D.C., to London and then switch carriers for the flight into Belgrade. His passport was in the name of Darrell Jackson. His business cards listed his title as a geologist employed by Capco Mining Company.

Once in Belgrade, his NIA contact would be a man named Steve Mather. Mather operated several franchised coffeehouses in Belgrade whose start-up costs had been funded by the NIA. Like several of the cover businesses the NIA had set up in the world, this operation was quite profitable.

Cappuccinos and biscotti were becoming a frontline information-gathering station.

Taft had considered asking for a transfer to a city, like Mather. An assignment like that had to be more stable and easier on the soul. With Taft's seniority he could probably have his pick of locations. Maybe a nice posting on some South Sea island where he could finish his time out with the company napping on a hammock and filing occasional reports.

Maybe somewhere like Liechtenstein or Norway where he could resume the sport of snow skiing he had enjoyed so much when younger.

Taft would be forty-five years old this year and was eligible for retirement. The NIA used the same system to calculate retirement benefits as the U.S. military. If you somehow lasted twenty years, and so far Taft had, you could retire at that time at half pay. Taft had socked away some money that could supplement his monthly checks.

In addition, Taft had managed to ride the real-estate appreciation train on his house in Virginia near D.C., and owned a nice parcel of land in Arizona free and clear. He figured he could live pretty well on half pay. Maybe he could repair his karma before he left this Earth, maybe he could spend more time worrying about the state of his garden and not the state of world affairs. Maybe he could meet a nice lady and settle down. Maybe he could find love again.

These were the thoughts Taft had as the onboard movie finished and he pulled his blanket closer around his torso. Waving away the steward who was walking down the isle with fresh cookies on a tray, Taft settled down to sleep.

His nap high above the ocean would prove to be his last sound sleep for some time.


GALADIN RATZOVIK COULD never clear his karma. He had tortured his countrymen during the war, ordered the widespread ethnic cleansing of entire villages, and had personally killed dozens of men and women in cold blood. Currently wanted by the UN War Crimes Commission, Ratzovik was a man on the edge of both madness and hell.

At a private hospital suite hidden in downtown Belgrade, Ratzovik was in a twilight.

As the surgeon carefully bonded the skin back together under Ratzovik's chin, a Mozart concerto was softly playing in the background. Pausing to examine his work and deciding there was nothing else to be done, the surgeon turned to the nurse.

"Pack his face in ice," the surgeon said.

Bending over, he placed his face in Ratzovik's field of view. "The procedure went fine," he said in an even tone. "Three down and only three to go."

Ratzovik did not attempt to shake his head in reply; he merely moved one hand out from under the surgical sheet and made a thumbs-up sign. Later today he would be taken by several of his men to a nearby safe house for recuperation.

In another week or so he would undergo liposuction and pectoral implants. The last thing he would do before he escaped into the world was a penis enlargement. But that was not to disguise his appearance—that was just for future fun.

Ratzovik's plan was to leave Serbia with a new smile, a new face, and a new body.

The Serb was planning to cheat both God and the devil. And no one, or nothing, could stand in his way. In the chaos he would create he would simply slip away, and the people hunting him would pay the heaviest price.

STEVE MATHER GLANCED up from his computer as the last person in line was served by his counter help. He was in a corner of his coffee shop with his back against the wall and using a wireless connection for his laptop. Reading the communication from his handler at NIA head-quarters, he memorized the information, then watched as the image dissolved and was erased from his computer's internals.

"So number seven is paying a visit," Mather said under his breath.

He nodded slightly to himself. Mather had met Taft twice. The first time was when the senior agent had spoken at Mather's commencement ceremony from spy craft school. The second time at a briefing when Mather was aide to a senior NIA official after Taft had cracked the Einstein Papers case.

Taft was somewhat of a legend in the NIA.

An early recruit to the agency, as was evidenced by his agent number, the lucky number seven, he was often the go-to guy when Benson was faced with a serious threat. But that seemed to be changing as of late. Mather had heard that Taft had been on light duty for the past few months, allowing the younger and more gung-ho agents to take the dangerous assignments.

Taft coming to Belgrade meant one of two things. The first was that the NIA was not taking the power surges very seriously. The second was that they were. Mather had no way to know which was the case—he could only wait until Taft arrived and briefed him further. Folding the laptop closed, Mather rose from his seat.

"Milosec," he said, walking over to the counter and speaking to the manager in charge, "I'll be gone the rest of the day. If you need me, call my cell phone."

Milosec was wiping out a cooler where the diary products were stored with a solution of bleach and water. He rose as Mather spoke, then nodded. "Okay, boss," he said, smiling, "but can you make sure the bakery order will be delivered as promised?"

Mather nodded and flipped open his cell phone. The number at the bakery was ringing as he walked out the door. Ordering pastries, Mather thought. Had he missed this part of the job when the recruiter had come calling?


TAFT HAD REACHED the point where he hated flying. Usually when he flew within the United States his ticket was tagged and he did not need to undergo any security checks. Overseas and undercover he was just another person. At Heathrow they scanned his body with a wand, then motioned him out of the line for a more through search.

He smiled, bit his tongue, and said nothing.

The irony was astounding, but it brought Taft no laughter. Here he was one of the premier antiterrorist agents in the world, and a security guard who was paid a salary equivalent to that of a sanitation worker was checking his shoes for bombs. If Taft wanted to blow up a plane, he knew a dozen or so undetectable ways that were a lot more subtle than a shoe bomb.

"Sorry about the delay, sir," the guard said, finishing his inspection. "You can put your shoes and socks back on."

"Belt, too?" Taft said, smiling.

"Sure," the guard said. "You're clean."

Taft finished dressing, retrieved his briefcase, and walked down the concourse toward the plane to Belgrade. Stopping at a stand to buy a meat pie, he made his way to the gate where nearly a hundred people were milling about, waiting to board the plane.

"I'm filing the papers when I get home," he muttered to himself.

"Pardon?" the man standing next to him said.


VOJISLAV PESTIC MOVED the secondary coil a few inches closer to the third, then tuned the coil by raising it a few centimeters higher in its stand. Twisting the nut tight with a wrench, he stared at the device and nodded. Walking over to a bench in the workshop, he picked up a rag and wiped his hands, then glanced out the window.

Two guards in black military uniforms were standing alongside an off-road vehicle in the courtyard, smoking cigarettes and talking. Pestic knew that two more were around the back of the building.

Pestic had been given no helper. That bothered him. If the people holding his family wanted him to work alone, there must have been a reason—and the only reason that made any sense considering the tight timetable was that they wanted but one witness.

If the need for secrecy was that tight, Pestic knew they would never allow him or his family to live once he was finished. His only chance was to figure out the settings, then hold the information for ransom in exchange for his family's freedom. And to pull that off Pestic would need to prove to them that he was on the right track. Once he offered some proof, he'd figure a way to escape, then offer to give up the settings if they released his family unharmed.


GIUSEPPE FIORENINI STARED down in the hole from atop his backhoe.

"Measure the depth!" he shouted in Italian to one of his workers.

Edging over to the hole, the worker ran a tape measure down the side of the shaft until it reached the bottom, then stared at the measurement. "Ten meters!" the worker shouted up to Fiorenini in the backhoe.

"In feet!" Fiorenini shouted. "This is for Americans—the specifications are in feet!"

Fiorenini ran a small construction company based in Avezzano, Italy, an industrial town some fifty miles east of Rome. Avezzano is in a picturesque location, surrounded by mountains and ancient Roman ruins. Nearly decimated by an earthquake in 1915, when thirty thousand people lost their lives, the city was also heavily damaged in World War II. Rebuilt from the edge of ruin twice, the town more recently had become a magnet for various multinational companies that built factories in the area.

Fiorenini had been hired by an American firm that owned a large chip fabrication facility on the outskirts of the town.

"Thirty-three feet!" the worker replied.

"Good!" Fiorenini said.

Swinging the bucket away from the hole, Fiorenini raised the hydraulic supports on the machine, then backed it away from the hole and shut off the diesel engine. Now it was quiet, save for the grinding sound of the nearby cement mixer. Reaching behind the seat of the backhoe, Fiorenini removed the set of blueprints and unrolled them.

A giant flagpole was to rise from the center of the hole and stretch a hundred feet into the air. The flags of Italy and the United States as well as the company's flag would fly from the top, in descending order. Surrounding the pole would be a meditation area constructed of flat stone platforms in levels. There was a water feature off to one side, a slow-moving river that stepped down over several flat sections to the lowest level, as well as a fountain and flower gardens near the upper level.

The flag relaxation area, as it was called, would be a fine addition to the building.

"The cement is ready," his worker said, walking over.

"Okay," Fiorenini said, rolling up the blueprints and setting them back behind the seat.

He climbed from the backhoe and began walking over to the hole.

"We want three feet of cement in the bottom—measure it with a weighted line. Once that's in place I'll hook the harness on the backhoe bucket and raise it into place. Once the pole is in place, I'm going to shake it up and down so some of the cement goes up into the pole. Keep filling the hole and keep the cement level at three feet."

"I understand," his worker said.

An hour later the pole was in place. Fiorenini left the backhoe supporting the pole until the cement could dry. The men sat down for lunch near the hole.


VOJISLAV PESTIC OPENED the door and shouted at the guard.

"Call your boss," he said, "and tell him I'm attempting another test!"

Pestic waited outside, smoking a cigarette, as the guard slid in the SUV and called on the secure telephone. A few moments later he climbed back out of the truck and walked over to Pestic.

"He said to go ahead," the guard said.

Pestic turned and started to walk back inside.

"Should we take any precautions?" the guard asked.

"How the hell would I know?" Pestic said loudly.

Walking back inside, Pestic checked the lead that was hooked directly into the main power line for the southern region. Finding it tight, he walked over to the control panel. Alongside the panel was a thick rubber mat to shield Pestic from charges. Fiddling with the adjustment to the coils once again, he opened a notebook and recorded the settings and the exact time.

Then he started the flow of power. Pestic had yet to make it past the halfway point before random electrical discharges had started to disintegrate the outer edges of the coils and he'd been forced to stop the test.

Right now, however, Pestic was at one-quarter, and the plasma and lightning bolts were flowing smoothly. He moved the lever to one-half. Puffballs of plasma, like chunks of goose down blown in a wind, leaped from coil one to coil two in a steady stream. The lightning bolts flowing from coil two to coil three were forming an almost constant stream across the space. Pestic scanned the fixtures and found all in order.

He flipped the lever to three-quarters power.

Dust devils rose from the floor as the glow from the lightning grew brighter. Pestic flipped a welding helmet over his head and lowered the shield. He stared at the visual display. The display of plasma leaping and lightning streaming was almost hypnotic.

It was as if the powers of the universe were been harnessed and directed.

Scanning the coils, Pestic could see none of the glowing red edges that had plagued the earlier experiments. Making a notation as to the time in the notebook, he flipped the lever to full power.

Inside the building the windows and doors began to vibrate and pulse. A sound like that of a distant wind across the prairie began to fill the air. Down into the shaft the electricity poured like water in a river flowing into an opening in the earth.

Even though he was standing atop the thick rubber pad, Pestic's limbs began to twitch. His brain was flashing images to his conscious memory like a supercharged slide projector. The plasma balls began to shape into a stream of what looked like bright white slime. The lightning bolts grew as thick as a man's wrist and then a leg.

Still the power flowed.

Outside the building, the guards began to hop from foot to foot as the ground began to feel as if thousands of needles were poking out. One of the guards to the rear made the mistake of touching the door handle to his truck, thinking he could climb inside and be insulated by the rubber tires. He was thrown through the air a distance of forty feet.

Deep underground the massive flow of electricity found a highway. The beam began to stream east in the direction the bend on the pipe at the bottom of the hole directed. The electricity slipped through the earth like a greased snake through a slick, smooth hole.

All it needed now was an outlet. Some receptor that could receive its blessing.


"WHAT'S TH——" FIORENINI started to say.

A howl that sounded like a thousand electric trains filled the air. The buried pipe began to glow a bright red and shake against the harness at-tached to the backhoe like a salmon on a light line. Large bolts of light-ning shot from the end of the flagpole and leaped across the distance to the microchip fabrication factory.

One by one the machines inside began to explode in a shower of sparks.

Under Fiorenini's feet the ground began to shake. He and his helper both managed to take a few steps toward safety before being flung in the air and tossed nearly one hundred feet. They landed in a heap, twitching like marionettes controlled by an evil master.


AT THE NATIONAL Earthquake Center in Golden, Colorado, one of the technicians noticed a waving gauge and reached for a telephone.

"We have an incident in Italy," he said.

# 3

MATHER WAS ON the way to the airport to pick up Taft when the lights in the shops along the streets of Belgrade flickered out. At the same instant, his automobile began to misfire and sputter. Mather pulled over to the side of the road, placed the vehicle in park, then pumped the gas pedal with his foot. The engine hesitated and missed, then began to run smoothly again. Mather slid the gear lever into drive and pulled away.

Worried about the rough running, he failed to notice that his car had started running smoothly exactly when the electrical lights in the shops nearby quit flickering and settled back into a steady glow. It was not bad gas that had made Mather's vehicle misfire—it was something far more complex.

Ten minutes later, and without further incident, Mather pulled into a parking spot at Belgrade International Airport, then locked the door and walked across the street to the main terminal. Entering the structure, Mather passed a pair of soldiers carrying assault rifles who were working security. They were headed for a break and brushed past quickly without a sideways glance. Walking further down the building, Mather found the checkpoint where the gates leading from the planes spilled out. He blended in with a throng of people awaiting their arrivals. Several minutes passed until he saw a blond-haired head above the crowd exiting security.

Taft did not bother to glance left or right—he just walked slowly ahead, toward the baggage claim area. Experience had taught him that his contact would find him before he could ever pick him out himself. Mather paced Taft's walk, then spoke.

"I'm here to pick you up," he said. "Do you have much luggage?"

"Just this," Taft said, yanking on his rolling carry-on bag.

"Follow me."

Taft walked along with Mather. They exited the terminal, made their way across the street, then stopped at Mather's van before talking again. Once they had stopped at the van and Taft's bag was stowed in the rear, Mather reached out his hand.

"Steve Mather."

"My name is Taft," John said, smiling and shaking. "John Taft."

"Hop in," Mather said. "I'll fill you in as we go."

Mather slid behind the wheel, and Taft climbed in the front passenger seat. Mather started the car and drove out of the garage, then turned on the road away from the airport.

"So," Mather said when they were up to speed on the road leading from the airport, "as I wrote in my report, we have been experiencing intermittent surges of electrical power throughout Serbia, Croatia, and Montenegro."

"They have been all throughout the region," Taft disclosed, "with the Carpathian Mountains forming an arc on the eastern border, the farthest southern part of the Czech Republic the northern border, the top of Greece is the southern limit, and most of Italy as the western terminus of the disruption."

"What is causing this?"

Taft glanced out at the hills near Belgrade before answering. "We don't know, but for right now I'm here to poke around and see what I can find out. Our scientists have almost certainly ruled out a natural phenomenon; that leaves some type of man-made disruption. The theories the scientists offered me ranged from an antiquated electrical grid that is overtaxed, to someone trying to siphon off the power illegally. Needless to say, as usual, our scientists were less than creative. Sometimes . . ."

Mather listened to Taft carefully and was somewhat surprised by what he was hearing. He had expected the NIA's most famous agent to sweep off the plane wrapped in the Stars and Stripes and whistling "America the Beautiful." While Taft certainly looked like a poster child for Nordic genetics, he was a little more cynical than Mather expected.

Taft looked over and noticed that Mather's mind was drifting. "Hoss," Taft said, "what's on your mind? You're somewhere else right now."

"Sorry," Mather muttered, "I was just . . ."

And then it happened. Taft gave Mather a little of what he had expected.

"No sweat," Taft said, flashing a grin, "but I'm here to save the world, and I don't have much time. I'm going to need you to pay close attention so I can pull this off."

Mather nodded; this was more like it.

"Right away I'm going to need a car to use," Taft noted, "with local maps—as many as you have. Also weapons, one or two handguns, a rifle or a shotgun if you have one, and knives. I prefer the folding type."

"I can do that," Mather said.

"Good," Taft said, glancing down the road they were on. "Our people back home plotted the route they thought you'd drive from the airport back to your cover business. It takes me right past my first stop. When I tell you, pull over and let me out. Then you go back to your business and round up what I'll need. I'll meet you there at your shop later this evening or call."

"Vehicle and weapons," Mather noted as Taft motioned to an open spot ahead.

They were near downtown Belgrade in an area of older brick and stone buildings.

"This is fine," Taft said as Mather slid to a stop. "Please make sure you take my bag inside and lock it in your office."

Taft quickly slid from the passenger seat and started moving along the street. Mather started to say something else, but when he glanced up, Taft had already blended into the crowd and was gone. Mather placed the car in gear and pulled back onto the street.

BELGRADE IS A beautiful city. The Danube River is to the north, with the Sava River to the west forming the line that denotes Old Belgrade to the east and New Belgrade to the west. The downtown area in Old Belgrade has hundreds of old stone and brick buildings, half a dozen parks, and an occasional newer skyscraper that had been built when President Tito was running Communist Yugoslavia.

Outside the stately mansion at 51 Krunska Street, schoolchildren formed up into lines outside an ornate wrought-iron gate set between a pair of carved stone supports. The teacher waited until they had settled down and were evenly spaced; then she led them up the stone walkway toward the front door, where the museum curator stood waiting.

The curator was tall for a woman, nearly six feet in height, with jet black hair and piercing blue eyes. She was lean and long and dressed in a white top and navy blue skirt. The pointy-toed, high-heeled shoes she wore below her skirt only adding to the image that she was constructed of all straight lines and sharp angles. For all the severity of her appearance, her smile was warm and welcoming.

"Good morning children," the curator said, smiling. "My name is Miss Slavja, and I'll be taking you on today's tour."

"Children," the teacher said.

"Good morning, Miss Slavja," the voices rang out.

Slavja turned and started to lead the line of children inside the museum. As she walked, she spoke loudly back over her shoulder.

"Welcome to the Nikola Tesla Museum. Mr. Tesla was one of the most famous Serbians of all time," she began, "and one of the pioneers in the use of electrical energy. As we pass through the museum today we will see many . . ."

Taft, walking past on the sidewalk, strained to hear, but Miss Slavja was entering the front door, which was crowned with the stone railings that surrounded the second level of the beautiful ex-mansion. Behind the railings and soaring above the children's heads was a domed window framed by massive stone pillars. Founded in 1952, nine years after Tesla's death, and opened to the public in 1955, the museum housed the most complete collection of Tesla's mechanical devices and personal papers anywhere in the world.

As the schoolchildren filtered inside, Taft slowed his walk and stared at the building, which sat inside a stone wall that faced the sidewalk. The mansion was of a type that had not been constructed in the past hundred years. Stately, elegant, and built to last for generations, the mansion was a fitting edifice to house the works of a man who had changed history.

It also looked to Taft to be relatively unprotected.

He continued his reconnaissance.

Turning the corner, he walked down the sidewalk along the far side of the museum. Taft guessed the building had been constructed prior to electricity, the forest of chimneys from the fireplaces that had formerly warmed the rooms indicating that. That meant that the junction box from the main line on the street should be easy to find and disable if needed. Scanning the doors and windows carefully, Taft could see no sign of any type of security system. That led him to believe that the building used a night watchman, hardly uncommon in former Communist countries where full employment had been the watchword. That was something he'd need to deal with.

The doors and windows on the lower level had wrought-iron gates and shutters that Taft imagined were fastened at night, but the locks looked flimsy and easily broached. The second story, set back from the first and surrounded by the walkway outlined by the stone railings, featured a forest of windows and doors without shutters or gates. Taft doubted if they were even locked.

This was probably the best place to make entry.

Taft reached the end of the property and continued along the street. After walking a few blocks farther, he entered the lobby of the Hotel Park and secured a room. He explained to the desk clerk that his bags were overdue at the airport and he would bring them along later, then took the old-style brass key in hand and rode the elevator up to his floor. After checking his room and finding it adequate, he rode down and walked through the lobby again. Once back in front, Taft flagged down a taxicab and gave the driver instructions to Mather's coffee shop.

"Could you please drive past the Tesla Museum on the way?" Taft instructed the driver.

The man grunted a reply.

Taft scanned the building again as they drove past. By the time he'd reached Mather's shop he'd formed a rudimentary plan. Paying the cab-driver, Taft walked across the sidewalk and opened the door. Half a dozen people were seated inside, one lone man behind the counter, but Mather was not visible.

Taft walked over to the counter. "I'm a friend of Steve's," Taft said. "He around?"

"I'm Milosec," the man said, extending his hand.

Taft shook it as the man continued, "Mr. Mather is in back. He told me to keep an eye out for you and direct you there when you arrived."

Milosec raised a folding section of the counter in the air, and Taft stepped behind the counter. The two men walked around a corner of the counter away from the front seating area. Once out of sight of the customers, Milosec swept back a curtain and knocked on a door. Then he stepped away and started back to the front. Mather opened the door a second later and motioned Taft inside. Mather slid the curtain back in place, then closed the door behind him.

"Hiding in plain view," Taft said, smiling.

"The company just reinforced the existing office back here and added the necessary security. It's actually more secure. If anyone wanted to try to storm the door, they would need to get past both the workers outside and the counter. Plus, let's face it, if someone is after you they can get you in a regular office just as easy."

Mather was making his way into the room as he spoke. The lack of windows in the space, the bank of computers to the side, and locked metal doors on one wall made the room seem more like an underground

bunker than an office. Mather slid behind a gray metal desk and mo-
tioned to a chair for Taft.

"Who is your decorator, NORAD?" Taft joked as he sat down.

The nervousness Mather had felt upon first meeting Taft was dissi-
pating.

"Makes a prison cell look inviting," Mather noted.

"I've been in submarines more pleasant than this."

"Shipping containers."

"Dungeons," Taft said.

"Want any coffee?" Mather asked. "It's free to company employees."

Taft glanced around the crowded room until he caught sight of his
carry-on bag, "Not right now," he said. "But how are you coming on
acquiring the weapons?"

Mather smiled; then he reached under his desk and pushed a but-
ton. The metal doors built into the far side of the office slid back on
tracks inside the wall as a single fluorescent strip light overhead lit up.

Dozen of rifles, shotguns, and handguns hung from hooks.

"Regular," Mather asked, "or decaf?"

Taft stood up, then walked over to the weapons locker. "Any of
these rifles fold?"

Mather removed a strange-looking rifle that featured a bent metal
rod for the stock. "This is custom built in Austria. Fires a 7.62 NATO
round; scope is a Leopold. The case is down here."

Mather removed a leather case from a drawer below. It looked like
a suitcase, even down to the stickers from various hotels and destina-
tions plastered on the side.

"Nice," Taft said.

Mather opened the case on one side. Black foam rubber was cut to
fit the weapon. There was room for multiple clips and even a cleaning
kit. He slid the rifle inside, tossed in enough ammunition and extra clips
to launch a small war, then closed it and flipped it over. Unbuckling the
clasp on this side, Mather raised the top, revealing another compart-
ment. Reaching up, he removed a knife from a row.

"Carbon fiber, folding, and glare-resistant."

"I'll take it," Taft said, smiling.

"Take two or three," Mather said, reaching for various sizes and placing them in the case. "Now we should talk about handguns—automatic or revolver type?"

"As you know," Taft said, acting serious, "the real advantage of an automatic is more loads in the clip. The disadvantage is the possibility of jamming. As I only shoot people as a last resort, they are usually very close before I use a handgun."

"No shooting at fleeing cars?" Mather asked. "That sort of thing."

"That's only in the movies."

"Then I recommend this fine Colt Combat model in black with black grips."

"A .357?" Taft asked.

"I would use a 10-millimeter instead," Mather said, "being we're in Europe and all."

Mather set it in the case along with a box of ammunition.

"That should do it," Taft said.

"Have a few stun grenades," Mather said, adding them to the case, "and this portable high-temperature torch suitable for cutting metal."

"There's more?"

"Order today and you also receive this thin wire garrote suitable for strangulation," Mather said, tossing a thin wrapped wire in the box.

"Anything else?" Taft asked.

"Take a bag of these plastic ties in case you need to handcuff someone." Mather tossed them in the case, then shut the lid and fastened the snaps. He handed the case to Taft. Then the two walked back toward the desk.

"What else will you need to perform your mission?" Mather asked.

"I need to be able to see and hear," Taft noted.

"Night vision as well as magnification?"

"That would be nice," Taft said.

Mather reached into a desk drawer and removed a set of goggles. "Do me a favor and don't lose these," he said. "They are new and I waited almost a year to get them."

Taft nodded.

"Standard ears?"

"That'll work," Taft said.

Mather removed a small box the size of a cigarette pack from the desk. Inside was a small parabolic dish that folded out and a listening clip that went over the ear. The pack itself housed the noise amplifier.

"That it?" Mather asked.

"That should do it," Taft said.

"Then if you will just sign the form stating I transferred this company property to you, we'll be done."

Mather sat down and listed the equipment. Taft signed it quickly, and Mather fed it into a secure fax machine and sent it to the NIA headquarters.

"Here's my cell phone number as well as a pager number," Mather said. "If you need anything, call day or night."

Taft smiled. "Pleasure doing business with you."

Then he gathered up the weapons case and his rolling carry-on and left the office. A few minutes later he was in a cab heading back to the Park Hotel. Pulling up in front, Taft carried his bags through the lobby and rode up the elevator to his room. Unlocking the door, he made his way inside.

Late tonight he would visit the museum. But first he needed to clean up and change. If all worked as he planned, Taft had a date tonight. The problem was, his intended was not yet aware that she had been selected. The two had yet to meet.

**4**

NADIA SLAVJA LOCKED the front wrought-iron gate and turned. It was dusk in Belgrade, and a light breeze was blowing leaves down the street. Slavja walked north from the museum and soon entered an area where the streets were crowded with small retail shops and food stores. She slowed, then stopped next to some waist-high wooden boxes and bent down.

STOPPING TO SMELL the roses, Taft thought—a nice touch. The first thing he had done this evening was reverify what he had noticed this afternoon—that Slavja was not wearing a wedding or engagement ring. The second thing was to again notice the Serbian's striking good looks. Slavja would never be a fashion model—her face and body just didn't fit the mold. Her nose had a small bump in the center, and her teeth were not perfect; still, her cheekbones could dice carrots and her eyes penetrate granite. Her body was a different matter. First was her height—nearly six feet tall. Second, she was larger in the upper body than a fashion model, and bigger in the waist. She had hourglass figure, all right—but it was like two triangles placed atop one another.

Taft moved closer behind her.

SLAVJA SENSED RATHER than viewed someone growing closer. She watched as an arm swept past her and removed a single rose from the bucket. She turned and looked.

"I think this one is an American Beauty," a blond-haired man said in English.

"Ameri—" Slavja said in halting English.

"American Beauty," Taft said. "It's a variety of rose."

The shopkeeper, a Serb with thinning black hair and bushy eyebrows that looked like caterpillars above his eyes, stepped outside his shop. He was dressed in a white canvas apron, with pockets below the waist for tools and clippers. He smiled, but there was wariness, as if worried that he would need to defend the woman's honor.

"How much for the rose?" Taft asked in halting Serbo-Croatian, the native language.

The shop owner quoted a price.

Taft reached in his front pocket, removed a clip filled with the local currency, and peeled off a bill. He handed it and the rose to the shop owner and said, again in the local language, "Could you wrap it in paper, please?"

The man nodded, then stepped back inside with the rose.

Nadia turned and stared up at the taller American. "I'm Nadia Slavja," she said in English.

"Darrell Jackson," Taft said, using his cover name, "but everyone calls me by my middle name: John."

Slavja held out her hand, palm down. Taft bent over and pecked the back of her hand.

"Pleasure to meet you John," Slavja said easily. "Visiting Belgrade for the first time?"

"Yes," Taft said. "I'm a geologist, and my company sent me over to assess future mining prospects south of here."

Slavja smiled. The blond American was handsome. And, like most of the Americans she had met, he seemed to be a go-getter—the type of man used to taking what he wanted. Right now, for whatever reason, it seemed he wanted Slavja. And Nadia was interested in being taken. It had been nearly two months since she had broken up with her last boyfriend. He had turned out to be married—and at just over the hump of thirty years old, Slavja was finding the local pickings slim. Maybe a fling with the man named John might just be good for both of them.

"In America," Slavja asked, "do you often buy roses for women you just met?"

The shopkeeper opened the door of the shop and walked out. He handed Taft the rose wrapped in butcher paper, and his change. After Taft thanked him, he walked back inside.

"Who said," Taft said, "I was buying this for you?"

Slavja smiled. "I was stopping for a drink on the way home," she said boldly. "Perhaps you and the rose might like to join me?"

Taft smiled. Sometimes things just came easy. He nodded and took Slavja's hand.

"ANOTHER AMERICAN SHOWED up at the coffee shop."

Galadin Ratzovik nodded. The skin where it had been stapled and glued back together behind the hairlines on the side of his face itched. This, combined with the fact that his eyes were watering slightly more because of the eyelid lift, were his only major complaints from the plastic surgery.

"Do we know who it is?" Ratzovik asked.

"No," the man who had been watching the coffee shop said. "He might just be a friend of the owner."

"Where did he go?"

"Has a room at the Park Hotel," the man said. "He went back there with his suitcases a few hours ago."

Ratzovik nodded. The well-developed sense of paranoia he had developed over the years had kept him alive so far. Even so, he had learned not to overreact.

"Keep watching Mather," Ratzovik said. "If the other man is involved, he'll soon start turning up in places he shouldn't be. If not, then we'll know he's just a friend or acquaintance."

"So you still think that Mather is American intelligence?"

"I don't know what agency," Ratzovik said, "but I do smell a rat."

"What else do you want me to do, sir?"

"Just do what you're doing," Ratzovik said. "I'll call if there are changes."

The man rose from his chair at the edge of the hospital bed inside Ratzovik's rented mansion on the outskirts of Old Belgrade. Reaching down, he shook Ratzovik's hand.

"To a pure Serb nation," he said.

"To Serbia," Ratzovik replied.


"YOU'RE KIDDING," TAFT said.

They were halfway through icy pints of local beer. A waitress brought an appetizer plate Taft had ordered and slid it onto the table. Cheese, tiny pickles, some sausage, and brown bread and butter. The waitress started to leave. Taft caught her and ordered two more beers.

"No, it's been my only job," Slavja said. "I've been with the museum since I graduated from university almost ten years ago."

"I've read a little about Tesla," Taft offered. "He was an amazing man."

The pub Slavja had selected was a local establishment that had existed on this site for more than a hundred years. The walls were dark wood, as were the round tables and heavy chairs with leather seatpads. Red candles were scattered about, and polished brass light fixtures gave light to the walls and overhead. When they'd first arrived the pub was busy. Now it was starting to clear out as people made their way home.

"Truly amazing," Slavja agreed.

The waitress walked over, placed the fresh beers on the table, and retreated.

Taft asked, "Was your building damaged during the NATO bombings of Belgrade?"

"It came through unharmed," Slavja said. "Thank heavens."

Slavja was starting to feel the alcohol, and her inhibitions were starting to fall faster than snow in winter. She reached over and placed her hand on Taft's arm.

"But enough about me," she said. "Let's talk about you."

"All right," Taft said. "What do you want to know?"

"Let's begin with, are you married?"

"Single, free, and over twenty-one," Taft said.

"Gay, or any social diseases?"

Taft laughed. "You don't mince words—I like that."

"Well?"

"No and no."

"Interested in having dinner?" Slavja asked.

"Could be," Taft admitted.

"Do you have any questions for me?"

"Just one," Taft said quietly. "What do you look like under those clothes?"

"Be nice," Slavja said, "and you might just find out."

Taft smiled.

"Now drink up," Slavja said. "I have to work tomorrow, so that only gives us twelve hours or so for dinner and whatever else."

They had a quick dinner at a restaurant nearby, then walked to Slavja's apartment. Once they reached the bedroom, they grabbed for each other like Greco-Roman wrestlers. Taft did some of his best work. Slavja quite kindly reciprocated.

AS TAFT AND Slavja were working off their dinner, thousands of miles across Earth and six times zones away at the NIA headquarters, Benson and Allbright were holding a meeting in the general's office.

"So this surge or drop in electricity in Europe was followed by a small-scale earthquake?" Benson asked.

"That's the consensus, sir," Allbright said. "It could have been a co-incidence, but the timing is suspiciously close."

"So this case has moved from someone possibly siphoning off power from the European grid, to some person or party that is trying to create an earthquake machine?"

Allbright nodded slowly. "It's a possibility."

"It just doesn't make any sense," Benson continued. "As a weapon, an earthquake has no accuracy. It's too random—not targetable."

Allbright nodded, and the men sat silent for a few moments. "But what if they could, sir? What if some group has figured out how to deliver pinpoint accuracy with earthquakes?"

"The target would still need to be along a fault line," Benson said, "or they would have no effect. That leaves a lot of the Earth far from any danger."

"I had one of the analysts assemble a short list of major earthquakes in the past ten or fifteen years so you would have some idea where the active faults are currently," Allbright said, removing a sheet of paper from a folder, "Afghanistan, Iran, Turkey, South and Central America, Taiwan, Japan, along what's called the Asian Ring of Fire, along with the occasional California earthquake are the majors. The most 'quakes were probably in the first two countries."

"Well," Benson said, "if whoever was doing this was targeting Afghanistan and Iran, we might just have to leave them alone."

"Not a bad idea," Allbright agreed.

Benson thought for a moment before speaking. "What if this device, or whatever it is we're talking about here, instead could create a tremor where one has never existed. What if it could create its own fault line, so to speak."

"That would be catastrophic," Allbright said slowly. "In areas not prone to earthquakes, the building codes are all different—the structures would quickly crumble from even light shaking. Not only that; wherever it was—and I'm speaking of the United States here—they would not have adequate emergency preparedness plans to handle such an event. You don't prepare for what should never happen."

"But I still come back to, why?" Benson said. "Even as a weapon of sheer terror, it's simply too crude. If the purpose of terror is to bring a grievance to light—like the bastards who hit New York City veiling their actions as some kind of religious war—why build a weapon whose destructive power can be blamed on nature?"

Benson paused, then resumed.

"Dick, think about this for a moment. It would be like if I wanted to kill the president to prove a point or bring myself glory. Then my plan was to have him choke of a piece of steak. Even if it worked and I claimed credit, everyone would think it was just a coincidence. It would simply not have the desired effect."

Allbright nodded. "You have a valid point, General."

"I want to get the thinking right before I brief the president," Benson said. "For this thing to be effective as a weapon of terror against the United States, we both agree that whoever was behind the action would need to be able to hit our entire country at once."

"At least a few different spots across the country, yes."

"Then if we have our scientists calculate the energy drop on the European grid and the size of the tremor in Italy, we would have some idea of the energy necessary to strike—"

Allbright interrupted. "I see where you are going, sir," he blurted out. "If our scientists can figure how much electrical energy it would take to strike at multiple targets inside the United States from Europe, we have a basis to work from."

Benson smiled and nodded. "Let's say, for example, that it takes a billion watts or whatever to somehow trigger earthquakes on the Eastern Seaboard and California at the same time—and you and I agree that terrorists would need to make simultaneous strikes for the exercise to be believable as an act of terror—then if we find there is insufficient power available in Serbia for such an action, I think we can safely rule out terrorism."

"Makes sense," Allbright said. "Can I make a suggestion, sir?"

"By all means."

"We should ask the president to make security teams available at all the European power plants for the near term. Then if whoever is behind this moves to acquire more electricity to make a move against us, we can shut them down before they get started."

"Excellent idea," Benson said.

"So first we figure out what is needed in terms of electrical power to be a multiple threat to the United States," Allbright noted. "Then we systematically start to eliminate the ability for whoever is behind this to be able to do anything."

Benson nodded. "We move in ever decreasing circles toward Serbia until we have secured the electrical facilities throughout Europe."

"That would eliminate the possibility of a terrorist threat to the United States," Allbright agreed.

"And that, Dick," Benson said, reaching into his humidor, removing a cigar, and clipping off the end, "is our job." Nodding to Allbright, who shook his head no, Benson sat back and puffed the stogie to life.

"I feel better," Allbright said.

"Me, too," Benson said from behind a cloud of smoke.

The men sat quietly for a few moments.

"There would still, of course, be the threat to our allies," Allbright noted.

"And any U.S. installations on European soil," Benson added.

"Maybe they could do a pinpoint attack on the Middle Eastern oil fields," Allbright offered. "That would send the world economy into a tailspin."

"What if they directed the strike on one of our overseas military bases housing nuclear weapons?" Benson said.

"This case might have a lot more facets than we first thought," Allbright said.

Benson shifted in his chair. "Do you have time to go over this all right now?"

"I'll make time," Allbright said.

"You need to call home?"

"I should," Allbright agreed.

"You do that," Benson said. "I'll have my receptionist call down to the cafeteria and have a tray of sandwiches sent up."

"Sounds like we're in for a long night," Allbright said, rising to walk over to a telephone on the side table.

"I think so," Benson said, reaching for the telephone on his desk to place the order.

# 5

THE TIME WAS just past 2:00 A.M. Taft huddled in Slavja's small convenience kitchen scrawling a note by the light from the bulb she left lit over the stove. Once that was finished, he walked a few feet through the kitchen to the dining room. There, on the half wall dividing the small dining room from the rest of the apartment, sat Slavja's keys.

Taft was lucky. Unlike many, Slavja had but three keys on her ring. Quietly opening her front door, Taft tried them in the lock. As soon as he found the front door key, he made a small scratch on the metal so he could identify it. Next, he closed the door and returned to the kitchen. Removing a plastic device not much wider than two or three keys stacked atop themselves from his wallet, Taft slid the door key in a slot on the end and then waited a few seconds until a small green light illuminated on the side. Removing the front door key, he marked it and placed it in his pocket, then slid in the second and then the third, repeating the procedure.

Once a record of the keys was in the computer, Taft flipped a switch embedded in the side and waited while the first key was formed from hard plastic inside the case. When it was finished, the end slid out of the slot on the side. Taft pulled it the rest of the way out, then picked a few plastic slivers from the edge as the other formed. He placed the front door key in the left front pocket of his pants.

Once the other two keys were done, Taft placed these in his right pants pocket, returning Slavja's set of keys to their place atop the half wall.

With that done, he looked around the apartment once, listened to make sure Slavja was still sleeping, then slipped out of the apartment. Once in the hallway, he locked the door behind him so Slavja would be safe.

A light wind blew down the streets of downtown Belgrade, scattering cigarette butts, litter, and dust. There were a few people still out at this hour—the late-night bargoers, night shift workers, and cabdrivers who frequent the night and shun the daylight.

Taft passed a pair of men in an alley just outside the pub he and Slavja had visited earlier that evening. One was hunched over at the waist retching into a trash can; the second man was peeing a stream against the brick wall and singing. A few blocks farther along, a street sweeper passed on the street. Twice cabs drove past him and slowed, seeking a fare. No police cars intruded on the night. It was midweek, and the department was not fully staffed. Taft was almost to his hotel when a lone dog trotted slowly down the middle of the street, as if intent on going somewhere. The dog turned his head to stare at Taft but kept trotting at the same methodical pace.

Riding the elevator to his room, Taft retrieved the sight and sound devices. Assembling the small parabolic dish for the listening device, he placed it in a paper grocery bag that he had secured earlier, then slid the earpiece into his ear. Taft turned on the goggles, then checked to see that they were working by scanning the hotel room. On full magnification, he could read the artist's name on the lithograph across the room. Sliding the goggles into the bag, he left the room and rode the elevator down.

The front desk clerk was in the rear doing the night accounting and the lobby was empty. No one saw Taft leave.

It was only a few blocks to the museum, and Taft made fast time.

Once alongside the Tesla Museum, Taft slowed and peered toward the windows to determine where the guard might be. At the same time he removed the two keys from the right front pocket of his pants as he approached the gate. Swinging his head in an arc, he scanned the street.

Finding it deserted, Taft approached the gate and tried the first key. It slid into the lock and turned. Taft removed the key, bit the end to make a mark so he knew which key opened what door, then slid it back into his pants pocket. Then he crept inside and hid alongside the wall that fronted the street. Pulling the parabolic dish from the bag, he swept it across the front of the building. On the far end of the building, where a light was burning from a corner room, he heard snoring.

The guard was inside his office, asleep.

Removing the goggles, Taft turned a switch on the frames that adjusted them to read infrared and checked for motion detectors. Then he scanned the area between him and the front door. Nothing. Switching on magnification and night vision, he scanned the windows and doors. Those were clear—no wires or anything extraordinary.

It seemed that the Tesla Museum was about as well protected as a Dairy Queen.

Taft put the dish and the goggles back in the bag and clutched it in his hand. Next he removed the remaining key from his pocket and approached the front door. The key slid in, and the lock twisted open. Taft slowly crept inside.

AT THE FAR end of the museum in a small office barely large enough for a desk, the guard slept contentedly. He was old, sixty-two years of age, and heavy-set. His small office smelled of the goulash the guard had eaten a few hours earlier for dinner, the schnapps he drank with his coffee, and his sweaty feet. His boots had been unlaced and removed and sat to the side of his desk. His feet were encased in socks, once white, now gray, atop the desk. The guard's chair was crammed against a corner wall. His mouth was slightly open, periodically erupting with snores, and a thin stream of drool ran from his mouth to his chin.

Someone would need to hit him with a bat to wake him up anytime soon.

Taft's seemingly innocuous conversation with Slavja over drinks and dinner had provided the clues he needed now. Making his way past the exhibits of Tesla's coils and inventions, past his death mask and the urn containing his ashes, Taft headed directly for the archives, which were in a separate room.

Inside the room were thousands of documents, letters, patent applications, and photographs. Almost all of Tesla's papers were contained inside. It was 2:47 A.M. when Taft entered the room. A quick perusal of the inventory revealed that the documents were arranged by the year of their creation. Taft picked the years in which he had the highest interest and began to scan through the files.

It was almost 5:00 A.M. when the parabolic dish Taft had left in the hall outside signaled to Taft's earpiece that the guard was stirring. Placing the papers he was examining back in their files, Taft went down the hall, retrieved the dish, then made his way to the front door and slipped back out onto the street.

He walked quickly away from the museum. The sky was growing light in the east when Taft entered his hotel room and placed the dish and goggles back in their secure case. Checking the room for intruders and finding it untouched, he slipped out again.

Walking back toward Slavja's apartment, he found a bakery that was open early and purchased coffee in paper cups and an assortment of baked goods. Carrying the tray back to her building, Taft entered and walked up the stairs to her apartment. Stopping to listen at the door, Taft heard water running.

He knocked quietly at the door and waited until Slavja opened it.

"Did you read my note?" Taft said as he walked in carrying the paper tray.

Slavja reached over and kissed him on the lips. "Jet lag," she said. "What is that?"

"It's when you fly a long ways and your body is still on the time zone from the place that you left," Taft said. "For you, it's night, for me, it's day."

"I've never been on a plane," Slavja noted.

Taft stared at the Serbian. She looked as good today as yesterday—

maybe better. Her robe was partially open, and Taft caught another sight of her long legs below and a hint of her bosom from above. Strangely, in contrast to the thick black hair on her head, the remainder of Slavja's body was nearly hairless.

Taft placed the tray on the small dining room table, and the two sampled the pastries as the sun came up over Belgrade. The feeling was almost suburban, as if they were a couple—not strangers who had met only yesterday.

"I'm starting to get tired," Taft noted.

"Then sleep," Slavja said. "I have to get ready for work, but I can be quiet."

Taft considered this. On one hand, if he chose to leave, Slavja would want to know where he was staying, and that had yet to come up. On the other hand, him staying here—or even letting her believe he was, and leaving later—built a commitment he was not sure was fair to create.

"Nadia, I'll need to go south soon for my work," Taft said. "Maybe later today even."

"Well," Slavja noted, "you can't go if you are tired, so why not sleep here a few hours, then come down to the museum and take me to lunch. Then you can do whatever, later."

It all made perfect sense.

They made love for another hour, and then Slavja left for work just before 8:00 A.M.

IN THE OFFICES of the Serbian Security and Intelligence Agency (BIA), Zoran Slavja sipped coffee from a glass cup, then set it back on his desk and reached for a large manila envelope. Slitting the end open with a knife, he removed the contents and began to read the first page. The sheets contained the nightly intelligence reports for the country.

There was nothing much to report from the prior night. Records of truck traffic along the border with Bosnia, some reports of Albanian traffickers crossing a few mountain passes. All in all a quiet night. Just then Zoran's intercom buzzed.

"Sir," his secretary said, "your sister is on the line."

"Put her through."

Nadia was standing at a pay telephone on the street a few blocks from her apartment.

"Do you have time to see me this morning?" she asked when Zoran came on the line.

"Always," Zoran said. "When?"

"Do you have time right now?"

"Certainly."

"I'll be right over," Nadia said.

Zoran's office was eight blocks away, and Nadia covered the distance in fifteen minutes. Once she had passed through security she rode up the elevator. Zoran, who had been called by the security desk at the front door, met her as soon as the elevator opened.

"Come on down to my office," he said, taking her by the hand.

Once inside and seated, Zoran offered coffee, which Nadia waved away.

"What is it?" Zoran asked.

"I think NATO sent an American to remove more Tesla documents from the museum," Nadia blurted out. "I met a man yesterday. . . ."

Nadia told Zoran all the details about meeting Taft right up until now.

"Now, sister," Zoran said, "you have never had any proof that the documents that are missing were taken by NATO forces—in fact, I checked into your allegations at the time, as I've told you before. Then, as now, they proved groundless."

"I can't think of who else might want them," Nadia said logically, "and NATO *was* bombing Belgrade and killing our citizens at the time. Maybe that was just a cover to create chaos so the museum could be pillaged."

"You don't even know for sure if anything was actually removed," Zoran said quietly. "You said yourself the dates match on the files in question."

"But the contents of those dates are different," Nadia said. "Over the years I have read most all those files. The ones in the times from

1899 to 1904 have been switched—I know this as a fact, even if you don't believe me."

"Why would NATO want to steal the documents?"

"It's the *Americans*," Nadia said loudly, "they are always trying to build bigger and better ways to kill people. The sections missing concern the Colorado experiments and Wardenclyff. Those were perhaps Tesla's finest accomplishments—the transmission of power without lines."

"Forget that for a moment, sister," Zoran said. "Why do you think this American you met—and, I guess bedded—is in on the theft?"

"Because he slipped from my apartment last night."

"But you said he came back. He claimed he had jet lag and went out for a walk. That makes sense to me, particularly if he just arrived here yesterday."

"But the dead bolt was locked when I awoke," Nadia said.

"He took the keys," Zoran said in exasperation.

"My keys were on the half wall next to the dining room in the ash-tray, where I always leave them."

"Then how did he lock the front door upon leaving?" Zoran said slowly.

"Exactly," Nadia said.

"I think I'd better talk to this man," Zoran said. "What did you say his name was?"

"Darrell Jackson," Nadia said, handing her brother his business card, "but he goes by his middle name: John."

"Where is he now?"

"Sleeping at my apartment," Nadia said, "but he's supposed to come to the museum at noon and take me to lunch."

Zoran rose from behind his desk. "I'm sure this is nothing," he said, "but I'll come by at lunch and meet him. In the meantime, I'll check out the company he says he works for, this Capco Mining, and see what else I can learn about him. Did he say where he is staying in Belgrade?"

"I never asked," Nadia admitted.

"I'll run through the hotel database and find out where his room is," Zoran said. "You just head into work, and I'll meet you at noon. By then I'll know the whole story, and if we need to, we can confront this man then."

Nadia stood up. "If it's nothing," she said quietly, "just call me and stay away."

"Sister," Zoran said easily as he made his way over to the door to open it, "do I detect you have a passion for this American?"

"Sometimes lust," Nadia said, "knows no loyalty."


ONCE HE HAD seen his sister to the elevator, Zoran walked back to his office. Logging onto an intelligence database maintained by INTER-POL, he punched in Capco Mining. There was no file. Next, Zoran did a Dun & Bradstreet search for the company's credit rating. The rating was perfect. Not only did Capco pay their bills on time, they also had relationships with several large private banks in the world. One was in Liechtenstein, at a bank where Zoran had a contact. He found the number in his computer files and dialed.

After greeting his contact, Zoran made his inquiry.

"Are you familiar with a company named Capco Mining?" Zoran asked.

"Sure," the contact said. "Excellent company. I think they concentrate on gold and copper primarily, medium-sized 50 to 100 million in yearly sales."

"Anything out of the ordinary about them?"

"Nothing I know," the contact said.

"Thanks," Zoran noted.

"Not a problem," the contact said easily.

Once the phone went dead, the bank officer waited a second, then dialed a number at the NIA in the United States.

"A BIA officer just inquired about Capco," the banker noted.

"The Serb Secret Police? What was his name?" the voice at the other end asked.

"Zoran Slavja."

"I'll alert our principal so he can take precautions."

"Fair enough. Now would you please check into my request for rotation," the man in Liechtenstein said. "I'm tired of playing banker."

"Hold on," the man at the NIA said.

He punched some information into his computer, then waited.

"Fifty-eight more days will make three years," the man noted, "and you have been approved for transfer. What, is Liechtenstein that bad?"

"No," the faux banker said. "It's beautiful and mountainous and snowy in winter. I'm just tired of it all."

"Well," the voice said, "you should be happy with your next assignment, then—you got the Cayman Islands, like you requested."

"Excellent."

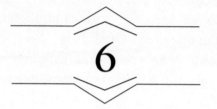

# 6

TWO MINUTES AFTER the call alerting him came in from NIA head-quarters, just over five minutes after Zoran Slavja made the call to Liechtenstein, John Taft was exiting the back door of Nadia's apartment complex. Twenty minutes later, he had packed and removed his bags from the Park Hotel and left through the rear door without checking out. Ten minutes after that he was checking into an entirely new hotel using a different set of false identification. Darrell Jackson, it seemed, had become a liability. Once situated again, he called Martinez on the secure satellite telephone.

"I'm repositioned," he said, "and safe. Do you mind explaining what happened?"

"We received an inquiry about Capco Mining at the cutout," Martinez said.

"So it was just ordinary procedure," Taft said, "Move and assess the risks. Do you know who made the inquiry?"

Martinez looked down at his notes. "An agent working for the Serbian Intelligence and Security Agency."

"The BIA?" Taft said. "That's odd. Let me ask you something. Did the inquiry come from an agent we suspect of something?"

Martinez opened the file on his desk and read the summary quickly. "No," he said quickly. "There's no dirt on him—in fact, he seems like a competent agent. His name is Zoran Slavja. Do you want his particulars?"

"No," Taft said quietly. "I know what this is about."

"Care to fill me in?"

"I banged his sister last night," Taft said sheepishly.

Martinez laughed. "Now you see why I stay married. One date with someone and the woman is having her spy brother check you out. Where's the trust?"

"She works as a curator at the Tesla Museum here in Belgrade," Taft said with a hint of defensiveness. "I needed to copy her keys to make entry. I went in last night."

"I'm sure there was no other way to lift her keys," Martinez said, "like steal them from her purse at dinner or maybe just break into the place without keys—like always. I think you're getting sloppy, old buddy—and I'm beginning to worry about your safety."

"I've decided to retire," Taft admitted.

Martinez was quiet for a moment.

"You want me to pull you out?" Martinez asked. "Send someone else over?"

"No," Taft said easily, "I'm okay—I can finish this up."

The line was silent for a second, and both men contemplated Taft's disclosure.

"So," Martinez said finally, "as long as you are staying, what did you find when you entered the museum?"

"Someone removed and swapped the files pertaining to the years from just before 1900 to about five years later."

"How do you know?"

"The paper appears to be from a different age," Taft said, "I clipped samples we can test to be sure—but mainly because the text had been written on a different typewriter. The documents switched to a courier font, and that did not come into use until decades later. Plus the pages were not indented, like from a typewriter—"

"So they were printed off a computer," Martinez interrupted. "Maybe they are simply copies and the originals are out being preserved or something."

"That's possible," Taft said, "but if that was the case, why place the copies in the files? Wouldn't you just explain to any researchers that the dates I mentioned were currently unavailable and leave it at that?"

"You have a point."

"I think we need to pull back the veil a bit," Taft said, "and allow me to openly speak to the museum staff and the agent with the BIA."

"I'll call General Benson and ask for clearance," Martinez said. "You sit tight."


AN HOUR AFTER Zoran had called Liechtenstein, he stood outside his sister's apartment.

Since Nadia's visit, Zoran had been busy. He'd made a host of other inquiries that also led nowhere. He was beginning to smell a rat. Capco Mining, at least according to their credit report, earned and spent millions each year. But in spite of this fact, no one knew anything about them that could be considered concrete.

Capco Mining was a wraith of a company that moved across Earth leaving no tracks.

Zoran crept up to his sister's door and listened. It was quiet. Using his spare key, he slowly unlocked the door, then entered. Making his way to the bedroom, he found it empty. Coming back through the small kitchen, he found a note on the half wall.

*Nadia dear, if you are reading this, I'm gone. Hope to see you soon. J.*

Zoran pocketed the note and walked out the front door. The BIA's hotel database showed that Darrell Jackson was staying at the Park Hotel. Zoran headed there.


TAFT TURNED THE satellite phone on at the first ring.

"Yo," he said.

"You're good to go," Martinez said. "Benson approved you coming out to Slavja if need be, but ordered that you not disclose anything to the BIA headquarters. Apparently we've had some trouble with them and leaks. He also asks that you keep this low-key. The story that you give Slavja is that there are power surges on the European electrical grid. At this time we don't want to alert the Serbs that there might be more to this than just that. Tell them you are looking into Tesla just as an aside."

"I understand," Taft said breezily. "What's the status of the BIA?"

"According to our files," Martinez said, "after the NATO bombings and the fall of Milosevic, the agency was revamped and new officers placed in charge. There may be some of the old guard still around, however, so tread lightly—the U.S. is not their favorite."

"Slavja?"

"From what we have on him, he's clean," Martinez said. "He wasn't involved in the ethnic cleansing and has no ties to socialist or Communist countries that we know."

"I guess, then," Taft said easily, "I should go give him a big howdy. Do you have his mobile number?"

Martinez read off the mobile and office extensions for Zoran from the file.

"I don't know how accurate the numbers are," Martinez said slowly. "It's been two weeks since Mather ran the last scans."

"I guess I'll see," Taft said.

"One more thing," Martinez said. "If I were you, I'd bring some roses for his sister."

"Larry," Taft said before hanging up, "you are such a romantic."


AFTER FLASHING HIS badge and taking the manager aside, Zoran was approaching Taft's room with key in hand. He passed a room service waiter pushing a cart along the hall. The man nodded and continued on toward the elevator. He was waiting for the elevator when Zoran stopped at the door. Listening carefully and hearing nothing, Zoran slowly opened the door and entered.

Empty. On top of the dresser was another note.

*Sorry to be a bother—but I was called away.*

Zoran was folding the note and slipping it into his pocket when his cell phone rang.


TAFT REMOVED THE flowers from the vase on the room service cart with his free hand while holding his portable phone in the other. He had not bothered to push the elevator button and instead made his way toward the emergency stairway, leaving the empty cart behind. Sliding the flowers into his jacket pocket, he opened the door to the stairs just as Zoran answered. Closing the door behind him, Taft stood on the landing and peeked through the window leading back out to the hallway.

"I hear you've been checking up one me," Taft said.

"Who is this?" Zoran demanded.

"Well, I'm not Darrell Jackson," Taft said.

"Oh, this must be the man my sister calls John," Zoran said. "Strangely enough, I've been looking for you."

"Yes," Taft said, "I know."

"I think we should meet," Zoran said. "What do you say?"

"So do I," Taft said. "In fact, I'm down in the lobby right now."

"Be right down."

The phone went dead and Taft considered his options. If he was Zoran, there was no way he would take the elevator—Taft could simply push the button from any lower floor and open the door. Then Zoran would be at his mercy.

The stairway was the obvious choice, but Zoran was smart enough to enter through the door carefully and then check each landing as he walked down. Taft peered out the window from the landing of the stairs. Zoran was just exiting the hotel room.

Taft climbed up a flight, walked through the door leading to the hallway, and pushed the elevator button. Luckily the elevator was but a floor above and quickly arrived. Taft reached in and pushed the button for the floor below. Then he raced back downstairs to wait.

Zoran was almost to the elevator and making his way toward the stairway when the bell chimed and the door of the elevator slid open.

Zoran slid a handgun from a holster slung under his arm, and, gun drawn, turned to face the elevator.

Right then, Taft opened the door to the stairway and pointed his Colt 10mm at the side of Zoran's body facing him. "Hey, cowboy, I have the jump on you."

Zoran stood quietly as he tried to decide how to turn and fire.

"John Taft, Special Agent, United States National Intelligence Agency."

"Zoran Slavja, BIA."

"I know," Taft said. "Now turn toward me. But do it slowly."

Zoran pivoted on his heel.

"I'm putting mine away," Taft said easily. "Then I'll reach in and retrieve my badge."

Zoran kept his weapon trained on Taft as he placed the Colt on the ground and removed an ID card from his pocket. Stepping forward slowly, he held up the ID card so Zoran could see. He read it, then slowly lowered his weapon.

Taft nodded at Zoran. Then he spoke. "Sorry about your sister."

"Don't worry," Zoran said, extending his hand. "There is still time to marry her."

THIRTY MINUTES LATER, Taft and Zoran were sitting in Nadia's office at the Tesla Museum. Nadia had overcome her initial anger at Taft's deceit. Now she was more interested in what he was telling her about the files he had examined.

"I told Zoran the same thing," she said. "I first noticed the change sometime in the months after the NATO bombing of Belgrade."

"That was in 1999," Taft noted.

"I first noticed the change probably early 2000," Nadia said. "I was doing a contents summary and rereading a series of documents. Once I began reading the ones from 1899, they did not seem to make much sense."

"What do you mean?" Zoran asked.

"Tesla was very precise," Nadia said, "compulsively so in both life and his work. But at that point in the files the records began to wander, as if large pieces of the research were left out. For five years or so in the files it's like a jigsaw puzzle with some pieces hidden under the couch."

"Weird," Taft said.

Nadia's office was quiet.

"I still don't get it," Zoran said. "You tell me you are looking into what you believe is simply some glitches in the European power grid. I don't see where Tesla ties into this."

"Quite frankly," Taft said, "it was a shot in the dark. I just thought that since we feel the power surges might be coming from Serbia, and Tesla was born here, it should be looked into. Now, after what Nadia has told me, I think there might be more to it than that."

"I'm certain someone has stolen a set of Tesla's documents," Nadia said.

The room was silent for a moment.

"Zoran," Taft said, "can you work with me on this? Off the books?"

Zoran asked, "Why?"

"The NIA has reason to distrust the BIA," Taft said easily. "There are still a lot of Ilic's men in positions of power."

Zoran nodded. What Taft had said was true, and the entire ethnic cleansing policy Ilic espoused had been a blot on Serbia's history. Zoran's opposition to that time was strong. "I'll need to clear my schedule of what I'm working on currently—but I think I can do this."

"If you can," Taft said, "I could use your help."

Zoran nodded.

"I won't ask you to do anything that smacks of treason toward Serbia," Taft said. "Just work with me until we can sort this out and know who is behind these power drains."

"Once we solve this mystery," Zoran said, "I'll need to report the findings to my superiors."

"What if we find they are in on it?" Taft asked, "and it poses a threat to Serbia's independence?"

"How so?" Zoran asked.

"If this electrical glitch has anything to do with a threat to the

United States," Taft said quietly, "the new policy is to shoot first and ask questions later."

"So to save my country," Zoran said, "I have to conspire with you?"

"Might come to that," Taft admitted.

"Will you guarantee my safety?" Zoran asked. "And that of my family?"

"My word," Taft said.

"I'll help you," Zoran said slowly, "but I'm sure this is nothing."

Taft reached over and shook his hand. The room was quiet again.

"As for you and me," Nadia said, "you recover the papers I think are missing and all is forgiven."

"So," Taft said, "you'd go out with me again."

7

GALADIN RATZOVIK STARED at his new face in the mirror. The swelling was going down and the redness finally receding. His nose had diminished in size, his chinline strengthened and cheeks accentuated, his eyelids redone. His lips were injected with silicone to make them larger. Contact lenses changed his eye color and cosmetic bonding the appearance of his teeth. For all intents and purposes, the face staring back at him in the mirror was that of a different man.

He smiled at the image of himself. At that instant the intercom buzzed.

"Sir," one of his aides said, "you have a call."

Ratzovik sat down on the edge of his bed and lifted the receiver. "Go ahead," he said.

"You asked me to call if anything unusual came up."

"I did."

"The BIA agent whose sister runs the Tesla Museum showed up there with an unknown man."

"Do you know why?" Ratzovik asked, staring back toward the mirror and rubbing his chin as he spoke.

"No," the voice said. "Just that they are still inside."

"Can you try to take a photograph of them together?"

"I'll try," the voice answered.

"It's probably nothing," Ratzovik noted.

"Anything else you would like me to do?"

"No, just call me if you can get a photograph," Ratzovik said.

"Very good," the voice said.

The telephone went dead in Ratzovik's ear. He placed the receiver in the cradle. Then he cursed long and loud while staring into the mirror. But his face had changed, and the fury that so many had seen before was gone. Ratzovik looked more like a happy clown with a dirty mouth than a cold-blooded killer. He tried to screw his mouth into a grimace, but his plumped-up lips would not cooperate.


ZORAN AND TAFT walked down Krunska Street, away from the museum.

"You ask who in my country might be behind this," Zoran said slowly, "but that's hard to say. Serbia is again increasingly unstable. Once Prime Minister Djindjic was assassinated, the old wounds started to open again."

"He was the first democratically elected leader in Serbia since World War II, correct?"

"Exactly," Zoran said, "and he was moving quickly to bring Serbia into the European Community. It was Djindjic who allowed Ilic to be extradited to face trial in The Hague. And he was promising more extraditions of those involved in the ethnic cleansing plus cracking down on the criminal elements and working with the West to improve Serbia's economy."

"Shot through the heart by an assassin," Taft said. "When was that—spring of 2003?"

"March twelfth, to be exact," Zoran noted.

"And Ilic has still not been convicted."

"The UN War Crimes Tribunal estimates that the trial might last years more."

"And reforms?" Taft asked.

"They died with Djindjic," Zoran admitted. "The new prime minister, Kostunica, was elected with the support of Ilic's old allies. For their help he agreed to stop any further extraditions as well as stop the movement of Serbia into the European Union. The prosecution of the Muslims has started again—it just has not yet grown so large as to attract the attention of the West yet."

"Will it?" Taft asked.

"Most certainly," Zoran said. "The Ilic supporters are growing in power again. It's just like Iraq after the First Persian Gulf War—the West never went all the way. They made a token gesture with NATO, and now the problems are resurfacing."

Taft reached down and placed his arm on Zoran's arm.

"You are telling me that Serbia is ready to explode again?"

"Like with your President Kennedy," Zoran said quietly, "any planned reforms were snuffed out by an assassin's bullet."

Zoran and Taft were standing motionless on the sidewalk now. "I wonder just how close your country's problems are tied to the electrical surges," Taft said quietly.

"Well," Zoran said, starting to walk again, "that's the million-dollar question, isn't it?"


MARTINEZ WAS IN his office reading the classified files on Nikola Tesla. From what Martinez was reading, it seemed like both the United States and the old Soviet Union had used some of his theories in an attempt to produce particle beam weapons. Perhaps the much-heralded death ray that Tesla spoke of in his later years was not just the ramblings of an old man seeking lost fame, as history had reported. But there was more.

Back in the late 1930s Tesla, down on his luck and short of cash, had sold some plans and documents to a company in New York named Amtorg Trading Company. It was later discovered that Amtorg, based in New York City, was a front for the Soviet Union. Those plans and documents had never been recovered.

The files went on and on.

Courts in the 1940s ruled that Marconi infringed on Tesla's patents to develop radio. The HAARP project in Alaska, a U.S. project currently testing propelling beams of electricity off the inosphere, is based on Tesla's theories. And the true purpose of his works at Wardenclyffe on Long Island are still being debated.

Tesla, it seemed, had his hands in everything electrical.

Martinez signed and dated the tag on the files that related to Wardenclyffe. He was the third signatory. The files had last been examined by a scientist with the Department of the Navy in 1964. He was seeking a method of low-frequency radio transmission to contact submarines but found nothing. Prior to that was the originator. The file had been started not long after Tesla's death in 1943 by an agent with the Office of Naval Intelligence tasked with analyzing this file as well as all papers that had been recovered from Tesla's hotel suite after his death. The few items that interested the agent had been noted; then the documents had been microfilmed. He found nothing Earth-shattering.

In 1952 the originals were released and sent to Belgrade to the museum.

Breaking the seal on the file, Martinez started to read.


FORMER SERBIAN COMMANDER Radko Ilic was sitting in the conference room just down the hall from his cell. He was conversing with one of his newly hired Serbian lawyers. During the first years of his incarceration Ilic had represented himself. Then the presiding judge was forced to resign for health problems in May 2004. Ilic saw an opportunity. Assembling a team of attorneys, he managed to force a mistrial and started the long process over.

The delaying tactic meant that any decision on his fate might still be years away.

Of the three dozen attorneys currently on Ilic's payroll, only thirty or so provided actual legal advice and defense. The remaining men were factotums, who Iilic used as errand runners. Operating under the rule that conversations between a client and his attorney were private and protected, Ilic had began to rebuild power within his country through his lawyer-emissaries. Now there was a snag.

"What in the hell do you mean," Ilic said loudly, "we're running low on money? Just call Ratzovik and tell him to transfer some."

"We're having some trouble reaching him," the lawyer admitted.

"Trouble reaching him?" Ilic thundered. "Have my people hunt him down and bring him here. I'll straighten him out."

At the sound of Ilic yelling, the guard started to enter the conference room. Ilic waved him away.

"This is priviliged communication," he said.

The guard retreated to his chair outside the door and sat down once again.

"Of course we cannot bring him here," the lawyer said quietly. "He's indicted himself."

Ilic nodded slowly. "Make notes," he said quietly.

The lawyer uncapped a gold pen and held it poised over a yellow paper pad.

"Contact Radko Bucdl," Ilic noted, "and have him—"

"I don't know who that is," the lawyer interrupted.

"No," Ilic said loudly, "but if you'd let me finish, I'll give you all the details. You are not familiar with Bucdl. When you return to Serbia my wife will give you the contact information. I want you to give him this note."

Ilic reached for a separate pad and scribbled a message with a pen. Then he folded the note in quarters and handed it to the attorney.

"I take it I should not read this message," the lawyer said quietly.

Ilic shook his head no. "Once Ratzovik has turned over the location of my funds, I want them split up and transferred to new private banks. I don't want anything like this to happen again."

The lawyer sat quietly for a moment, folding the sheet with Bucdl's name into thirds, then sliding the note from Ilic inside. "You seem confident this man will be able to do what you need done."

"That's why I was a commander and you were just hired help," Ilic said coldly.

• • •

INSIDE THE BARN in southern Serbia, Vojislav Pestic stared at the diagrams taken from the Tesla Museum. Everything he needed was there, but Pestic could feel it—something was just wrong with the order and direction of the diagrams. He was sketching changes on a pad of paper when one of the guards opened the door and entered.

"The boss wants to know your progress," he said coldly.

Pestic stared up at the guard, whose head was topped with a thick pelt of black hair, and whose eyes were a watery brown. When he spoke, his lower teeth were exposed; they were crooked and stained by coffee and cigarettes. A thin scar ran along one cheek, and Pestic had the feeling that the man that had inflicted this had suffered a far worse fate.

"Tell him," Pestic said, "I seem to be missing some documents. Without them I doubt I can control the device properly."

The guard nodded, then reached for his cellular telephone. He dialed a number and explained. Nodding as the party at the other end spoke, he paused. "He wants to talk to you," he said, handing Pestic the phone.

"What documents are you missing?" the voice said coldly.

"I'm not sure."

"That's a pretty vague statement," the voice said, "considering our deal."

"If I could see all the documents at the museum," Pestic said, "I would have a clearer picture. Take me there. I'll find what I am missing."

Pestic was playing a dangerous game. If he made it to Belgrade, he might find what he needed to complete the device; more importantly, he might find a way to escape, then rescue his family and go into hiding. The telephone was silent as the man at the other end thought.

"I'll consider that, Vojislav," the voice said coldly, "and let you know soon. In the meantime, continue working."

While the man was speaking, Pestic stared at the documents on the table in front. The diagrams were being reflected off a polished metal toolbox. The scribbles looked as if they were being held in front of a mirror.

"I understand, sir," he said, staring at the reflection. "How long until I will know one way or the other?"

"If I decide to honor your request it will take time to plan your transfer and entry into the museum," the voice said. "The danger of being caught is great. I'll need to decide if it is worth the risk."

"Sir, I think I can do what you need," Pestic said, "with the missing information."

"I'll let you know."

The telephone went silent.

Pestic handed the cell phone back to the guard, who slid it into his pocket and exited the barn. Once the guard was outside, Pestic held one of Tesla's documents closer to the toolbox. The image was reversed. Suddenly the diagrams became clearer.

Pestic started quickly making notes.

TAFT AND ZORAN reached a park in downtown Belgrade. A large marble fountain sat in the center, the sound of falling water muffling sound. Taft pointed to an empty bench, and the two men sat down.

"Here's how I see it," Taft started. "You are, of course, loyal to your country and probably have some distrust toward me and the United States."

Zoran nodded.

"That's going to get in the way of what I think we need to do," Taft said.

Zoran continued nodding.

"I'm sure the BIA could handle this themselves," Taft said easily, "but I believe your organization might be infiltrated with Ilic supporters, so I'm just going to ask you: How do you personally stand on him and what he was doing?"

Zoran stared at Taft before answering. "I oppose what he was doing with every fiber of my being. Contrary to what the world community might feel, Serbia is not populated by genocidal maniacs. Ilic and his types are nothing more than butchers."

"But the United States is not your favorite either?"

"I think your country meddles in the affairs of sovereign nations much too frequently," Zoran admitted. "What's right for the United States is not right for the world."

Taft nodded and stared at the water in the fountain. A bird was bathing in the pool.

"On that score," Taft said slowly, "I tend to agree with you. Our problem is this: Even if the BIA was not infiltrated with Ilic loyalists, I don't believe you have either the manpower or the resources to solve this yourselves."

"Which means?" Zoran asked.

"Which means if a terrorist attack occurs using something Tesla invented," Taft said quietly, "and it is traced back to Serbia, the United States will move swiftly and decisively to counter the source of the threat."

"Your country would attack?"

Taft nodded. "The rules have changed of late. Any strike against the United States or her allies opens the door to full-scale retaliation and retribution."

"So, in a nutshell," Zoran said, "what you are offering is a choice between capitulation or destruction."

"It could go that way," Taft admitted.

"Not much of a choice," Zoran said slowly.

The two men were silent as the ramifications of Taft's assessment settled.

Finally Zoran spoke. "So what are you proposing?"

"I need you to go off the farm," Taft said. "Work with me to solve this and do not notify your superiors of what we are doing."

Zoran stared at Taft. "That could cost me my job."

"But save your country," Taft said.

"A nice thought," Zoran said, "but it doesn't feed my family."

"If I can guarantee that you and your family are properly taken care of," Taft said, "will you go the distance with me?"

A light wind swept across the oak tree off to the side of the fountain. Another bird landed in the fountain and began to bathe. From a distance away on the Danube River, the horn from a cargo barge signaled its presence.

"You leave me little choice," Zoran said at last.

"I wish," Taft said, "there was some other way."

"What about my sister?"

Taft removed a small notebook from his pocket. "Write down the names of your immediate family."

Zoran took the notebook and listed a few names, then handed it back.

Taft read the names. "What about your mother?"

"Killed in the bombings," Zoran said quietly.

Taft paused. "I'm sorry," he said at last.

"Now do you see," Zoran said, "why I have agreed to your plan?"

Taft nodded and scanned the list again. Zoran's father, only Slavja as a sibling, a wife, and a single child age two. The extrication, if it came, would be easy.

"If it comes to it and we have to relocate you and your family to the United States," Taft said, "do you have a state in mind?"

"I hear Colorado is beautiful," Zoran said, "and the schools are good."

"Wait here," Taft said. "I need to make a telephone call."

Walking around the fountain where the water would muffle his words, Taft opened his secure telephone and dialed. There was a lag as the signal bounced off a Department of Defense satellite, then down to the NIA headquarters. Martinez answered.

"Yo," he said.

"I need you to have Benson okay charges for a relocation if needed."

"Zoran and family?"

"Great minds think alike," Taft noted.

"Identities, government jobs, the full package?"

"Yes."

"How many?"

"Four adults, one child."

"Preferred location?"

"Colorado."

"I'll get it in the works," Martinez said. "What else?"

"A few other items," Taft said. "I'll need three high-speed scanners transported to Serbia. The scanners need to be able to randomly change text. Plus a box of microlocators and the hardware to follow the signals. Last, line up as many experts on electrical engineering and Tesla's work as we can find."

Martinez snorted. "It doesn't take a rocket scientist to figure this one out. It looks like you're planning to switch, then remove the Tesla files from Belgrade."

"That's the plan."

"Then what, big boy?"

Taft paused. "How do you find a needle in a haystack?"

"Ah," Martinez said, "the old NIA exam question."

"Remember my answer?"

"Who could forget?" Martinez said.

"Burn it down," Taft said, disconnecting.

# 8

WITHIN AN HOUR of Taft's conversation with Martinez, the scanners were programmed and loaded on a U.S. Air Force C-19 cargo jet at a base in Germany. The plane took off heading south to a KFOR base controlled by the United States inside Kosovo. As soon as they arrived, they would be immediately trucked up to Belgrade. Inside the cover of one of the machines was a box containing the microsize tracking devices.

The cargo would arrive at the museum early this evening.

TAFT AND ZORAN walked through Belgrade toward another park.

"We keep moving?" Zoran asked.

"If someone is tracking us," Taft said, "It makes it harder for them to pick up any audibles. By the time someone sets up any type of listening device, we're on the move."

Taft reached for his telephone and called Martinez again. "What's the status?"

"The equipment is airborne," he said, "and should touch down later this afternoon. I contacted Mather and he arranged a truck to bring them to Belgrade."

"What type of truck?" Taft asked. "We have to assume the museum may be watched."

"Damn, partner," Martinez said easily, "do you think you're the only spy with a brain? Mather and I discussed that—it's just a plain white truck. He has a contact with a shop on the outskirts of Belgrade that will paint the sides with whatever you want."

"Okay main brain," Taft said, "what business do you think we should use as a cover?"

Martinez laughed. "Survey says, heating and air conditioning."

"That's good," Taft noted. "A little ductwork gone awry."

"I though the cover could be that maybe some welding on ductwork on the upper floors leaves a smoldering fire that sweeps through the upper floors."

"Why are they working late?" Taft asked.

"Perhaps because of the report of smoke that is called into the fire department sometime in the next hour or so?"

"So the firemen find nothing," Taft said, "but the report they checked is on file. Damn, you're good."

"Have Zoran talk to his sister and set it up," Martinez said. "That lends credence."

"Done," Taft replied. "Now how are you coming on the Tesla research?"

"I'm working on the Colorado portion of his experiments," Martinez said. "It seems his main thrust was the wireless transmission of electricity through the Earth."

"What about the death ray he announced to the newspapers?

"I'm not buying it," Martinez said.

"What's the boss say?"

"They have determined the minor earthquake in Italy and the surge on the power grid are probably linked. He's coordinated with the various European countries' power facilities to increase security and be on standby to cut themselves off the interconnected grid if it comes down to it. The idea is a terrorist organization would need to strike multiple targets inside the United States to have any effect. To do that they need power from outside Serbia."

"So they believe the threat can be isolated to Europe?"

"If this is *even* a threat," Martinez said, "we still have no real link to Tesla. Papers may have been lifted from the museum, but there could be many explanations for that. As far as who, and why, someone could benefit from creating earthquakes, so far we have came up blank. In the absence of any real reason this still could just be nothing."

Taft paused before speaking. "Larry, old buddy, I've got a feeling there is more to this than that."

"Know what?" Martinez said. "I hate when you say that."

"Anyway," Taft said, preparing to disconnect, "I'm glad you got to talk to me."

"Yeah, I'm sure you'll call if I can do anything for you."

The phone went dead, and Taft turned to Zoran.

"We need to talk to Nadia—there's been a fire inside the museum."

"When?" Zoran asked quickly.

"The first report will be in about an hour," Taft replied.


MATHER STOOD ABOVE a hole cut in the floor inside his secure office. Ten minutes before, he had removed a section of the wooden flooring, then unlocked and opened a manhole cover. He had dropped a microphone on a cord down in the hole, and the sound of footsteps was coming closer. Suddenly a head came into view.

"Afternoon," Taft said breezily. "Mind if I play through?"

Taft climbed up the metal ladder and stood inside the office. Zoran scurried up the ladder after him.

"This is Zoran Slavja," Taft said once they were both out of the hole.

"You're BIA," Mather said with a slight surprise in his voice.

"He's going to be working with us now," Taft said easily.

Zoran shook Mather's hand and stared around the room. "Where are we?"

Taft made a slight movement with his head.

"Sorry," Mather said, "but that needs to remain our little secret for now."

"Nothing personal," Taft said, "but my agency spent a great deal of time and money setting up this cover. If something should happen, it's best you don't know exactly where this office is located. If you are in danger—I'll let you know then."

Zoran nodded.

"It looks like my directions worked," Mather said easily. "Any problems?"

"The storm drain cover was loose just like you said," Taft noted, "and the directions were excellent."

"Good," Mather said. "Now what can I do for you?"

"We need another truck," Taft said, "painted with the same company as the one you and my partner arranged for earlier."

"How soon?"

"Five minutes ago," Taft said, smiling.

"Hold on," Mather said, walking over to his desk and starting his computer.

A few minutes passed as he scanned.

"All we have is a small van," Mather said a minute later.

"That would do it," Taft said.

"Hold on," Mather said. He reached for his telephone, then paused. "Can I speak in front of him?"

"Go ahead," Taft said.

Mather pushed a button on his phone, then began speaking in Serbo-Croation when it was answered. The conversation went back and forth for a few minutes. Then Mather hung up and turned to the two men.

"About an hour," he said as he scribbled an address on a pad of paper. He then tore it off and walked over to Taft and handed it to him.

"This is the address," Mather said. "You will also pick up the cargo truck there."

"Have you set up telephone answering if someone calls the company number?"

"I'll do that next," Mather said, "but if someone digs deep, the cover won't stand. This company is a brand-new creation—if someone checks references, it will collapse."

"I understand," Taft said.

"What else?" Mather asked.

"That should do it for now," Taft said. "But just so you know—from now on I think I'd better use this back door. I don't think you and I should be seen together just in case."

"If this helps any," Zoran said to Mather, "as far as I am aware, the BIA has no file on you. If there was a file with a photograph of you, I would probably remember. My specialty was North American agents."

Mather smiled and nodded. "Thanks. That's good to know."

"One last thing," Taft said as he started for the hole in the floor. "Ask your guys at the paint shop for two sets of coveralls. We'll need to cover our street clothes before we enter the building in the off chance it is being watched."

"I've got some here," Mather said, walking over and opening a closet on one side of the office. "What do you think? Large for you and a medium for our new friend?"

He pulled two sets of tan one-piece coveralls from a shelf and handed them over.

Taft grinned at Mather. "Ah, my good man. I want you to know you can expect a little extra in your pay envelope this next week."

"Just doing my job," Mather said quietly.

A few seconds later Zoran started down the ladder. Taft dropped the coveralls down to him, then followed behind. Once they were back in the storm sewer, Mather set the manhole cover back in place and re-assembled the floor. Then he sent an e-mail to the NIA headquarters outlining his actions.


ONE HOUR AND eleven minutes later, dressed in the coveralls, Taft and Zoran pulled up in front of the Tesla Museum. Making their way to the front door and carefully hiding their faces, they entered and located Nadia. Taft explained the plan.

"Okay," she said when he had finished, "so once you two take off I call the fire department and report I smelled smoke."

"Right," Taft said. "Tell the firemen we were working on the furnace ducts, then took off for a break. You smelled smoke and called right away."

"Then they will check and find nothing and leave."

"Correct," Taft said.

"Then what?"

"Later this afternoon into the early evening another truck will arrive. It will appear as if the heating company has called in more help. At this point I want you to go home as usual. Zoran and I will do what we need to do—that will take several hours, and then we'll leave. The fire will start soon after."

"I'm not very comfortable with you destroying the museum," Nadia admitted.

"It will be a controlled fire," Taft said easily, "with only limited damage to the upper floor. That I can promise you."

"And the guard?"

"I have something to put in his vodka that will make him sleep while the work is in progress. I'll also leave his window open. Once we leave, the timed charges will start the fire. One of my people, posing as a passerby, will phone it in. As the emergency contact person the fire department will contact you immediately. Come here then and make sure the guard is safe; then demand the fire department remove the files and take them to a safe location."

"You are sure this will work?"

Zoran nodded toward his sister. "John here has a sound plan. It gives us a chance to see who has an interest in the files—and possibly lead us toward whoever is behind the power surges. If we don't, and a terrorist attack is launched from Serbia aimed at Europe or the West, our citizens could face massive retaliations."

"But what if it is nothing?" Nadia said logically. "Then my museum is damaged and we don't have the money for repairs."

"My government will pay for any repairs," Taft said. "You have my word."

"Since my first meeting with you was when you promised me you were a geologist," Nadia said, "your veracity is in question."

"Well," Taft said easily, "you've got me there."

# 9

ON THE TOP floor of the Tesla Museum, Taft lit a fire in a metal trash can, then waited as smoke filled the room. Extinguishing the fire with water, he carried the can downstairs, then nodded at Nadia to telephone the fire department. With Zoran following behind, he walked out to the van, slid the trash can into the rear, then walked off the museum grounds. One block and a few minutes later, Taft and Zoran heard the sirens.

AT THE SAME instant, thousands of miles away, Martinez was running the names he had found in the Tesla files through a screening program on the NIA computer. Iver Esbenson was showed as receiving Social Security payments until 1963. That had to make him at least ninety years old when he passed away. Digging through a genealogy program, he found that Ivar had two daughters and a son named Karl, who had been born in 1917. Karl had one child, a boy named Erich, who had been born in 1947.

Martinez punched Erich's name in a database and retrieved his address from the Colorado tax record. It showed that Erich was living in a suburb of Denver. Martinez located the telephone number and dialed. Martinez could track the progress of the signal on his computer. He watched as the signal reached the home number he had located, then bounced to a cellular connection automatically.

"Erich," the voice said a minute later.

In the background Martinez could hear the sound of a power saw.

"This is Larry Martinez, I'm a special agent with the National Intelligence Agency. I'd like to—"

"Watch that crane!" Erich shouted just away from the phone. "That hits you and you'll feel it for sure! Sorry," he said to Martinez a second later.

"Like I said," Martinez began again.

"You said you are with the National Intelligence Agency," Erich said. "I caught that. Listen, Mr. Martinez, I can assure you all my workers are U.S. citizens—we don't hire illegals. And if you check with the state I think you'll find all my permits and legal documentation up to date and in order. Would you like the number for my main office? The manager there can provide anything else you might need. Back away from the cement bucket!" he shouted to someone on the site.

"Mr. Esbenson," Martinez said, "I can assure you this had nothing to do with your business. Why I called concerns your grandfather."

"Grandfather, " Erich said loudly. "He's been gone since '63."

"I know," Martinez said. "We're doing research into his work with Nikola Tesla."

"I don't know about that," Erich shouted, "but my dad might."

"Your father is still with us?" Martinez asked.

"My family has long genes, Mr. Martinez," Erich said, "and my dad won't even be ninety until next year. You got a pen?"

"Yes," Martinez said.

"Watch the swing of the bucket!" he shouted to someone on the job site. "You're too close to the pillar!"

"Sorry," Erich said again. "You're ready?"

"Fire away."

Erich read off a telephone number. "My dad's name is Karl. He'd be the one to talk to—he has all of Grandpa's things."

Martinez hesitated before speaking. "How's your father's memory?" he asked at last.

"Better than yours," Erich said quickly. "But you'd better catch him today—he told me he's going to Cabo tomorrow to golf for a week."

"Okay," Martinez started to say, "I'll give—"

"I'm sorry, Mr. Martinez," Erich said, "but it's a busy day here. If you call my dad I'm sure he can help with whatever you need. I need to take care of something here."

The telephone went dead, and Martinez stared at the number he had written down. He dialed the number and waited while it rang.

Halfway across the continent, Karl Esbenson was driving down Colfax Avenue in a 1967 Corvette convertible. The top was down, the sun was shining, and a Beach Boys disc was playing in the player set on the ledge just behind the front seats.

"Karl Esbenson," he answered.

Martinez went through his introductions again.

"Hold on," Karl said as he pulled into a parking lot.

Martinez waited.

"Trying to steer this beast, shift gears, and talk on the telephone take more hands than I've got," Karl noted as he slid to a stop. "Now, what's the NIA, and what do you need from me?"

"We're like the CIA," Martinez said, "only smaller and more secretive."

"Fair enough. You're straight to the point. I like that," Karl said. "Now, what do you need?"

"Did your father ever speak about his work with Nikola Tesla?"

"Quite a bit, actually," Karl said. "What in particular do you need?"

"Information about his work in Colorado."

"Come out here, Mr. Martinez," Karl said, "and I'd be glad to share what I remember."

"I talked to your son," Martinez said. "He said you were leaving tomorrow for Mexico."

"So come today," Karl said. "I assume the government has jet airplanes."

"We do," Martinez noted.

"Good enough," Karl noted. "You mosey on out here and I'd be glad to talk to you and show you the files."

"Files?" Martinez asked.

"Dad was a compulsive record keeper," Karl said. "I've got boxes of billing records, notes, design diagrams, photographs, and whatnot."

"Has anybody asked to see them before?" Martinez asked.

"Just a local friend," Karl said. "He's a historian of sorts."

Martinez was starting to feel a tinge of excitement. "I have to arrange the plane, but I'll be out there this afternoon."

"Private or commercial?"

"Probably private," Martinez said.

"Then you'll want to land at the Jefferson County Airport," Karl noted. "That's closer to my home. You just call me when you're close and I'll come get you in the 'vette."

"You're almost ninety years old and you drive a Corvette?"

"Always remember, Mr. Martinez," Karl said as he revved up the engine, "it's a great life if you don't weaken."

The telephone went dead. Martinez hit a number on his speed dial and connected with the NIA's aviation wing. He arranged to tag along on one of the agency's flights heading for the West Coast. They could drop him in Colorado before continuing onward. He had less than an hour to make the flight. After e-mailing General Benson, he set off for the airport.

AT ABOUT THE same time as the Gulfstream carrying Martinez lifted off from the runway near Washington, D.C., Taft and Zoran were inside the paint shop in Belgrade, examining the lettering that had just been added to the truck that would carry the scanners and other equipment. The paint was drying when Mather came into the shop.

He set down several jumpsuits and a box, then handed Taft a vial with an eyedropper built into the top. "It's the standard issue," he said. "One drop for each hour of sleep."

Taft slid the vial into his pocket. Off to one side, several U.S. Army

KFOR troops dressed in civilian clothes were eating from a buffet meal Taft had secured.

"We're almost ready, men," Taft said. "When you finish mess, dress in the jumpsuits, and we'll get out of here."

"What else do you need me to do?" Mather asked.

"Just stand by in your office," Taft said. "We'll call if we need anything."

"The accelerant to start the fire is in the box," Mather said. "It burns down to an undetectable ash after use."

"Thanks," Taft said.

"I'll be waiting," Mather said as he headed for the door.

During the truck-lettering procedure, Taft and the others had secured the scanners in boxes marked as furnace equipment. Once the soldiers dressed and the boxes were loaded back aboard, they could leave.

It was early evening when the truck rolled from the shop.

"You'll need to handle the guard," Taft said to Zoran as the truck drove through the streets of Belgrade.

Zoran was clutching a bottle of vodka between his legs. "You want three drops into his glass, correct?"

"Yes," Taft said. "If we introduce it into the bottle itself, there is no way to know how much he will drink. With the glass, we can be reasonably assured he'll finish that."

"I understand," Zoran said.

The truck was in downtown Belgrade, only blocks from the museum now. Taft reached for his secure telephone, punched in a code, and turned to the driver. "Our man here in Belgrade placed several cars directly on the street in front of the museum. They will be pulling out now, leaving us a spot directly in front."

The driver nodded as they turned down Krunska Street. Just ahead, a trio of cars were pulling away from the curb. The driver slowed as they cleared the spot, then slid to a stop directly in front of the Tesla Museum.

"Take out the guard," Taft said to Zoran as he climbed from the truck. "We'll unload the cargo and bring it inside."

Twenty minutes later the scanners and the other equipment were inside and sitting near the file room. Ten minutes and a few drinks later and the guard was soundly sleeping.

"Okay, men," Taft said once the coast was clear, "feed everything through the scanners as fast as you can. Replace each box of documents with the fakes, but make sure you keep the originals separate."

The sergeant in charge nodded.

Taft and Zoran made their way to the top floor to rig up the fire. The hours passed as the files were scanned and replaced with fakes. Taft made sure each fake box was tagged with a locator, while Zoran periodically checked on the sleeping guard.

"WE'RE ABOUT HALF an hour out," Martinez said over his satellite telephone.

"I'll head out now," Karl Esbenson said. "Once you land, make your way to the private jet terminal. How will I recognize you?"

Martinez described himself to Karl, and they disconnected.

"Mr. Martinez," the pilot shouted back to the cabin a few minutes later, "that's Denver to the south side and Boulder directly ahead, at the base of the mountains. We'll be on the ground in fifteen."

Martinez stared at the sprawl on the ground below. It had been several years since he had visited the Denver metro area, and the growth since his last visit was evident in all directions. Flying over the town of Broomfield, Martinez listened as the pilot slowed the engines and lined up for an east-to-west approach. The mountains loomed in front as they headed for the mesa the airport sat atop.

A few minutes later, the pilot touched down and taxied over to the private jet terminal.

"Stay away from the engines!" he shouted back as they rolled to a stop. "Exit the stairs and around the front of the aircraft!"

Clutching an overnight bag with his briefcase strapped to the outside, Martinez moved away from the jet. Once free, he sat his bag down and rolled it toward the terminal. The jet began taxiing toward the runway to continue on to California.

Martinez opened the door to the terminal. A man was sandy-colored hair flecked with gray stood up from where he had been seated on a leather couch. He was thin and somewhere south of six feet in height.

"Mr. Martinez?"

"Call me Larry," Martinez said, extending his hand.

"Karl Esbenson," the man said, shaking hands. "Come on, my car is just outside."

The men made their way through the small terminal to the parking lot. Karl walked over to the red Corvette and unlocked the trunk.

"Slide your bags in there."

Martinez placed his bags in the trunk and secured it, then climbed into the passenger seat. Karl slid into the driver's seat and twisted the key. The Corvette roared to life, then settled into a rumble.

"Four twenty-seven," he said, smiling at Martinez.

They headed out of the airport and west toward the mountains. While they drove, Karl shouted above the noise from the open top. "I live on that flat-top mesa over there," he said, pointing to the south. "It's named North Table Mountain."

They slowed as he turned to the south.

"That's Rocky Flats!" he shouted, pointing to a large installation to the west. "It's the old nuclear bomb plant! They are going through the cleanup phase now!"

A few minutes later they slowed at a stop sign, then made a slight turn to the left and under a railroad bridge. Just ahead was an old limousine, with the driver sitting out in the open and the large passenger compartment enclosed. Shiny black with the passenger area enclosed in leather, the bodywork featured a thin red pinstripe down the side. Karl waited for the road to clear so he could pass. Once the road was clear, he pulled alongside. The old Packard was being driven by a gray-haired man with a mustache. An unlit cigar was clenched in his teeth. Karl paced the town car's speed and honked. The man looked over, then smiled and waved. Karl accelerated and pulled in front.

"That guy looked familiar," Martinez noted.

"He's a big-name author who has a car collection near here," Karl said.

"Driggs, right?"

"Yes, Malcolm Driggs," Karl noted, "and we ought to see if we can get him to stop by my house later. He's well versed on Tesla—he's the guy I told you read the files."

"You're kidding," Martinez said.

"No," Karl said. "Read everything one summer a few years ago. I don't know if he was working on a book plot or what, but I know he spent nearly a week up at my house reading it all."

"Can you call him now?"

"I don't have the number of his shop with me," Karl said, "but as soon as I get home we'll call him up."

"Think he'll stop by?"

Karl slowed and turned west. North Table Mountain was just off to the south.

"Don't worry," Karl said as they slowed and turned south for the last leg of the drive. "I have inducements."

A mile or two later, Karl turned west again and started up a winding road that led partway up the side of the mesa. A few minutes later he slowed, pushed a button that opened a metal gate at the end of a long driveway, then drove onto his property. On the plains below was most of Denver. Karl stopped in front of the house and set the emergency brake, then climbed out.

"Hell of a view," Martinez said as they removed his bags from the trunk.

"You should see it on the Fourth of July," Karl said. "You can see every fireworks display that takes place."

The two men walked inside the house. Karl went right to the telephone. When he finished the call, he turned to Martinez. "He'll stop by within the hour."

"How you do that?"

"Tequila," Karl said, leading Martinez to a back office in the house where the files were.

• • •

"HE'S STIRRING," ZORAN said.

"Is he sleeping with his mouth open?" Taft asked.

"He was last time I looked."

"Put one more dot directly on his tongue," Taft said. "We're almost finished here."

Zoran headed for the guard's office while Taft stared around the file room. Most of the fake files were back in place, and the originals were boxed outside the room in a hallway leading toward the front foyer.

"I'll start moving these out to the truck," he said to the sergeant in charge.

"We should be all done here in half an hour or so," the sergeant replied.

Forty-seven minutes later, Taft and his team triggered the timers on the pyrotechnic devices, then made their way to the truck. As they drove away from the museum they passed a man at a pay phone. The first tendrils of smoke were curling from a top-floor window Taft had left open when the man at the pay phone called the fire department.

Eight minutes later, the first truck arrived on the scene.


"THAT'S A FINE badge," Driggs said after he'd asked Martinez for identification, "but I need a little more."

Martinez nodded and handed him a card with a number. "Call this number and tell them you need to verify my identity."

Driggs walked over to Karl's telephone and dialed. "White House."

"I was given this number by a Larry Martinez."

"Hold on."

The telephone was switched over to another extension. "Verification."

"Larry Martinez," Driggs said, as if talking to a machine.

"Is this Karl Esbenson?" the operator said, reading the trace.

"No, this is Malcolm Driggs."

"Mr. Martinez is on direct assignment with presidential approval," the voice said. "Any assistance you can render would be considered a favor to the president."

"I understand," Driggs said.

"Is there anything else?"

"No," Driggs said.

"Just so you know," the voice said, "I enjoy the books."

"Thanks," Driggs said as the line went dead.

Driggs set the phone back in the cradle.

"Well," Martinez asked.

"He's real," Driggs said to Karl. "Now where is that special tequila you promised?"

"Coming up," Karl said, walking over to the bar. "Rocks, right?"

Driggs nodded.

An hour passed as the three men discussed the files. Driggs seemed to have a photographic memory for the contents. Martinez turned to Karl.

"I'll need to get a team in here to copy them all," Martinez said. "Do you have any problem with that?"

"No," Karl said, "but I'm going out of town tomorrow. It would need to be after that."

"I think I can get them in here tonight," Martinez said.

"I'll go along with that," Karl said.

"What exactly does this pertain to?" Driggs asked. "I could be of more help if I knew what this was all about."

Martinez was silent for a moment. "What I'm about to tell you is classified. Under the recent Patriots Act and other statutes, if what I'm about to tell you is discussed, you could face charges ranging up to treason."

"I understand," Driggs said. "It's secret. Don't worry, it's not going to appear in one of my books."

"Good," Martinez said. "We have detected electrical surges originating in Serbia. We believe they might be tied to someone creating a weapon using Tesla's technology or plans."

"Any idea what type of weapon?" Karl asked.

"It's all hazy at this point," Martinez admitted, "but we think a test of the device may have triggered a small earthquake nearby."

"Where?" Driggs asked.

"Avezzano, Italy."

"I'll need to ponder this," Driggs said. "Where can I reach you?"

Martinez handed him a card. "Day or night you can reach me on this."

Driggs took the card and slipped it into his pocket. "Are you going to be okay here tonight with spies racing around copying everything?"

"I'll use the back bedroom," Karl said.

"Mr. Martinez," Driggs said, "I'll be in touch."

With that, he walked out. Martinez dialed a number and arranged for a team to come over and do the copying. The work would not be completed until nearly sunrise.

# 10

FLAMES HAD MADE it out of the windows facing Krunska Street before the fire department extinguished the fire. As the emergency contact person, Nadia had been called as soon as the first truck arrived on the scene. She made it from her apartment to the museum in less than five minutes. The guard had inhaled some smoke but started stirring as soon as the firemen dragged him outside and administered oxygen. He was now sitting in the back of an ambulance and seemed to be better by the minute.

If the guard realized he'd been knocked out, he had yet to mention it to anyone.

Nadia was discussing the fire with the department captain when a black limousine pulled in front of the museum and a thin man in a suit climbed out, followed by a pair of bulky men dressed in black suits. The pair scanned the area for danger as the thin man stared for a second at the smoke stains on the stones lining the windows in front. Next he crossed through the gate into the courtyard and approached Nadia and the captain.

"Zarko Bodonavik," he said in introduction. "Special assistant to the president."

Nadia knew Bodonavik by reputation. As special assistant to the president of Serbia-Montenegro he was known to be the behind-the-scenes power broker. If someone wanted the president's ear they first needed to go through Bodonavik. Part bagman, part heavy, men like Bodonavik were close to every politician.

It seemed odd that a simple fire would stir him from his night slumber.

"Nadia Slavja. I'm the museum curator."

The captain introduced himself as well, then excused himself to go back inside.

"How much damage was incurred?" Bodonavik asked quietly.

"Lucky," Nadia said. "Not much, sir."

"Does the fire department know how it began?"

"They think it was from some work we had done yesterday on the furnace ducts."

"May I go inside?" Bodonavik asked, as if Nadia had any control over that.

"But of course," Nadia said, motioning for him to follow.

The pair walked across the courtyard and through the front door. A pair of firemen were pulling their hoses from the upper level and carefully rolling them back up into a ball. The air smelled of smoke and soot, and the marble floor was dotted with water and ash. Bodonavik motioned to the stairway.

"The fire was on the upper floor?"

"Yes," Nadia said, "luckily."

"And Mr. Tesla's files?"

"They are in a room on a lower level," Nadia said easily.

"So there was no damage?"

"Only slight smoke damage."

"Good," Bodonavik said.

Nadia paused before speaking. "Sir," she said after a few seconds, "may I ask you something?"

"By all means."

"Why would you rise from bed to visit a simple fire? It seems that you could just send one of your assistants?"

Bodonavik paused before answering. He stared at Nadia, as if trying to gauge her intentions. Then, as if deciding it was okay, he answered.

"Mr. Tesla is a Serbian national treasure," he said with a blank expression. "You surely know that. The president was worried that his important papers might have suffered destruction or damage. I'm here to report my findings directly to him."

Nadia nodded, then motioned toward the file room. Bodonavik followed as she led him inside. She motioned to the shelves containing the files.

"If the president is that concerned," she said slowly, "perhaps he could help the museum in two ways. Until we determined the exact cause of the fire and repair the damage plus ensure that this won't happen again, I think it would be best if the files were moved to a safer location."

"And the second item?"

"If we had some funds to install sprinklers," Nadia said, "that would help us in the future if something like this arises."


EIGHT BLOCKS AWAY, in a car borrowed from Mather, Taft and Zoran were listening to the conversation from a bug Mather had left behind. The frequency was tuned to an unused AM radio band, and the voices were playing over the car speakers.

"Damn," Taft said, "she's good. Hitting him up for money is brilliant."

"Since we had no idea who might show up," Zoran said, "this move was all an improvisation."

"She's good," Taft said, staring at a small device that registered stress in the voices coming through the airwaves. Nadia was barely registering any tension.

Taft and Zoran continued to listen.

• • •

"YOUR REQUESTS ARE are sound," Bodonavik said easily, "but your second request I will need to submit to a budget committee."

"But the files," Nadia said, pointing to the shelves. "That you can do now?"

This was working better than Bodonavik had hoped. The curator of the museum was practically begging him to take the files. No break-in, no covert copying would be necessary. It was as if Providence were shining down on him tonight.

"Allow me to make a call," Bodonavik said graciously.

Stepping away from Nadia and back out into the foyer, he removed a cell phone and made a call. A few minutes later he stepped back over to where she was standing.

"Soldiers from the Defense Department will be here within the hour," he said, smiling. "They will take the files to a secure location. I trust this alleviates your concerns?"

"Oh, yes, sir," Nadia said, smiling.

Bodonavik nodded, then spoke to the captain, who was just descending the stairs. "The president will expect a report on the fire by tomorrow morning."

"I understand," the captain said, "but don't expect much—it seems to be fairly straightforward. The heating company was welding on the ducts, and sparks must have lit a fire that smoldered for some time."

"Put it all in the report," Bodonavik said.

Then with a nod to Nadia, he walked back outside.

Thirty-seven minutes later, a olive drab truck with six soldiers inside parked in front. They immediately started carrying boxes outside and loading them in the back of the truck. High overhead, a U.S. satellite would track their movements.

AT THE SAME time the false documents were being removed from the museum, a C-130J Super Hercules was leaving on its regularly scheduled flight from the KFOR base in southern Serbia to Ramstein Air Force Base in Germany. Along with the usual food, weapons, and troops rotating out was a pallet containing the boxes of Tesla's documents taken earlier. Once in Germany the pallet would be unloaded and placed in a military Gulfstream for a fast flight across the Atlantic Ocean to Andrews Air Force Base, near Washington, D.C. In less than forty-eight hours from their removal from the museum, they would be at the NIA headquarters, undergoing examination.

"GET SOME SLEEP," Martinez said over the secure phone to Taft after he related the events surrounding the fire. "It'll be a while until the documents find their new home, and the satellites will watch them until then."

"How you coming?" Taft asked.

Martinez related meeting with Esbenson and Driggs, then concluded. "I'm on my way to the airport now with copies of all his files. Once we're airborne I'm going to nap until we reach the East Coast."

"Was there anything Earth-shattering in what you had a chance to read so far?"

"Only that Tesla may have also done experiments in Iowa at some time."

"Iowa," Taft said. "That's the first I've ever heard about that."

"I don't know," Martinez noted. "Esbenson wrote about the experiments in Ames. As soon as I get back I'll put the egghead battalion on the problem and see what turns up."

"You haven't received any further reports about power surges or anything like that, have you?"

"No," Martinez said. "It's all calm."

"Okay then," Taft said. "I'll grab a few hours and check back in later."

"Good job with the file switch, partner," Martinez said. "I have a feeling that will reap some positive results."

"That, my good friend," Taft said, "is why I get the big money."

The phone went dead, and Martinez motioned to the driver, who was entering the airport grounds. "It's that one," he said, motioning to a plane on the tarmac, "over there."

AT THE SAME time, in a home within twenty miles of the airport, Malcolm Driggs was drinking his first cup of coffee for the day. Reaching over, he turned on his computer and waited while it ran through the checks.

Once it was logged on to the Internet, he began searching a database.

"WHERE ARE WE?" General Benson asked Allbright.

"Here's the latest, sir," Allbright replied. "Taft has removed all of Tesla's files from the museum in Belgrade, copied them with a scanner that changes data to confuse anyone who uses them, and set up a ruse so the files were seized by the Serbian government."

"I assume he salted the fake files with trackers?"

"Exactly," Allbright said.

"I love that man," Benson said, puffing on a cigar. "He always comes through."

"Then this information will not make you too happy."

"What?"

"Taft had Martinez start his paperwork for retirement while he's been in Serbia. I guess our fair-haired boy has had his fill."

"Don't worry," Benson said. "I'll fix that when John returns. He's never turned down a request from me yet."

"If he wants out, sir," Allbright started, "then—"

"I'll worry about Taft," Benson interrupted. "What else?"

"Martinez is returning from Denver with documents and personal papers that were owned by one of the men who actually worked with Tesla on his Colorado experiments. Once he's on the ground I have a team of scientists standing by to read them and write you an overview."

"Excellent," Benson said. "Now what is the situation in Serbia itself?"

"It continues to slowly deteriorate," Allbright said, "ever since the unrest in 2004 and the Serbian government agreeing to fund Ilic's legal defense. Also in 2004, the ultranationalistic party hold over the country continued to strengthen. The citizens are increasingly calling for the UN to release Ilic from the Hague. Also, his stalling tactics and the replacement of the lead judge a few years ago have made the trial now stretch into the seventh year. In addition, attacks are escalating on the UN troops inside the country, and the analysts claim this will only become more frequent."

"It's a quagmire," Benson said, "that will only get worse. Whenever the trial does conclude, *if* Ilic is found guilty of war crimes, the ultranationalists are going to take up arms against anyone from the West. That's a military problem, it seems. I'm just worried about the terrorist elements. How does this impact the U.S.?"

"Our analysts seem to think that any acts will be concentrated first on The Netherlands, where he was tried, then on any of the seven countries that have agreed to hold him in prison," Allbright said, reading from his notes. "Those countries are: Norway, Sweden, Finland, France, Spain, Austria, and Italy. Norway and Finland are already housing convicted Serbs, so their chance of receiving Ilic are less."

"That leaves Sweden, France, Spain, Austria, and Italy," Benson noted.

"And Spain is out ever since the terrorist attacks in Madrid," Allbright said. "The new government has adopted a policy of isolationism. If it comes down to it they will turn the UN down cold."

"Only four left," Benson said slowly, "and coincidentally one of them has already suffered what we believe is a man-made earthquake."

"You're not thinking this is all tied to the release of Ilic?"

Benson puffed on his cigar before answering. "I don't know, Dick," he said slowly, "but it's what I might do if faced with a similar proposition. If there is no country that will imprison Ilic, then the outcome of the trial is a moot point."

"You know, sir," Allbright said, "that if it came down to it, the U.S. would step in and agree to house him."

"And that is what," Benson said, "we have to avoid at all costs. Along with the radical Muslim terrorists threatening our citizens, the last thing we need to add is a group of crazed Serbian radicals."

"Looking at it that way," Allbright said, "the stakes are much higher than we anticipated."

"Under every rock there's mud," Benson said.

"You're going to need to brief the president, sir."

"Prepare the briefing, Dick," Benson said, "and pray that Taft recovers this device."

Allbright rose from his chair. "How soon will you need the briefing?"

"The most I can stall is seventy-two hours."

"I'll start to work on it immediately," Allbright said, exiting.

Once Allbright had left, Benson sat back in his chair and puffed on his cigar. It was like the world was becoming infested with gophers. Just when you think you have killed them all off, more pop up out of the ground.

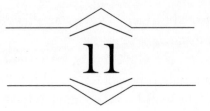

11

GALADIN RATZOVIK STARED at the ledgers showing the secret bank accounts he controlled.

A knock sounded on his office door, and Ratzovik yelled for the party to enter. "Word is Radko Bucdl is looking for you, sir. What should I do?"

Ratzovik swallowed hard. Having Bucdl seeking him was a bad sign. Ilic only called out Bucdl when a point was to be made—a point that usually entailed a knife, ice pick, or other sharp instrument.

"Bucdl doesn't know where we are hiding, correct?"

"No, sir," the aide said. "Since we moved you here after the last operation, no one outside our circle is privy to our location."

The aide was still standing in front of Ratzovik's desk.

"Double the guards and assign one of our men to track Bucdl's movements."

"That won't be easy, sir," the aide noted. "No one will want the assignment."

Ratzovik nodded slowly. "Then you do it."

The aide looked like he was ready to argue the order, but he stopped himself. "As you wish, sir," he said finally. "Should I report by telephone?"

"Yes," Ratzovik said. "And don't let him catch on you're around."

"Sir," the aide said, "could you tell me how long until we're finished?"

Ratzovik glanced at his face in a small mirror on his desk, then glanced at the ledger showing the bank balances. "Not long now, I hope."

"But—" the aide began to say.

"That's all!" Ratzovik said loudly. "Just find Bucdl and stake him out."

The aide nodded and started to retreat from the office. Once at the door he turned around. "Sir," he said, "there is one more thing."

"What?"

The aide explained about the fire at the Tesla Museum.

Ratzovik motioned the aide out, then quickly reached for the telephone.


DRESSED IN AN all-black suit that hung on his frame like clothes on a scarecrow, Zarko Bodonavik stared at the stacks of files taken from the museum.

"You and these men," he said to the sergeant in charge, pointing at the half-dozen guards inside the room, "are the only people who know this location?"

The sergeant nodded. "As per your instructions, sir," the sergeant said, "the operation was kept off the books."

Bodonavik nodded then walked over to a painting on the wall. Flipping the painting away from the wall on hinges, he revealed the dial for a safe. Shielding the numbers with his left hand, he spun the dial around until the safe opened; then he removed a stack of currency from inside. Closing the door to the safe, he folded the painting back in place, then broke the paper strap on the bills. Dividing the bills up, giving the sergeant the largest cut, he handed stacks to each man.

"I will call your commander and explain I need you all for a period of two more weeks," Bodonavik said. "You will be taken off the active-duty roster until then. I want each of you to take this money and go on a short vacation. If you have a family, I want you to call them and tell them that you will be away for a couple of weeks. Buy civilian clothes, then go to a hotel or resort outside of Belgrade and remain there."

Reaching in his pocket, he removed a stack of business cards.

"There is a number on this card. Once you've found a hotel, call and report your location. Do not tell anyone what you did here today. Any questions?"

The room was silent.

"Do what I ask," Bodonavik said quietly, "and when you're back at your unit you will receive a jump in pay and grade. That is all."

The soldiers began placing the bills and the card in their wallet. Then they slowly filed out of the room. Bodonavik stared at the files for a second, then walked over and poured himself a cup of coffee. Then he called the Serbian president.


RATZOVIK MADE A dozen calls but was not able to locate the Tesla files. His well-laid plan was beginning to unravel, and he could feel it. The walls were closing in—only days, perhaps a week, away from victory.

Ratzovik sat back and thought for a few moments. Suddenly an idea came into his head. It was dangerous and would attract attention—something he had wished to avoid. If it worked, however, it would buy him time with Ilic as well as divert attention from his primary objective. The more Ratzovik thought about it, the more he liked it.


IN THE BARN in southern Serbia, Vojislav Pestic was smiling. Tesla had been smart hiding his true equations in reverse images. But for a chance glance at the paper in the chrome toolbox, Pestic would have missed his opportunity entirely.

Now he just had to figure out the last few adjustments and he'd be home free. His first order of business was to ensure the safety of his family; then he would do what Ratzovik wanted. Time to make a deal.

Pestic walked over to a barn window and slid it up. The guard standing nearby jumped. "Call your boss," Pestic said. "I need to speak to him."

Pestic waited while the guard phoned Ratzovik. Once they were connected, the guard handed him the receiver. "How is my request to view the files progressing?" Pestic first asked Ratzovik.

"I'm still working on it," Ratzovik lied.

Pestic sensed tension. "Is there a problem?"

"There was a fire at the museum," Ratzovik admitted. "The files have been moved. We're trying to locate them now. We should know something soon."

It was as if the clouds had parted and a rainbow had appeared. Pestic was suddenly holding all the cards, and he knew this. With access to the files shut off—even if Ratzovik found another scientist—there was no way anyone would have time to perfect use of the device. The chance of someone else discovering the reverse image was little to none.

"I might be able to make this work," Pestic said slowly, "without examining the files. There is just one problem. I want my wife and son brought here. In addition, I want an iron-clad guarantee of our safety if we are successful."

Ratzovik realized he had his back in a corner. There was no time now to replace Pestic. Either he made the device work or the entire plan was doomed. "If I agree to your demands," Ratzovik said angrily, "how do I know you can pull this off?"

"Later today I'll perform another test," Pestic said, "target number two. As we discussed, that's the farthest we can go without blacking out most of eastern Europe and perhaps damaging the grid. If that test works, I want my family brought here and your personal guarantee we can all walk out of here alive."

Ratzovik thought for a second. "You have my word."

"Sorry," Pestic said, "but your word is not good enough."

"What do you want?"

"A signed confession from you that you orchestrated these events," Pestic said. "Take it or leave it."

The line was silent for a moment. "Call me after the test," Ratzovik said at last, "and we'll discuss your demands."

The phone went dead. Pestic walked over to the device and made an adjustment.


TAFT AWOKE TO the smell of fresh coffee and baked goods.

Reaching his arm across the bed, he felt the space next to him was cold. Without bothering to dress, he walked out toward the kitchen.

"Why are you still here?"

"I called down to the museum and asked them to cover for me until lunch," Nadia said, "since I was up most of the night dealing with the fire aftermath."

"Good." Taft smiled stumbling past the table and into the bathroom, where he relieved himself. Walking back out, he poured a cup of coffee.

"What's that scar on your shoulder from?"

"Gunshot wound," Taft said, "from a Chinese agent."

"What happened to him?" Nadia asked.

"My partner head-shot him," Taft said, leaning against the counter.

Nadia stared at Taft. His naked body showed the ravages of a dangerous life.

Taft stared at Nadia. She looked resplendent with her black hair spilling down onto the shoulders of her red silk robe. "My brother called," Nadia said. "He'll be over around lunchtime to collect you."

Taft stared at the clock on the stove. "That is almost two hours," he said easily. "I wonder how we should kill the time."

"I have an idea," Nadia said, unfastening the sash on her robe and sliding it open.

"I'll second that," Taft said, rising to the occasion.


IT WAS 9:30 A.M. in Palencia, Spain, when Felipe Garza strolled along the Pisuerga River. Garza was seventy-two and long retired. His primary exercise was his morning walk. Nodding to the shopkeepers he passed, Garza was lost in his thoughts. His hometown had a long history: It had been occupied by the Romans, and plundered by the Visigoths in the sixth century.

The main industries were iron foundries and textiles, with a smattering of chemical plants and high-tech manufacturing. Nearing the edge of town, Garza paused to watch a plume of dust from a nearby hill as a giant mining truck drove up a switchback road leading into the entrance of a mine. The truck slowed to await a radio call from inside to enter. Once another truck was clear, he could drive inside.

Garza stopped, sat down on a bench, and took in the view of the hills nearby.


PESTIC CHECKED THE settings one last time, then flipped the switch that allowed the electricity to flow off the grid into the device. The bolts of lightning began to arc from coil to coil. Then they fused into a thick blue-and-white bolt that coursed back and forth like a snake being teased.

Then the bolt headed straight down and into the earth.


INSIDE THE MINE near Palencia, a giant rotary drilling machine was boring through the soil at eight feet per second. As the spoil from the digging flowed out the rear of the machine it was deposited on conveyor belts that carried it to an area cleared out underground, where it was loaded onto waiting trucks.

Then, in an instant, the ground began to violently shake. The drilling machine ground to a stop and started to turn a bright cherry red. Bolts of lightning traveled up the shaft and burst from the opening just as the walls of the mine began to collapse around those left inside. The violent cataclysm continued for nearly a full minute.

Garza heard the noise and glanced up as the lighting receded back toward where the mine opening once was located. He watched as rocks began to tumble down the hillside, and he felt the earth shaking at his feet. Once the quake began to slow, he rose on unsteady feet and started toward town again.

• • •

PESTIC MADE SURE the power lever was locked back to off, then clipped a padlock over the clasp. Carefully examining the device from a few feet away, he waited for a few moments, then removed his welding goggles and looked again. The coils looked none the worse for wear. Then he logged onto a computer in the barn and tried to establish if the test had been successful.

IN GOLDEN, COLORADO, a technician stared at the graph on his computer. "We have a 5.8 in central Spain!" he shouted. "Aftershocks continuing!"

A second technician called the head of the laboratory to report the incident.

As he had been instructed, he telephoned the NIA.

FELIPE GARZA WALKED as fast as he could to the main police station to report what he had seen, but when he arrived, the station was in chaos. The earthquake had caused widespread damage among the old buildings of Palencia. By the time Garza could report what he had witnessed, the driver of the mining truck waiting to enter the mine had reached his office on his cell phone.

Rescue efforts for those trapped inside began at once, but it would be days before the rescuers would dig their way down to the boring machine, and days more before anyone pieced together what had happened.

WITH INFORMATION ON computers so readily available, Ratzovik could track the test almost as it happened. After he followed the event and the aftermath for close to an hour, he reached for the telephone and dialed Pestic's guard.

"Looks like it worked," Ratzovik said when Pestic came on the line.

"I saw that," Pestic noted. "I'm following it on the computer."

"Do you now think you can reach the objective?"

"It would help if you could find me those files," Pestic said. "Just to be sure."

"I'll do what I can."

"With or without, it's like I explained at the start," Pestic said. "I'll need a receiving unit buried deep. And I'll need you to agree to our deal first."

Ratzovik paused. "I'll agree to both."

"Then the next time I fire this up," Pestic said, "the lights should go dark."

## 12

MARTINEZ READ THE initial findings from the scientists tasked with analyzing the documents from Colorado. The first overview was not encouraging. From what the scientist had been able to glean, the Colorado experiments centered only on the wireless underground transmission of power. Earthquakes or death rays were not mentioned at all.

Suddenly his fax began printing, and he rolled his chair over and glanced at the sender.

The fax was from the earthquake center in Golden, Colorado. Waiting while it printed, he stared again at his notes. Each quake was stronger and farther from their estimated source, but other than that, he had little. The last power surge had blown a transformer in Albania, but other than that did only minor damage to the rest of the grid. In Hungary they had been reports of a series of high-tension wires glowing red as too much power transferred over the line. Austria reported flickering lights for a brief time.

"You told me to warn you when you had half an hour," Martinez's executive assistant said over the intercom.

Martinez thanked her and removed the first page of the fax. Before he could read the document, his direct line rang.

"Martinez."

"This is Driggs," a voice said.

"Yes, Mr. Driggs," Martinez answered.

"You can call me Malcolm. Everyone else does."

"What can I do for you?" Martinez asked.

"The incident in Spain?" Driggs asked. "Do you think it was tied to your situation?"

Martinez pondered how to answer. Driggs was a civilian—but he already knew some. "We think it might," he answered at last.

"Thanks," Driggs said. "If I work anything out, I'll call you back. I'm heading back to my house in Arizona if you need to reach me."

The phone went dead. Martinez pondered this for a moment, but his scheduled meeting with Benson and Allbright was drawing near, and he shut the call out of his mind for now. Martinez spent the next twenty minutes assembling his file; then he headed upstairs for his meeting. He had nothing—and he knew this.

"Afternoon, Mrs. M," he said to Benson's longtime assistant Mrs. Mindio.

"Hi, Larry," she said sweetly. "How's John?"

"He's overseas," Martinez admitted.

"The big dogs are inside already," Mrs. Mindio noted. "Let me buzz them and you can go inside."

Using the intercom, she reported Martinez's arrival, then motioned for the door. "Good luck," she said as Martinez started for the door.

Martinez nodded, opened the door, and entered.

Allbright and Benson were clustered around the desk, which had papers and maps filling most of the space. Cigar smoke made a blue haze in the room. They both turned as he entered.

"You need water or a Coke or something?" Benson asked.

"No," Martinez said. "I'm fine."

"Sit down then," Benson ordered, "and tell us what you have."

Martinez slid into the chair next to Allbright and opened his file. "The Spain event appears to be tied to the Tesla device. The earthquake center reports the area is a low-fault, low-risk area for natural occurrences. We have a few reports from other areas in Europe that suffered minor damage from the power drain, but other than that, the grid withstood the surge intact. There is no way to know what another event might do, however."

"What's the status with Taft?" Allbright asked.

"I reported Spain to him a little over an hour ago," Martinez said. "He recommended that he and the BIA agent assisting him start to search the countryside. I ordered him to hold off for now—until after this meeting."

"What's the status of the phony files?" Benson asked.

"They were moved to the apartment of the special assistant to the president of Serbia," Martinez reported, "a man named Zarko Bodonavik. They have not moved since."

"So if Bodonavik is not in on this," Allbright noted, "the people behind this have no idea where the flies are currently located."

"That seems a reasonable assumption," Martinez admitted.

"So bugging them is doing us no good," Benson said.

"But Taft did recover the originals," Martinez said in defense of his partner.

"That helps us in the event our scientists might be able to decipher the construction or intentions of the device," Allbright noted, "but our more immediate problem is the location and dismantling of the threat."

The room was quiet for a moment. Benson puffed on his cigar, while Allbright sipped from a large mug of coffee.

"We need to somehow leak the location of the files to the parties that have the device," Benson said at last, "to try and bring the wolves to the trap."

"Sine we don't know who that is, sir," Allbright noted, "how do you suggest we go about that?"

"The BIA," Benson said, "is a sieve. The group behind this must have someone inside. There are more overlapping loyalties in that organization than a congressman and a special-interest group."

"You want Taft to have his BIA partner do the leak?" Martinez asked.

"Have him figure out a way," Benson agreed.

Martinez made a note on his pad.

"What else do you have?" Benson asked.

"I received a call from the author I met in Colorado," Martinez admitted. "He inquired about Spain, and I went ahead and told him it might be tied to Tesla."

"Amateur help," Allbright said. "That's all we need."

"If this was a shipwreck," Benson concurred, "he might have value. But this is a whole different matter."

"Another brain can't hurt," Martinez said, "and he does know history."

The room was silent again.

"My call," Allbright said finally, "is that whoever is behind this will soon tip their hand. Whatever their motives, they should soon appear."

"Let's hope they do," Benson said, "because day after day tomorrow at 9:00 A.M. the president is going to want answers. Right now we've got nothing to give him."

"I'll call Taft and order the leak," Martinez said. "Our agent in Belgrade can handle the tracking if the leak works. I think Taft and the BIA agent should search southern Serbia, where we think this all originates."

"Taft will do what he wants anyway," Benson noted, "which brings up the question of his retirement. What's going on there?"

"I think he just tired and disillusioned," Martinez admitted.

"He's serious about this?" Allbright asked

"Seems to be," Martinez admitted.

"I'll handle Taft," Benson said. "You go order the leak."

Martinez gathered the file and exited the office. Once he was gone, Allbright spoke.

"Waiting for these mooks to move is like waiting for the guillotine to drop with our heads facing up."

Benson nodded slowly. There was little else he could do.


AT THE SAME time the meeting was taking place in Benson's office, Ratzovik was finalizing his latest plan. He was now fairly certain the ex-commander would buy his explanation wholesale. What Ratzovik had done required funds; surely Ilic would see that. Only an idiot would doubt the value of what he was doing.

If all went according to his plans, Ratzovik would soon be out of Serbia.

Finishing the document on his computer, Ratzovik printed it out and did a quick proofread. It was brilliant. After making a few copies, he slid them in envelopes, then shouted for an aide just outside the door.

"Take this to Ilic's Belgrade lawyer," Ratzovik said to the aide. "The address is on the card clipped to the envelope. Send in another man as you leave."

The aide headed out the door, and a few minutes later another man entered. "Call the man we have tracking Bucdl at this number," Ratzovik said, handing the man a slip of paper with a number written down, "then deliver him this envelope and tell him to give it to Bucdl immediately."

The aide took the papers and filed out.

Now Ratzovik just needed to wait for approval.

He had no doubt it would be forthcoming.


"CAN YOU LEAK it?" Taft asked Zoran as they walked through a park in Belgrade, "and make it appear you did not?"

"Standard stuff," Zoran said. "I'll just include it in my daily reports. They're due within the hour. If they have someone inside the BIA, that's the first place they will seek information."

"Do you fax or e-mail your reports?" Taft asked.

"E-mail usually."

"Send it to everyone on your list," Taft ordered, "then follow up a few minutes later, explaining your mistake and asking all those who received it in error to immediately delete the message. That raises the chances it goes to the double agent."

"What else?" Zoran asked.

"After that is done I want you to go home for a while," Taft said. "I have to meet Mather and discuss some business. As soon as the sun sets, I'll come over and pick you up. We're going to need to leave Belgrade for a time."

"How long should I tell my wife to expect?"

"One day, two," Taft said. "There is no way to predict."

"I understand," Zoran said.

Zoran started to walk away before Taft stopped him. "One more thing," Taft said. "Bring as many weapons as you feel comfortable carrying."

"So you expect trouble?"

"Trouble seems to expect me," Taft said as he turned and walked away.


IN THE NETHERLANDS, Radko Ilic read over the fax his lawyer in Belgrade had sent to his lawyer in The Hague, then handed it back.

"Make sure this is shredded immediately," he said, smiling.

"And your answer?"

"A most definite yes," Ilic said breezily. "Make sure we call off Bucdl immediately—I should never have doubted Ratzovik to begin with. All this time he's been making these arrangements—and I thought he was just after my money."

"Should I include an apology?" the lawyer asked.

"Absolutely," Ilic said.

"What else do you need done?"

"Have my tailor make me three new suits," Ilic said, smiling. "I want to look my best when the time comes."

The lawyer made a note on a pad of paper. "I did not read the message," the lawyer noted. "Would you like me to?"

"No," Ilic said quickly. "It's better you don't know."


TAFT WAS SITTING inside Mather's office. Mather was behind his desk.

"Zoran is sending out the leak now," Taft said, "so be ready to start surveillance as soon as I leave."

"The satellites can follow the movement," Mather said. "What would you like me to accomplish?"

"If the files are taken," Taft said, "we'll need photographs of the participants. In addition, if we have a glitch or sunspots that render the satellites ineffective, I don't want these files to disappear."

"Got it," Mather said.

"Stay out of harm's way," Taft said. "I'm not sure where I'll be or how fast I can respond if you run into trouble. Now swallow this."

Taft handed Mather a tiny plastic orb. Mather took it and stared at it for a second.

"It's a locator," Taft said. "Brand-new stuff. We're the only NIA agents in Serbia, so it will take some time to call in the cavalry if you are captured. I want to be able to find you fast if things go bad."

"How will you know I'm in trouble?"

"As soon as anything happens, hit the signal built into your watch."

"What if I can diffuse the situation myself?"

"Then signal again," Taft said.

"Anything starts, I signal?"

"Yep," Taft said. "But if we don't receive a follow-up within the hour, I'll come for you with both barrels blazing."

"What else?"

"If it comes to that," Taft said, "try and reach the floor—I tend to shoot first and ask questions later."

"I don't find that very reassuring," Mather said lightly.

"But it's the truth," Taft said, rising.


IT WAS NEAR the end of the workday when the e-mail ran through the system at BIA headquarters. The mole was reading it when his computer chimed that another message had arrived. Opening it, he read the mistake message, then printed the first and deleted the first and second.

Zoran's daily report was but a few paragraphs long. One sentence caught the mole's eye. Folding the paper in fourths, he slid it into his back pocket, then waited for his shift relief to arrive. As soon as the shift change was completed, the mole left his office, then made his way to a deserted pay phone.

"This one will cost you," the mole said when Ratzovik answered.

"How much?"

"Ten thousand Euros," the mole said. "No negotiation."

"What have you got?"

"Those files you were asking about," the mole said, "I think I have the location."

"Think?"

"If it proves wrong," the mole said, "I'll refund the fee."

"Well then," Ratzovik said easily, "we have a deal."

"Have your man meet me in the bar of the Metropol Hotel," the mole said. "We'll make the switch there."

"One hour?"

"I'll be there," the mole said.

The telephone went dead, and Ratzovik sat back in his chair. Things are suddenly looking up, he thought as he stared in the mirror. Removing a stack of Euros from his wall safe, Ratzovik summoned an aide and sent him on his way. He was just finishing that task when his telephone rang again.

"The commander wishes to thank you," the slick voice belonging to a lawyer said, "and apologizes for any doubts he might have had."

Ratzovik smiled. Today was coming up roses.

"So he liked my proposal?"

"Could not agree more with your plan."

"He'd like to have me meet with you," the lawyer said smoothly, "just to confirm you're all right. It has been some time since anyone in our group has laid eyes on you."

"With the War Crimes Tribunal still seeking my arrest," Ratzovik said, "I thought it best to go underground."

"But in the past," the lawyer said breezily, "we always knew where to find you."

Ratzovik thought for a moment before answering. "Tell the commander that with me starting to initiate the plan, I feel it is even more important that I remain safe and secure. Once this is all over, I'd be glad to meet with whoever he dictates I should."

"I'll tell him," the lawyer said.

"I'm preparing the demands now," Ratzovik said. "They should be ready to deliver sometime tomorrow."

"I'll notify the commander."

Ratzovik placed the receiver back in the cradle and sat back once again.

Then he chuckled to himself. It would not be long now.

## 13

THE COURIER HAND-CARRIED the document package from Belgrade to Rome. From Rome the courier flew directly to New York City. Arriving in early evening, he secured a hotel room, where he remained until morning. At 9:00 A.M. he delivered the packet, addressed to the secretary-general, to the front desk of the United Nations.

Catching the first flight east, the courier was in Amsterdam before the packet had been cleared through the extensive security screenings. It was late afternoon before the package landed on the desk of one of the many screeners employed by the secretary-general. Once the papers were read, they quickly traveled up the chain of command.

At 4:48 P.M. the secretary-general had them in his hands.

"Retrieve the films of the front desk," he ordered the head of security, "and determine who delivered these."

"Right away," the man said, leaving the office.

The aide to the secretary-general watched as the security chief left. Then he motioned to the package. "What is it, sir?"

The secretary-general slid the stack of papers across the desk.

"Good God," the aide said when he had finished.

"The worst of situations," the secretary-general agreed. "Compliance or destruction."

"We can't negotiate," the aide blurted out.

"Then what do we do, nothing?" the secretary-general said quickly. "The country threatened needs to be notified—and I can assure you they will not be willing to be sitting ducks for a cause most were not behind to begin with."

The aide stared at the documents again. Moving aside the sheets containing Richter scale graphs, he stared at the primary documents. The critical one read:

RELEASE RADKO ILIC
FROM ILLEGAL IMPRISONMENT NOW.

The enclosed graphs show evidence of our power. So far we have been gracious in our use of our weapon, but that will soon end. The Netherlands is our next target.

THE DESTRUCTION OF THIS COUNTRY IS IMMINENT.

Allow Commander Ilic to return to Serbia now and cancel all Serbian war crimes warrants or we will strike within seventy-two hours. These alleged crimes are an internal matter that shall be decided in the Serbian court, not the world court. The United Nations' actions over the past several years constitute an illegal act against the sovereign nation of Serbia and will no longer be tolerated. We hereby give notice that the continued detention of Commander Ilic constitutes an act of war against Serbia and will be dealt with as such. Do not think of transferring Mr. Ilic out of The Netherlands. Any country that offers to house Mr. Ilic will be targeted as well.

RELEASE RADKO ILIC
FROM ILLEGAL IMPRISONMENT NOW.

The aide stared at the document.

"Have the ambassador from The Netherlands come to my office as soon as possible," the secretary-general said into his intercom.

"One moment, sir," the receptionist said.

A few minutes later, just as the security chief was returning with discs from the front-desk camera, she buzzed.

"Mr. Secretary-General," the receptionist said, "he has gone home for the day. I telephoned his home but there was no answer."

"I understand," the secretary-general answered.

Turning to the security chief, he said, "Find me the ambassador from The Netherlands immediately. Then bring him here."

"What should I tell him?"

"Tell him we have a situation."

The security chief left the office once again.

"Next find me the ambassador from Serbia," the secretary-general ordered his receptionist.

The Serbian ambassador was still in his office and arrived at the secretary-general's office within minutes.

Quickly reading the documents, he sat them back on the desk. "I have no idea who is behind this," he said easily, "but they do appear serious."

"You are saying your government has nothing to do with this?" the secretary-general asked.

"If we did," the ambassador noted, "don't you think I would have delivered this packet myself?"

The secretary-general stared at the Serbian ambassador. If he was lying, he wasn't tipping his hand. "Could you please be available if we need to reach you?"

"Your office has my mobile number," the ambassador said. "Is that all?"

The secretary-general nodded, and the Serbian ambassador left.

"Call the members of the Security Council," he ordered the receptionist, "for an emergency meeting at 8:00 P.M."

TWENTY-FIVE MINUTES LATER the UN security chief was knocking on the door of a room at the Plaza Hotel in Manhattan. The door was answered by a blond-haired woman with Dresden blue eyes. A flight attendant with KLM Airlines, she was dressed in a robe and had a ten-dollar bill in her hand.

"I'll take—" she started to say.

But instead of the room service waiter, a man with a badge was at the door.

"I'm with the UN security detail," the man said. "I need to see the ambassador immediately."

The woman started to make a denial, but before she could finish, the ambassador came up behind her. "It's okay," he said.

"The secretary-general needs to see you immediately," the security chief said. "We have a situation."

The ambassador nodded. "I assume your discretion in this matter—" he started to say.

"Your personal life is no concern of ours, sir," the security chief said. "But we need to leave immediately."

"I'll get dressed," the ambassador said, closing the door.

Two minutes later the ambassador was riding down the elevator with the security chief. A black Lincoln Town Car was sitting just outside the front door, with the engine running and a driver behind the wheel.

"This way, sir," the security chief said, opening the door and helping the ambassador inside. Climbing in front with the driver, the security chief motioned to leave.

With the red lights behind the grille flashing, the Lincoln raced toward the UN.


THE UNITED NATIONS General Assembly Building is austere and modern from the outside, sleek and sweeping inside. The main chamber, where the General Assembly meets, looks like it was modeled after some Hollywood set designer's idea of what the future will look like.

The smaller meeting rooms are not much different.

The rooms are half-round in design and face a full screen hooked to audiovisual equipment. The seats are clustered around three different levels, with five stations each. In front of the participants are smaller screens that display the image on the main screen as well as a keyboard used for note-taking or voting.

Twenty minutes before 8:00 P.M. everyone was already in place.

The secretary-general approached a podium just off to the side of the massive screen and turned on the microphone. "If it is okay with everyone," he said, "since we are all here—I'd like to begin early."

As there were no objections, he continued. Motioning for the ultimatum to be displayed on the screen, he spoke again. "This was received this morning at the front-desk station. After security screenings it reached my aide late this afternoon."

The secretary-general waited as everyone read through the document. "The following pages will be displayed one at a time. They are graphs showing earthquakes this group claims to have initiated. In addition to the Security Council members here, I have also asked the ambassador of The Netherlands to join us, as it is his country facing the threat."

The secretary-general motioned to the ambassador, who was seated off to the side of the screen. The screen changed to a graph of the Spanish earthquake.

"Judging by the evidence sent in the package, we believe this threat to be valid," the secretary-general noted. "Let's begin the questions."

The ambassador from the United Kingdom lit his lamp. "When do we think the seventy-two-hour deadline will be reached?"

"We must assume the clock began at the time of delivery to the front desk," the secretary-general said, "so just after 9:00 A.M. New York time today."

"Do we have estimates of the possible damage to The Netherlands if another earthquake the size of the one that struck Spain occurs?" the French ambassador asked.

"I'll defer that question to the ambassador from The Netherlands," the secretary-general said, motioning him to approach the podium.

Holding several sheets of paper, the ambassador walked over to the podium. "I have been working with the UN security chief since being notified of the threat," he began, "and we have some limited appraisals.

As most of my country is low-lying and protected by a series of dikes and woven throughout by canals, any underground disturbance would be extremely serious. If the dikes are breeched we anticipate widespread flooding and loss of life from drowning and buildings collapsing. If the earthquake was to create a tsunami wave at a distance offshore, the entire country could be flooded, and depending on the size of the wave, threaten the western edge of Germany and perhaps Belgium. Loss-of-life estimates are difficult to determine. My country's population is nearly seventeen million, with more than a million living each in Amsterdam and Rotterdam and half a million in The Hague. All these cities are near the coast and risk heavy flooding."

"So we are potentially talking about millions dead?" the ambassador to the United States said.

"At the very least," the ambassador from The Netherlands noted.

"What about evacuations?" the Chinese ambassador asked.

"In less than seventy-two hours?" the ambassador from The Netherlands asked. "There is no way. The panic that would ensue would probably cost more lives than it would save."

A map was now being displayed that showed The Netherlands and the series of dikes. A computer simulation showed them being breeched and the sea rushing across the land. Next, the screen split, and another simulation showed a tsunami wave approaching the shoreline, then sweeping across The Netherlands all the way to Essen, Germany.

"Just what exactly is this device," the Russian ambassador asked, "that can create earthquakes at will?"

"We do not know," the secretary-general said, leaning into the microphone next to The Netherlands ambassador.

The United States ambassador lit his light. "May I request a five-minute recess," he asked, "so I might consult with my government?"

"Objections?" the secretary-general asked.

There were none, so the break was granted.

Making his way to a private office, the American ambassador dialed the number for the national security adviser and related the briefing. "Do we know anything about this?" he concluded.

"I'll need to check with the president and call you back."

The break was almost over when the ambassador's telephone rang.

"We've been working on this problem for a little over a week," the national security adviser said. "We believe the device may have been created using plans from the Serbian inventor Nikola Tesla. An agent is in Serbia now attempting to locate and disable the device. As of yet, he has had no luck."

The security adviser gave the ambassador a quick rundown of what had happened.

"So the United States discovered this threat and we notified no one?"

"Until just now," the security adviser said, "we were unsure of the intended use. No threats had been received, and the intended use of the device was still in question."

"But it was serious enough for us to dispatch an agent to destroy or recover the device?" the ambassador noted.

"It was an unknown," the security adviser said, "we wanted to make known."

"Can I report what you have just told me?"

"The president has okayed that," the national security adviser agreed.

The rest of the members were already seated when the U.S. ambassador entered the room. Making his way to his seat, he glanced around. The other members were waiting to hear what he had learned. He didn't even bother to signal with his light.

"Approximately one week ago," the ambassador started, "the United States began to learn that there might be a device that had been constructed using plans from the Serbian inventor Nikola Tesla. At first we believed we were just dealing with a threat to the European power grid and that the person or persons experimenting could be quickly located and the device disabled. Only after the mining disaster in Spain did we begin to put together the more wide-ranging possible danger to the world. Even then, my country had no clear picture of the intentions of the parties controlling the device—it might have been one of many things, and all of them were still unknown."

"So until my country was threatened," the ambassador to The Netherlands said, "you were doing nothing?"

"No," the ambassador from the United States said, "we dispatched an agent to recover or disable the device. As yet he has been unsuccessful."

"I can see how this could happen," the ambassador to the United Kingdom said, "and there is no use laying blame on anyone. Had any of the other countries here been faced with the same problem, chances are they would have reacted in a similar fashion. Our problem now is more immediate than the blame game. Do we back down and release Ilic or not?"

"I think my country has a say in that," the ambassador to The Netherlands said.

"This is a Security Council decision," the secretary-general said quickly. "The Netherlands is not a voting member."

"I'd like to consult with my government," the ambassador said. "Whatever the outcome, my country is the one in danger."

The secretary-general nodded, and the ambassador left.

"We back down and agree to the terms," one of the most recent appointees, the ambassador from Morocco, said, "and the entire power of the World Court becomes questionable."

The debate went back and forth for the next hour.

In a small office down the hall, the ambassador to The Netherlands was holding a conference call with his country's prime minister and queen. Almost from the start, the outcome had been determined. The risk to the population of The Netherlands was simply too great.

"We risk the chance of losing the World Court," the queen said finally, "but my first cause is to my people."

"Then," the prime minister said, "this is your decision?"

"We will return Mr. Ilic to Serbia," the queen said calmly, "or at least try to do that. Notify the appropriate parties we will comply, Mr. Ambassador. And do this as soon as possible."

"And what if the Security Council votes otherwise, Your Majesty?" the ambassador asked.

"Do not disclose out decision to them at this time," the queen noted. "This is an internal matter. When you return to the chamber merely stress how dangerous the threat is, and how your government wishes to comply with their decision but fears the attack. Then merely sit back, listen, and report back to us periodically. It will be at least tomorrow after-noon before the UN Security Council passes any resolution."

"And by then?" the prime minister said. "We shall have freed him?"

"Start making the arrangements," the queen said, "but wait until I so order."

The ambassador from The Netherlands made his way back to the Security Council chamber. He approached the podium.

"I have been in consultation with my country's officials," he said. "They are very concerned by this threat and ask that any and all mea-sures be taken to protest The Netherlands and its citizens."

The statement was standard diplomatic boilerplate, and the entire room knew this. Whatever had been decided, or not, would for now re-main secret. The ambassador from the United States took leave to use his telephone. When the national security adviser answered, the ambas-sador did not mince words.

"I think The Netherlands is going to cave," he said.

"We expected as much," the national security adviser said. "There is not much else they can do."

"What if the same threat was received by the United States?" the ambassador asked.

"Chances are we would do the same thing," the national security adviser noted.

"Would we?"

"Why not?" he answered. "We could always take care of Ilic later."

14

TAFT AND ZORAN drove south on the road leading from Belgrade through Montenegro. They would enter Kosovo, stay the night in Peja, and then continue on to Prizen at first light. Mather had procured them an old Nissan truck with a plywood shell over the cargo area. Crates of whiskey stuffed with straw were stacked inside. Their weapons and auxiliary equipment were at the bottom of the crates.

"Think we'll make it through the checkpoint?" Taft said quietly.

Zoran turned to glance across the cab of the truck. "If the checkpoint is manned by UN troops that are European, a few bottles and some well-placed bribes should get us in. If they are American, you can use your badge."

Taft nodded and steered around an old Russian truck stacked high with hay.

"What don't you give me the short course on your country as we drive," he asked, "since the dismantling of the Soviet bloc. I know most of the details, but I think a recap is in order."

"Fair enough," Zoran said as he lit a cigarette. "As you know, Marshal Tito came to power at the end of World War II. He then helped established the Yugoslavian Communist Party and abolished the monarchy. At that time, the republics of Macedonia, Montenegro, and Bosnia-Herzegovina became partially self-governing countries with the greater Yugoslavian Federal Republic. In 1948 Tito and Stalin had a falling out, and the United States offered Yugoslavia aid—which we accepted."

"At that time there were what in Yugoslavia?" Taft said. "Serbia, Slovenia, Croatia, and the countries you already mentioned?"

"Plus Vojvidina, Kosovo, and," Zoran said, "Dalmatia."

"So let's move it up a few years. Tito died in 1980?"

"Exactly," Zoran said taking a puff of his cigarette.

"That smells like burning shoes," Taft said. "The first American base we come to, I'm buying you some real smokes."

"You want one?"

"Quit years ago," Taft said, "except in extreme cases."

"The craving never fully goes away, does it?"

"I guess not."

"So after Tito," Zoran continued, "Yugoslavia was ruled by a rotating selection of presidents, all Communist until 1990, when the Communist Party stepped aside."

"Enter Radko Ilic."

"He really started to establish his power in the late 1980s by espousing a doctrine of a Greater Serbia. This, of course, frightened both Croatia and Slovenia, who, after seeing a vacuum after the fall of the Soviet Union, declared their independence. Ilic sent troops into Slovenia to bring them back into the fold, and this caused the European Community to begin an arms embargo. In 1992 the two countries were recognized as separate, and this caused Bosnia-Herzegovina and Macedonia to seek freedom. Montenegro, which borders the Adriatic Sea between Albania and Bosnia, chose to remain allied with Serbia."

"But what about Kosovo?" Taft asked.

"It's always been considered a province of Serbia by the leaders of

Yugoslavia, but quite frankly, as it is heavily populated by Albanians, it has always been treated like an outcast, and subjected to repression," Zoran said.

"Which led to the creation of the Kosovo Liberation Army in 1996."

"Right," Zoran said. "The KLA was the main force opposing Ilic."

"And there was no way Ilic was going to lose Kosovo after losing the other countries?"

"That's the short answer," Zoran agreed.

"So that brings us to the NATO bombings."

"After brokering a peace settlement that failed and in an effort to stop the widespread ethnic cleansing taking place in Kosovo, NATO bombarded Yugoslavia for seventy-eight days in 1999."

"Which led to the Serbian troops pulling out of Kosovo."

"Correct," Zoran said, tossing the cigarette butt out the window. "Then came the elections of 2000, when Kostunica won the vote but Ilic refused to step down."

"Citizens then surrounded Parliament and took over the state-owned television station, and the next day Russia recognized Kostunica as rightful president. Ilic had no choice then but to step aside."

"So then in April 2000, Ilic is arrested for misappropriating funds."

"Then in June he was extradited to The Netherlands to stand trial for war crimes relating to the entire Kosovo mess."

"What's the situation now?"

"Serbia and Montenegro are united in a union, and Kosovo is a UN protectorate."

Taft sped up and passed an old truck filled with melons; the truck was belching smoke from the tailpipe. "So the Albanians in Kosovo are primarily Muslim and the Serbs Orthodox. Is that the gist?"

"Basically."

"What do you think the future will bring?"

"In the region?" Zoran asked.

"Generally."

"I think Bosnia will continue to be a problem, since Radovan Karadzic, the Bosnia Serb leader, as well as his strong-arm man, Ratko

Mladic, have yet to be captured. The country is fractured internally. If Montenegro ever tries to split from Serbia, that will be trouble. Closer to home, Kosovo is the main threat. The UN will eventually tire of the duties and withdraw. Once they do—if Kosovo is not already a separate country—the entire thing will began anew."

Taft shifted down as they headed up an incline. "So by entering Kosovo, we're heading right into the hornet's nest."

Zoran slowly nodded.

RATZOVIK WAS BECOMING impatient. "Cut to the end," he said forcefully. "How can it be done?"

Ten of Ratzovik's aides were seated around the dining room table in his rented villa. The table was littered with liquor bottles, ashtrays filled with butts, and a few plates with half-eaten sandwiches.

"The units to all sides are occupied," the head of his security detail said. "There is no way to enter the Bodonavik apartment without being detected. Our only way in is through the front door."

"So our only choice is to do a smash and grab?"

"That's about it, boss," the man said. "We break down the door, race inside and snatch the files, then get out as fast as possible."

"What about the amount of files?" Ratzovik asked. "We can't have you running loads to the elevator or down the stairs. You'd be caught before you're halfway through."

"We have that handled," the man said, showing Ratzovik a diagram.

Ratzovik glanced at it and nodded his approval. "You will need to create a diversion—block the streets. As soon as someone calls the police to report and Bodonavik's apartment is mentioned as the location, a police will swarm into the area."

"There is one more problem," the man said, "if you want us to go in tonight. What do you want us to do with Bodonavik."

"Kill him," Ratzovik said coldly. "If any of you are caught stealing from his apartment, you'll be in prison the rest of your life anyway."

Everyone at the table turned and stared at Ratzovik.

"That's all, men," he said, rising. "Retrieve the files after midnight and have them headed south. I want the engineer to have them by to-morrow morning. Time is running short."

The men filed out. They would rest until early evening, then start their preparations.


"I'VE JUST BEEN called to an emergency meeting by the president," Benson said to Martinez, "and we have nothing?"

Seated in front of his desk were Allbright and Martinez. Benson was fastening the shirt of his uniform. He finished and straightened his tie.

"The scientists analyzed the drain on the grid from the Spanish in-cident," Martinez said, "and placed the source farther south than we thought. They think now it may be originating in Kosovo."

"You notified Taft?" Allbright asked.

"Yes, sir," Martinez said. "He was heading to southern Serbia for recon—I telephoned him about an hour ago and reported the new find-ings. He and the BIA agent that is assisting him are making their way to the protectorate as we speak."

"This is unwelcome," Benson said. "Along with the UN troops maintaining order, the largest contingent of other troops comes from Russia."

"Are you worried about the Russians recovering the device?" All-bright asked.

"Hell yes," Benson said, "and the president will be, too."

Just then the intercom buzzed.

"General," Mrs. Mindio said, "your car is downstairs. You'll need to leave now to be on time."

Benson squared his shoulders and started for the door. "You men stay here in the building," he said, stopping at the door. "I'll want to speak to you again when the briefing is completed."

Martinez glanced over at Allbright.

"What do you think will happen?" Martinez asked.

Allbright had spent decades in intelligence. His knowledge of the in-ner workings and agency politics was keen as a knife blade.

"Taft out," he said, "CIA in."

Allbright and Martinez stood and made their way to the door.

"Somehow," Martinez said, "if that happens, I don't think John will be crushed."

"If it does," Allbright said, reaching for the doorknob, "go down that way, I want you to send Taft on a vacation. Tell him to take one of those motorcycles of his for a tour. I want him to think this retirement idea through a little better."

"Sir," Martinez said, "it would be better if you told him that. He never listens to me."


GENERAL BENSON WAS seated on the side across from the president's chair several places to the left. Promptly at 9:00 A.M. the president entered and made his way to his chair.

Once seated he said, "Let's get under way."

First, the national security adviser explained the ransom letter received by the UN.

"Mr. Secretary of State," the president said when the security adviser had concluded, "what's your take?"

The secretary of state was known for his bluntness, and he did not disappoint. "Our read is The Netherlands has no choice but to comply with the demands."

"Thanks for not mincing words," the president said.

Reaching for a silver coffeepot in front of his chair, he poured some coffee into a china cup with a gold rim and the seal of the president of the United States on the side. "So," he said after a sip, "we now have forty-eight hours to recover the device or The Netherlands releases Ilic."

It was a statement, not a question. No one said anything.

"General Benson," the president said next, "what is the status of your agency's actions?

Benson reached for a folder and flipped it open. "The latest scientific analysis pins the source of the power drain farther south than originally estimated. At first we believed far south in Serbia. Now we believe it may be originating from south of the town of Prizren in the area bordered by Macedonia and Albania."

"Map, please," the president said.

On the far end of the conference room a video display flickered to life, and a map of the region was displayed.

"In that boot area?" the president asked.

"It's not definitive," Benson said, "but the analysis includes the area from Prizren south, an area of approximately forty miles in depth by twenty miles at the widest point."

"That at least gives us a workable area," the president noted. "What forces do we have in the area?"

The chairman of the Joint Chiefs of Staff fielded the question. "Mr. President, at present we have contributed just over 4,300 troops and personnel to the approximately 50,000 total force that makes up KFOR. We have another 250 or so in Macedonia."

"Remind me again," the president said, "the makeup of the rest of KFOR?"

"A variety of multinational forces, with the largest contingent from Russia," the chairman answered.

"So in effect we have a possible, more likely probable, weapon of mass destruction that is being used to threaten one of our allies. This weapon is inside the province of a country that has faced internal war for the past decade or so"—the president paused and looked around the table—"and there is a pretty good chance of the Russians grabbing it if they get wind of the entire affair."

"That's the down and dirty," the secretary of state answered.

"General Benson," the president asked, "how many men do you currently have on the ground there?"

"Our agency's liaison in Belgrade and an agent we dispatched from the States," Benson admitted.

"Two men?" the president said, astonished.

"Up until the ransom demand was received," Benson noted, "we were still not entirely sure there was a weapon. The earthquakes might have been coincidences, and there was no motive declared. In effect what we had was an unknown."

"Well," the president said, slightly cross, "we have one now. What the status of your two men?"

"The liaison is remaining in Belgrade. We removed files we believe the participants need to fine-tune the device from where they were being stored in a museum and bugged them with locators. If the files are retrieved we think they could lead us to the source. The U.S. agent is on his way south as we speak, in an attempt to identify the location of the device, disable it, and remove the threat," Benson said.

The president nodded and sat silent for a moment. "Have you kept the director of Central Intelligence appraised of this situation?" he asked Benson.

"He has, sir," the DCI answered, "and we have been formulating alternative plans."

Everyone stared at the president. The chopping block had been cleared, and everyone in the room knew.

"General Benson," the president said firmly, "I'm going to turn over the lead in this to the DCI. They have more men and resources to bring about the outcome we need in the time we have. Have your liaison in Belgrade coordinate with the incoming replacements, and call your agent back here for a debriefing."

"Yes, sir," Benson said quietly.

"Now the rest of you listen up," the president said. "As of right now the recovery or destruction of this device is our top priority. First, we want to protect The Netherlands; second, we do not want this to fall into Russian hands. Is that clear to everyone?"

The people around the table nodded.

"Okay," the president said, "one at a time, we're going to go over what each of your agencies can contribute."

It was twelve minutes past 11:00 A.M. before the meeting adjourned.

# 15

TAFT AND ZORAN were just driving through the outskirts of Rozaje. It was early evening, and they were within half an hour of entering Kosovo Province.

"We need fuel," Taft noted.

"I haven't been down this way in a few years," Zoran said, "but if I remember right, there used to be a station a few miles ahead just as we leave town."

For the past few hours they had traveled through the mountains of Montenegro. The scenery had been impressive. High mountains and gorges filled with fast-flowing rivers, with the architecture becoming more Turkish than the European style seen in Belgrade.

"There's the station," Zoran said, pointing ahead.

Taft was starting to slow down when his secure phone rang. Juggling the shifter and the brakes, he pushed the button and placed it to his ear just as he pulled off onto the gravel parking lot for the filling station.

"Yo," he said.

"Where are you?" Martinez asked.

"Just stopping for fuel," Taft said. "We should be in Kosovo within the hour."

"There is a change in plans."

"I never like to hear that," Taft said, pulling up in front of the pump and shutting off the engine. "What's up?"

"The big boss has placed the DCI in charge," Martinez said. "I'll fill you in on the details later; however, you've been ordered back home for an immediate debriefing."

"What?" Taft said, with his voice rising. "We're just entering the target area."

"I'm sorry, John," Martinez said. "It's politics. I'll fill you in as soon as you return."

Zoran had climbed from the cab and was instructing the attendant to fill the tank.

"So I'm supposed to turn around and drive back to Belgrade? It took us all day to reach here."

"I'll arrange a helicopter out to a KFOR base in Kosovo," Martinez said. "They want you on a fast plane back here. Have Zoran drive back to Belgrade alone. Mather is now liaison with the new team. He'll take care of Zoran."

"Man," Taft said, "I've put this guy's ass on the line. He'd better be taken care of properly."

"I've handled it with Mather," Martinez said. "You just explain the situation and then make your way to a open field nearby."

"We have weapons and operation equipment in the truck," Taft noted. "What should we do with that?"

"Have him drop you off away from prying eyes with the equipment," Martinez said. "We'll helicopter it out with you."

"Son of a bitch, man," Taft said, exasperated. "What happened?"

"I'll explain when you return," Martinez said. "Right now, just do what I say. I just fired up the locator." Martinez was staring at his computer screen. A map of Montenegro was displayed, with Taft's location shown by a flashing red dot. "I've already called in the helicopter for a pickup. They are airborne now. Make your way to a safe spot and await extraction."

The telephone went dead. The attendant had finished filling the tank. Zoran handed him a few bills, then climbed back into the cab. He looked over at Taft and nodded.

"I take it that you received some unwelcome news?"

Taft twisted the key and started the engine. Then he slid the Nissan into gear and pulled away from the pumps. A few seconds later he steered back onto the blacktop.

"I've been ordered home," Taft said flatly. "There is a helicopter on its way for me as we speak. I'm sorry there has been a change in plans."

Zoran was unable to hide the surprise on his face. "What am I supposed to do?"

"Drive the truck back to Belgrade," Taft said. "The agent who gave us the weapons will be your control agent now. He'll contact you on your return with instructions."

Taft caught sight of a dirt road that angled off into a meadow that was surrounded by forest. He slowed and turned off the pavement, then drove into the clearing and shut off the engine and climbed out. Zoran climbed from the passenger seat and watched as Taft opened the door over the cargo area.

"I've been ordered to secure the weapons," he said, as Zoran watched him digging through the crates, "and take them out with me."

"So you're dumping me here," Zoran said, "unarmed and with my ass flapping in the wind? What happened to you taking care of me if I helped the U.S.?"

Taft had moved the weapons into a single crate. He reached in the top and removed a handgun. "Compliments of the U.S. government," he said.

The thumping sound of a helicopter rotor blade was growing louder. A few seconds later, a military Blackhawk appeared over the treetops and set down on the meadow. A pair of marines clutching automatic assault rifles jumped from the open door and raced over to Taft.

"Sir," the first one said as the other kept his weapon trained on Zoran, "you have to come with us."

"Zoran," Taft shouted over the noise from the Blackhawk, "make your way back to Belgrade! Someone will contact you upon your return!"

Taft lifted the crate.

"You made a deal!" Zoran yelled. "You'd allow me and my family to immigrate if I helped you!"

Taft looked directly into Zoran's eyes. "That deal," he said as the marine took him by the arm and started to lead him to the helicopter, "still stands. Don't worry, my friend, I always honor my deals."

With the second marine covering their exit, Taft and the first stowed the crate, then climbed through the side door. The second marine followed them into the interior. With his rifle still pointed out the open door, the Blackhawk lifted off.

As they flew east, Taft watched as Zoran stood next to the Nissan until he disappeared from view. He felt like he had betrayed a friend. The feeling lingered like a bad smell. There had to be a good explanation. But right now Taft was more than mad.

He was livid.


AT THE SAME instant Taft was lifting off the meadow, Malcolm Driggs was in a private plane flying across the Navajo Nation in northern Arizona.

"In a minute or two we'll be over Colorado!" the pilot shouted back to the cabin. "Then about twenty minutes more until we reach Telluride!"

Driggs stared at the manila folder of research he'd been accumulating on Tesla since returning to Arizona earlier. A big piece of the puzzle was missing, and he hoped to find it in the library of his mountain home.

"Sounds good, John," Driggs answered.

"You need anything back there?" the pilot asked.

"No," Driggs said. "I'm good."

Driggs stared out the window at the tops of the mountains. Other than a few pockets above twelve thousand feet, the snow had melted.

High mountain lakes were visible, and he caught sight of a herd of elk bedded down in a meadow. He watched as the plane flew up the valley and over Gunnison, Colorado. Driggs was lost in thought.

AT THE SAME time, in Geneva, Marcus Bernal was preparing to go home for the night. He was sliding his overcoat atop his suit when his private line rang. Walking to the phone, he answered it without sitting down.

"Bernal."

"Eighty more are coming in on a wire," the voice said. "Check to see if they have arrived."

"Hold on," Bernal said, sitting down at his desk.

Turning on his computer again, he waited as it ran through checks; then he entered his password and logged onto the account. The new wire showed as being received only a few minutes before.

"I have it, sir," he said.

"Good," the voice said.

"Same instructions as before?"

"No," the voice said quietly. "Use the entire wire proceeds to short the dollar."

Bernal was staring at the streaming data that ran alongside the account information. The request was not a trade he'd order if this was his own money. In the past few days the dollar had shown strength, not weakness.

"Sir," he said quietly. "I would not recommend that at this time."

"Marcus," the voice said coldly, "I pay you for execution not discussion. At the open of the market tomorrow morning, start shorting as ordered."

"That size order," Bernal said, "might take tomorrow and the next day to place properly."

"Perfect," the voice said.

The telephone went dead, and Bernal sat staring at his computer screen. The size of purchases he had already made for this client should have drawn some attention. Once he started to short the dollar, he was sure someone would notice.

BY 9:00 P.M. East Coast time that same day the new operations center at Langley, Virginia, was in full swing. The assistant to the DCI was heading the 6:00 P.M. to 6:00 A.M. shift.

"This is thirty-six hours into the deadline," he said to his team. "We're at the halfway point. Let's review our status until now."

He pointed to one of the women at the table.

"We have a total of ten Special Forces teams, comprised of six men each, on a U.S. Navy vessel in the Adriatic Sea. In just under an hour they will be transported on Special Operations helicopters across Albania and into southern Kosovo at various locations to begin the search for the device."

"What's the chance of detection?" the assistant DCI asked.

"We're jamming Albanian radar, and the routes are plotted to avoid populated areas. The chance of detection is minimal. Any detection that might occur once inside Kosovo will be explained as the movements of U.S. soldiers assigned to KFOR."

"What if the Russians raise flags?"

"Luckily there are currently no Russian troops assigned to the target area," she replied. "South of Prizren is a no-man's-land. There are isolated pockets of militia loyal to the KLA, but they are clustered village to village. What we have is mainly small farms and a few ranches. The area is hilly and allows our troops ample opportunities to hide."

"Good," the assistant DCI said. "Now what about the method of search?"

An official with the science directorate answered. "We have distributed detailed maps to each team for the specific area they are tasked with searching. These have the power transmission lines clearly marked. As the device needs a feed of electrical energy, any of the countryside void of power lines was excluded. If they systematically search the grids as they are ordered, they should be able to cover the areas just before the deadline. In addition, if the threat is real, we don't believe it has to occur at the exact expiration of the deadline. That might buy us a few more hours on the far end."

"And the Special Forces operatives are trained what to look for?"

"They have photographs and diagrams of the possible device taken from our files on Tesla," the scientist answered.

"Plus," the woman chimed in, "we would have to imagine that the location of the device will be guarded and secured. If they come across a farm with armed men—then it's a pretty good chance that's the location."

"And the orders are to engage any resistance, correct?"

"If a firefight should occur, we have retained two teams of six on the ship in the Adriatic," the woman answered, "to use as support."

"Excellent," the assistant DCI said. "What is the status of the NIA agent?"

"Right now it's 3:00 A.M. London time," another man answered. "He was transported on a military fighter jet to Italy earlier and was then transferred to a B-52 headed back to her base in England. Once there we had him transferred to a U.S. Air Force C-37A, which is also known as a Gulfstream V. He left England just under an hour ago and will arrive back here early morning our time."

"So he will be available for the 9:00 A.M. briefing?"

"Yes, he will," the man answered.

"What about the situation in The Netherlands?"

The assistant to the operations director answered. "Our agents on the ground report witnessing preparations for the release of Ilic progressing. Numerous meetings have taken place at the Royal Palace. In addition, our contact in the Dutch Royal Air Force is reporting the schedule for Falcon 2000EX, which is designated for executive transport, has been cleared until further notice. This, of course, leads us to believe this will be the plane that will fly Ilic to Serbia if it comes to that."

"Good. It sounds like we're progressing nicely," the assistant DCI said. "But now is the time to take it up a notch. At this point the game truly begins—and like all games, there can only be one winner."

• • •

THEY CAME DOWN the street like a pack of wild dogs, lacking subtlety or stealth.

Two black Mercedes sedans to the front and rear of a high-box cargo van. Squealing to a stop in front of Bodonavik's apartment, four men jumped out of the second sedan and raced toward the door, brandishing handguns. Barely slowing to shoot the doorman as they passed, they raced up the stairs to Bodonavik's floor.

As the first team was making their way up the stairs, two men from inside the van raced around to the rear cargo area and opened the door. Each man slid out a section of flat aluminum and raced toward Bodonavik's window. Quickly assembling the sections into one, they hoisted it up to the window for a ramp. They had just gotten the ramp situated when two flashes of light came from inside.

A few seconds later, the window was yanked open.

The four men from the sedan in front of the van walked over to the ramp and waited. A few seconds later the first box came sliding down. Standing in a line leading to the rear of the van, the four men passed the boxes from the ramp to the rear of the truck, where the men who arrived in the van quickly stowed them inside.

Bodonavik was gravely wounded but not dead yet. He lay at the side of his bed, staring underneath at the team shoveling the boxes of files out the window. They were dressed in black with wool hoods disguising their features. Bodonavik drifted in and out of consciousness.

"Six more, then pull the ramp," the leader of the men inside the apartment said.

Far in the distance, the plaintive wail of a siren could just be heard.

Bodonavik struggled to open his eyes. With what little strength he had remaining, he reached for the handgun he had taped under his box spring.

"Go, everybody out!" the leader yelled.

On the ground, the ramp was retracted and dismantled, then shoved in the rear of the van. The four men raced for the first Mercedes and climbed inside, while at the same time the two other men climbed into the van. Both the lead Mercedes and the van started moving as the sirens grew louder. Upstairs the first three men ran through the door and raced to the stairwell. The leader paused for a second to see if Bodonavik was dead.

Bodonavik shot him in his left eye.

Then it was silent. Silent and black.

"I'm going back in," the man in the passenger side of the Mercedes said.

He had just opened his door to race back inside when a flashing light appeared in the Mercedes' rearview mirror.

"Get in," the driver said. "He's on his own."

Before the front-seat passenger could argue or step outside, the driver slammed the Mercedes into drive and stepped on the accelerator. The door slammed shut and the black Mercedes rocketed down the street.

"Now!" the driver shouted as they reached the end of the street.

One of the rear-seat passengers flipped a switch on a timer open. Two charges placed on the power lines on each side of the street exploded. The poles and live wires tumbled down, blocking the road.

# 16

GALADIN RATZOVIK SAT in the study in his rented villa, staring at photographs of dead bodies piled in an open pit. Ratzovik had ordered the village in Kosovo razed, and he personally participated in the machine gun massacre. The photographs, some of hundreds he owned, gave him excitement. Ratzovik enjoyed inflicting pain.

Terrorizing people gave him pleasure.

He loved the feeling of power he felt when people pleaded for their life, loved the sense of destiny he received when he decided their fate. More than once, during the dark days when he led his army against the KLA and the citizens of Kosovo, he had randomly spared a lone person to tell the tale. The feeling of relief mixed with guilt he could see on those people's face gave him sexual excitement.

And the only way he could relive the feelings now was through his photographs.

A psychiatrist would classify Ratzovik as a sadist with delusions of grandeur, but no psychiatrist had ever examined the Serb. His disorder had started at a young age with an abusive father and savage beatings leading to a rift in his personality. By age nine he was abusing and torturing small mammals. By his teen years, already nearly at his full height and weight, he had taken to robbing and beating ethnic shopkeepers. The sadism he displayed once he rose through the ranks of the Serbian Army was merely an extension of an already growing problem.

Ratzovik had never formed close relationships. His sexual dalliances with members of both sexes were always based on control and the other party's submission to his will. But as the years passed, the strange vibes he emitted made most men and women he approached feel vary. Few would have anything to do with him. His sexual tension was relieved by masturbation and an occasional prostitute but, over time, even the whores had learned to avoid him. There was no amount of money worth the savage beatings he'd inflict.

Ratzovik only hoped that after he had reaped his rewards and relocated to another area, he could find a way to have his needs met once again. Somewhere where life was cheap and lives cheaper. Somewhere where bribes could handle the trouble he caused. Somewhere where he could live out his sick fantasies without distraction.

Whatever it took to achieve this was not of his concern.

A knock sounded on his door, and Ratzovik quickly slid the photographs back into a folder and slid them into the top drawer of his desk. "Come in," he said.

It was one of the men he had sent to steal the files. He poked his head through the door warily. His boss's violent outbursts were well known.

"Where's Maladric?" Ratzovik inquired about the leader of the team.

"Sir," the man said quietly, "there was a problem. Mr. Maladric never made it out of the apartment."

"What?" Ratzovik said loudly. "What happened?"

The man stood just inside the open door. He had no desire to enter any farther. "We don't know, sir. We all made it out but him. Then a police car was coming and we needed to leave or we would have all been captured."

"You did not bring back a body?"

Ratzovik had no guilt from one of the men who followed him being killed; he was worried about someone tying Maladric to him.

"No, sir," the man admitted. "We don't know if he was killed or escaped through another exit."

Ratzovik stared at the man with unconcealed fury. "Get out!" he spat.

WRESTED FROM A sound sleep by the ringing telephone, Belgrade's chief of police had quickly dressed in his uniform and made his way over to Bodonavik's apartment. Upon arriving he noticed four police cruisers, two unmarked detectives' cars, and a single sedan lacking identification.

"Whose car is that?" he asked a detective walking out of the lobby.

"BIA, sir," the detective noted. "They are up at the crime scene now."

The police chief nodded, quickly walked through the lobby, and climbed the stairs. Walking down the hallway, he could see the door to other apartments open and the residents being questioned. Peering inside Bodonavik's apartment, he could see half a dozen men at work.

"Who is with BIA?" he asked loudly.

A man dressed in a dark suit was bent down over the bodies. He rose to his full height while at the same time slipping his hands into his pants pockets.

"That's me," the man said.

"Stand back from the bodies," the police chief said loudly, "Belgrade Police is in charge of this investigation. Please wait out in the hall."

The man said nothing. He merely slid past the chief with a glare into his eyes.

"Which one of you is the lead detective?"

A man exited the bathroom of the apartment and walked over. "Detective Pavic," the man said. "I have seniority."

The chief knew Pavic; he had presided at his promotion. "Over here," the chief said, motioning to a corner of the apartment. Behind him a photographer was snapping pictures with a flash camera. Two other men were dusting surfaces for fingerprints. One man was on the floor at the side of the bed, staring underneath. Another was staring out the open window.

"When did BIA arrive?" the chief whispered to Pavic without preamble.

"Just after the second patrol car," Pavic answered. "The men in the first car entered and found the bodies. As soon as the second car arrived, the first team ordered them to call it in. Almost before the radio call had ended, the BIA agent arrived."

"And the officers let him examine the bodies?"

"I just arrived shortly before you," Pavic said. "I guess the patrolmen first on the scene allowed that to happen—the agent probably pulled rank on them. I was just preparing to exclude him when you showed up."

The chief nodded. "So what have we got?"

"The dead are the presidential adviser Zarko Bodonavik and an unidentified male."

"Oh, Christ," the chief muttered.

"Looks like robbery was the motive," the detective said. "A neighbor reported the robbers slid boxes down a ramp that was set up next to the window. Then the boxes were loaded into a truck that sped away."

The chief nodded and motioned for Pavic to follow him over to the corpses.

"If I had to guess," Pavic said, "Bodonavik was shot immediately upon entry, then somehow got to a weapon and shot the other man."

"Set up a command center," the chief said quietly, "and start logging everything you do. Next, I want an ID on the robber ASAP as well as a description of the truck used in the robbery."

"Very good, sir," Pavic noted.

"I'm going to go talk to the BIA agent and see what he knows."

But when the chief walked out into the hall, the BIA agent was nowhere to be found. Like a wisp on the wind, the man had disappeared.


THE UNKNOWN CONDITION of Maladric placed a huge kink in Ratzovik's plan. With just over one full day before his deadline for Ilic's release, Ratzovik was working on borrowed time. If Maladric had been killed, the authorities would soon learn his identity; as an officer under Ratzovik, the Serbian Army had Maladric's fingerprint and dental records. If they learned his identity, they would soon learn his employer for the past few years. Then it would not be just the UN War Crimes Tribunal seeking Ratzovik, but also the entire Serbian presidential apparatus. Until now, most of the Serbs in his country had helped shield Ratzovik from detection. Most citizens considered the matters in Kosovo an internal issue and found the UN intrusion into internal policies unwelcome.

If the people found out he was behind the assassination of the president's adviser, all that would instantly change. Everyone in Serbia would be on the lookout for Ratzovik.

"Come in here!" he shouted to an aide just outside the door.

The man opened the door and entered. "Where are the files?"

"The team managed to make it to the safe garage without detection," the aide answered. "They are there still inside the truck, sir."

"Go there now," Ratzovik ordered, "and prepare to move them again. Once you are there, call me. I'll arrange for a helicopter to take them south."

"Very good, sir," the aide said, leaving.


IN THE COMMAND center at the CIA, the assistant DCI was briefing the DCI at shift change. "The NIA agent made a good move bugging the boxes," the assistant said. "We had movement a few hours ago, but now the files are stationary again."

"Here's the latest, sir," an agent said, handing a sheet of paper to the assistant DCI.

He read it quickly and handed it to the DCI.

"We've been monitoring the radio traffic through any of the Serbian emergency services for the past few hours," the assistant said. "The Belgrade police received a call about shots fired at a residence, and we traced the address. The building was the residence of one Zarko Bodonavik, who is listed as adviser to the Serbian president. Judging by the response—the chief of police was summoned—we believe that Bodonavik was the target of the operation."

"Do we have any agent in Belgrade?" the DCI asked.

"Not yet," the assistant admitted. "They are due on the ground in the next few hours."

"Turkey and Greece?" the DCI asked.

"We diverted them from Turkey, Greece, Rome, and Hungary," the assistant noted. "You ordered the area flooded."

"Good," the DCI said, staring down at his watch. "Listen, I have to prepare for the presidential briefing in a few hours. Do you mind remaining in command until the meeting concludes? I should be back here by ten or ten-thirty at the latest."

"Are you kidding?" the assistant DCI said, smiling, "I live for this stuff."

IT WAS A few minutes past 7:00 A.M. when the plane carrying Taft touched down at Andrews Air Force Base. He walked down the ramp to see Martinez leaning against the rear fender of an NIA sedan. Seeing Taft, Martinez slid over the opened the passenger door. As Taft walked toward the door, Martinez walked around the front of the vehicle, then opened the driver's door. Taft tossed his carry-on bag on the floor, and both men hit their seats at roughly the same time.

Martinez looked over at his partner and grinned. Then he twisted the key, started the engine, and placed the car in drive. Driving down the concrete skirt leading to the hangars, he steered over to a gate built into the chain-link fence and flashed his badge at the guard who opened the door.

"I need food," Taft said as the gate rolled back. "They didn't have shit to eat on the plane, and I'm starved."

Martinez accelerated through the gate. "What," he said, "did you wake up on the wrong side of the bed?"

"Wrong side of the world's more like it," Taft said. "I've been on one plane or another for the past ten hours or so, and I haven't taken a shower in longer than that."

"How's about," Martinez asked, "we head back to the office so you can shower and change and I'll get you some grub from the cafeteria?"

"Oh, boy," Taft said sarcastically, "sounds swell."

"You pissed off they pulled you off?" Martinez asked as he hit the main road outside Andrews and started down the turnpike toward the NIA headquarters.

Taft rolled down the window and spit out a piece of gum he had been chewing.

"Wouldn't you be?" he asked, pushing the button to roll the window up.

Martinez was silent. At times like this it was better to just let Taft stew.

"SIR!" A POLICE medical technician shouted to Pavic.

Pavic walked over.

"We undressed the unknown man," the technician said, reaching down and hosting the limp leg, "and found this on the sole of his foot."

There was a twelve-digit number tattooed lengthwise.

Pavic wrote the number down on his pad.

"You know what that means, sir?" the technician asked.

"Some of the Serbian Army officers did that," Pavic said, "so if they were killed their bodies would be quickly identified. That's his military ID number—it's on the sole of his foot so if he's in a morgue on a slab it will not be missed."

"So we know who this is now," the technician noted.

"Well," Pavic said, "at least soon we will."

Walking out of Bodonavik's apartment, Pavic slid into his car and called the chief with the information. An hour later the number was matched to Maladric. Another forty-five minutes and fingerprint records confirmed his identity.


TAFT AND MARTINEZ had arrived at NIA headquarters and had immediately gone to Taft's office, where they'd retrieved his extra shaving kit. Next they made their way to the locker room in the health center in the building for Taft to shower.

Taft was shaving prior to his shower, while Martinez sat on a bench nearby.

"I'm going to need some clean clothes," Taft noted.

"Looked like there was a fresh suit and shirt in your office," Martinez said.

"Yeah," Taft said, "but no socks and underwear."

"I have clean underwear and socks in my office," Martinez said.

"That ought to work," Taft said. "I'm about eight inches taller than you and outweigh you by forty pounds."

"Beggars can't be choosers," Martinez said.

Taft glanced up into the mirror at Martinez and rolled his eyes.

"Allbright is going to order you on vacation," Martinez said, "and they have been pressuring me about your retirement plans."

Taft bent down and rinsed his face off in the sink, then stood back up and stared at the results. "You got any eyedrops?" he asked. "It looks like I've been on a bender."

"Back in my office," Martinez said.

"Do me a favor," Taft asked. "Bring the bottle back here when you grab those extra skivvies."

"Will do," Martinez said.

Taft spread some toothpaste on his brush and started brushing.

"So what's the deal?" Martinez asked. "A little forced vacation and then maybe a reassessment of your career goals?"

Taft's mouth was full of toothpaste, and his answer was garbled, but the letter *f* seemed to have a prominent place in the utterance.

"I'll be back," Martinez said.

Taft peeled off his clothes and stepped into the shower. He adjusted the temperature to hot and let the water wash away his tensions.

17

TAFT WAS WELL aware that he was simply a prop. The case had been wrested away from his and his agency's control. His only mission now was to fill time as others decided the course of action. After showering he had filled General Benson in on his actions thus far. Now they were riding over to the White House in an NIA staff vehicle.

"There is a good chance that after your questioning they will dismiss you," Benson said from the rear.

Taft was seated in front, next to the driver. "I understand, sir," he said moodily.

"Jim," Benson said to the driver, "if that happens, go ahead and take John back to the office. I'm sure you'll have time to drop him off and then come back before I'm finished. This briefing will probably take a few hours."

"Whatever you say, sir," the driver said as he pulled up to the gate of the White House. The men waited while the underside of the vehicle was scanned for explosives. A few moments later the guard waved them through.

The driver pulled to the far end of the driveway and stopped. Benson and Taft climbed out and started for the door.

"You've been in front of this president before, John," Benson said quietly as they approached the marine guard at the door, "so you know to give it to him straight."

"Yes, sir," Taft said as he stopped and raised his arms for the guard to wave a wand across his body.

When Taft's inspection was finished he took a few steps toward the door to wait while Benson was scanned. Once that was completed, he let Benson pass in front and followed him down the hall to the briefing room.

Just before 9:00 A.M. they were seated and waiting. Taft poured a cup of coffee from the silver pitcher in front of his seat, then glanced over at Benson and raised an eyebrow. Benson shook his head no. A few moments later the president entered the room.

"Okay, people," the president said, making his way to his seat, "we have a lot to do and a short time to get it done. Let's get under way. Who wants to go first?"

The room was quiet. "Mr. President," Benson said a second later, "perhaps the NIA should lead. Mr. Taft, the agent we assigned to Serbia, has returned as ordered. Would you like him to start?"

The president stared over at Taft. "Go ahead," he motioned with his hand. "It's John, right?"

"Yes, Mr. President."

"Let's hear it," the president said.

"A few days ago our agency detected power surges on the European electrical grid we have come to believe were emanating from Serbia. I was assigned to—"

"We have the background, Mr. Taft," the president interrupted. "Just cut to the chase."

"Since we believed this might be tied to technology linked to Serbian inventor Nikola Tesla, my priority was attempting to establish who might have an interest in Tesla's documents. To bring that about, I created a diversion that would ensure that his files and documents would need to be moved while at the same time copying the files with changes to the texts so they could not be utilized again. Then I bugged the fakes to trace their movement."

"We understand that," the president said.

Taft said, "I was awaiting any movements so I decided to make my way to the Serbian province of Kosovo for a field examination. I had just arrived in Kosovo when I was contacted and ordered to return here."

"So prior to your extraction," the president asked, "you were unable to determine who might be behind the surges or the possible location of the device?"

"Correct, sir," Taft said.

"Any clues, anything that might shed some light on this?"

"Would you like conjecture, Mr. President?" Taft asked.

"If that is all you have."

"From what I've learned recently," Taft said, "I'd suspect supporters of Radko Ilic."

The obvious statement was Taft's way of repayment for the extraction. The president did not take the bait. He simply nodded.

"Okay, John," the president said, "thank you for your efforts in this matter. If you have nothing else to add, you may be dismissed."

"Thank you, sir," Taft said, rising and walking to the door, "and good day."

A marine guard opened the door, and Taft walked into the hall.

Three minutes later he climbed back in the NIA sedan. "Home, James," he said.

The driver started the sedan and placed it in gear. "We know each other well enough," the driver said, slowly driving toward the gate, "you can call me Jim."

Taft looked over and loosened his tie. Suddenly the tension of the past few days began to lift. Whatever was going to happen was no longer his responsibility. Bigger forces were now in charge. His part in the proceedings was finished.

"Sounds fair," Taft said easily. "I know you need to return here and wait for Benson. I have a few things to wrap up, then I'm taking some time off."

The driver stopped and waited for the gate to open. "So how did it go in there?" he asked as he drove through the gate.

"About what I expected," Taft said, removing his tie completely and opening the top button of his shirt, "about what I expected."

SIXTEEN MINUTES LATER, Taft was seated in Allbright's office. Taft could sense a pep talk coming, and Allbright did not disappoint.

"John," he began, "you did what you were supposed to do—don't second-guess yourself. Once the ransom demand came through it was a foregone conclusion the case would be expanded and our agency's participation reduced. It's politics—nothing more."

"That's all fine and dandy," Taft said, "but I have a BIA agent over there who stuck his neck out for me. I promised him and his family a safe harbor, and I want to ensure that is handled."

"You have my word," Allbright said, "that the deal stands and I will personally make sure it happens. Right now, however, there is the matter of your state of mind. I'm aware of the filing of your retirement papers and I want to discuss them with you. In spite of this little mess, the NIA and the U.S. in general still need your services."

"My actual retirement date is still a month away," Taft said, "but right now I'm inclined to go ahead with my plans."

The room was silent.

"What's your main beef?" Allbright asked. "Maybe I can do something to effect a change, smooth things over, and make some changes to keep you with the agency."

Taft exhaled. "Boss," he said quietly, "I'm just not sure about this entire thing anymore. When I first started around here my work seemed like it truly mattered. The stakes were high, and there was little or no politics. Now, more and more, I just feel like a cog in the wheel of a system. This Serbian affair is just icing on the cake."

Allbright nodded.

"This is an unusual event, John," Allbright said quietly. "Why don't you just take some time off and consider your future. I'll authorize two weeks' paid vacation that won't count against your normal allotment—why don't you use the time to think. Maybe you're just burned out and tired."

"Thanks, boss," Taft said, "but I want you to think of something as well. If I had been captured or killed in Serbia, what good would it have done? I'd be gone and the case would be proceeding exactly as it is now. All the risks I took would have been in vain. Within days I'd be merely a footnote—and whatever is going to happen will happen—and it would be like I never existed at all."

Taft stared directly into Allbright's eyes. What he said was the honest truth.

"I understand what you're feeling, but at least for me, if nothing else, take the time off, John, and do some reflection. What you do here *is* critically important," Allbright said, concluding the meeting, "and talk to me in two weeks."

It was a sound plan—but at this second neither man had any way to know that a lot would happen before the two weeks was up, and that their next meeting would not take place for much longer time than that.


TAFT WAS SITTING in Martinez's office, leaning back on the chair with his feet up on the desk. Martinez was behind the desk with his legs draped across the corner. Both men were sipping coffee.

"Something about this is not right," Taft said.

"How so?"

"Well, to start with," Taft noted, "if the intention was to secure Ilic's release, why did they wait so long to place the operation in effect? If, like Nadia theorizes, the plans were first stolen in 1999, what has been the delay?"

"Well, to begin with, Nadia's wrong. She claimed Tesla's plans were stolen by NATO secret agents," Martinez said. "We know that's not true."

"That NATO idea was just a theory," Taft said. "What she is sure of is that the plans were stolen by *someone* around that time."

"So," Martinez said, "some Ilic supporter grabs the documents in

1999 and he has spent the time since then perfecting the device. Makes complete sense."

"Then why not target The Netherlands first?" Taft asked. "Give them a little shock to let them know they were serious. If they did that, Ilic would be free by now and they could have safely secured the device before anyone tried to recover it. It just doesn't make any sense. It's like being mad at a bully and slapping his brother. They must know that any preliminary action, any tests of the system, like Italy and Spain, would just lead to increased scrutiny and the chance someone could locate the device and disable it."

"What if whoever is behind this wanted to show their power first," Martinez theorized, "by striking other countries?"

"Doesn't jibe," Taft said easily. "It's like bombing Bakersfield to prove you can hit Los Angeles. The terrorists would just do the strike— that's how they think."

Martinez nodded. "They were worried Ilic would be hurt if they hit The Netherlands?"

"Maybe," Taft said.

"Both Italy and Spain agreed to house Ilic if he was convicted," Martinez noted. "Maybe it was to show the other countries they wouldn't be safe if they agreed to hold him as a prisoner as well."

"If he is ever convicted," Taft said quietly, "and no one else will house him, I'd have to believe he'd remain in The Netherlands. Or the U.S. would step up and supply a cell."

Martinez slowly nodded. "So you're thinking Ilic is just a patsy in a far greater scheme?"

"Think about that for a moment," Taft said, "and it changes the picture."

Martinez smiled. "No way," he said, laughing. "Then what's this whole thing with the release of Ilic about?"

"I don't know," Taft said. "An elaborate cover?"

"I think you're reaching now," Martinez said quietly.

Taft nodded. "We both know that when motive is in doubt, it's always one of two things."

"Love or money."

"Love or money," Taft agreed.

The men were silently thinking when the direct line rang.

"Martinez."

"This is Driggs," the voice said. "I hope I'm not bothering you."

"It's the author," Martinez said to Taft while holding his hand over the receiver. Martinez removed his hand, "No, you're not bothering me at all, Mr. Driggs. What can I do for you today?"

"I came across some things in my research I think you should know about," he said quietly, "but I'm not comfortable discussing them over the phone. These discrepancies may be nothing , but they are something you should be aware of. Is there any chance we could meet again? In person."

Martinez stared at the caller ID and noticed the area code and number. "It looks from the caller ID like you're still in Colorado. Or are you on a cell phone?"

"I don't use those damn things," Driggs noted. "They're a pain in the ass. I headed down to Arizona, then I discovered the information I needed was up at my house in Telluride. So I flew up here earlier. I'm at my home there now."

"Can you give me some idea of what you've come across?"

"Like I said," Driggs said quietly, "it's a little far-fetched but not something we should talk about over an open line. If I'm right, you might have a much bigger problem than you thought. Whatever the case, it's worth discussing."

"Can you hold on a second?" Martinez said.

"Sure," Driggs said.

Martinez placed his hand over the receiver. "Driggs is up in Telluride, Colorado. He's come across some information, and he needs to meet with someone in private. I think we can kill two birds with one stone here. You go up and feel him out—see what's he's uncovered. We can take care of the vacation issue while at the same time expensing the trip to the NIA. You spend some time with him—it shouldn't take long—then you cruise around Colorado and take your vacation for the rest of the time."

"Telluride, huh," Taft said. "I've always wanted to visit there. There are some hot springs nearby where I can take a soak."

Martinez smiled and nodded.

"Throw in a Harley rental and it's a done deal," Taft said.

"Mr. Driggs—" Martinez started to say.

"Call me Malcolm."

"Okay Malcolm," Martinez continued, "I can't leave the office at this time. However, my partner John Taft is free and could head out west later this afternoon."

"That's fine," Driggs said. "Whoever you think is right."

"Where do you want him to meet you?"

"Just call and tell me his flight information once you have it," Driggs said, "and I'll pick him up at the airport. Just be sure he's wearing hiking boots, because as soon as he arrives I need to take him to an area nearby where we'll need to tramp around."

"So you want me to call you at this number with the flight information?"

"Unless I go into town to pick up the mail," Driggs said, "I'll be right here waiting."

The phone went dead, and Martinez glanced up at Taft.

"Go home and pack a bag," Martinez said, "and make sure you take your hiking boots. Then just drive over to Dulles. I have the arrangements made by then."

Taft smiled and rose from his seat. "See if you can bump me to first class."

"I'll tell the airline it's a matter of national security," Martinez agreed.

"And work on the Harley," Taft said, stopping at the door. "I'm not sure where the nearest rental agency is, but I'd like to take a little ride when this is finished."

"I'll do it. Now get out," Martinez said easily.

"I'm getting," Taft said.

As Taft walked down the hallway to the elevator, his mood began to improve. The greatest minds in the United States were working on the Tesla case, so he was certain whatever Driggs had turned up would amount to nothing. He'd do a quick meet-and-greet, hear the author's story and dismiss it, then do a soak and a cycle ride. Things were beginning to look up, he thought, as the elevator door opened. Maybe some rest and relaxation *were* just what he needed.

INSIDE A WAREHOUSE near the Belgrade airport, the boxes containing the files were reloaded into a clean van emblazoned with the name and numbers of a catering company.

"This truck should not arouse suspicion," one of Ratzovik's aides said to the man who would do the delivery. "Drive directly to the helicopter—it'll be off to the side of the east-to-west runway—the pilot and copilot will help you with the loading."

"Got it," the driver said, making his way to the driver's door.

The aide motioned to a man standing next to the electric garage door button, and he flipped the switch. The door rose, and the van started. Next the aide reached for his cell phone and placed a call.

AT THE BELGRADE airport the copilot was supervising the fueling when the pilot's telephone rang. The pilot uttered a few words, then disconnected.

"The passengers are on their way!" he shouted to the copilot.

The helicopter was a Russian-made MIL Mi-17, also known as a Hip-H. Powered by a pair of TV3-117MT engines each producing 2,000 horsepower, the cargo helicopter had a rotor diameter of nearly 70 feet, a top speed of 155 miles an hour, and a range 370 miles. Designed to carry as many as three dozen troops when used in military operations, this unit had the seats removed and the inside hull converted for cargo hauling.

Old and showing her age, the airship had been sold as military surplus by the Russians five years prior. Now owned by a front company controlled by Ratzovik, she was normally hired out to whoever might need her services. Mining companies, logging firms, she had even held lift towers in place while they were bolted down at a Bulgarian ski resort last year. The Mi-17 was an old workhorse, and she looked it.

The pilot climbed into his seat and ran through the preflight check-list as he waited.

Six minutes later, the van pulled up alongside, and he climbed out to help with the loading. It took the three men a little over fifteen minutes to secure the load inside. Once that was done, the van pulled away, and the pilot started the engines. Right then a sedan pulled up nearby, and Pestic's wife and son climbed out. Led to the rear compartment by the copilot, he handed them cotton to stuff in their ears for the noise, then shut the door and fastened the latch. Next the copilot walked forward and climbed into his seat.

The pilot called the tower for permission to lift off.

## 18

"I WANT A satellite shot on Serbia and Kosovo," the DCI ordered, "ASAP." The operator glanced up at the DCI. "I was ordered by the air force to divert to southern Iraq about forty minutes ago," he said quietly. "It'll take about forty minutes to reposition."

The DCI stared at the mark left by Taft's tracking bugs. The files had left the Belgrade airport a few minutes before, heading due south. "Track speed?" the DCI shouted.

The operator punched some numbers in a calculator. "One twenty-seven."

"That'll be cutting in close," the DCI said, "but if they maintain the same speed, we should be okay."

"If the intended destination is Kosovo," the operator said, "we can catch them before they land."

"Then," the DCI said, "quit talking and start typing."

• • •

IN THE REAR of the unmarked C-17A Globemaster 3 flying over Kosovo, the loadmaster stood in the center of the pallet and waited. Hooked to a harness that was attached to the forward bulkhead to prevent him from flying out the rear of the plane, and wearing a parachute as a backup, he stared at the remaining cargo.

Seventeen down; thirteen to go.

At that instant the red light in the rear compartment began flashing, and the horn sounded. Pushing the crate along the rollers attached to the floor of the cargo area, the loadmaster increased the speed until the five-by-five-by-four-foot-tall crate flew out of the rear. Holding on to the side of the aircraft, the loadmaster watched to make sure the parachute opened properly. Once he verified it was open, he walked back to the forward bulkhead and flipped a switch near the light turning it off. The pilot lined up for another pass. The loadmaster lined up behind another crate to await the signal.


FOURTEEN MILES DUE west of Brezovica, Kosovo, about ten miles from the border with Macedonia, the crate drifted to Earth, then struck the dirt. A pair of army rangers raced over and began to pry the crate open while their lieutenant stared skyward.

Off to one side, two other rangers were rolling the camouflaged quad off the bottom of the first crate to land. One of them began to drag the wooden sides of the crate into the trees while the other pushed the starter. The quad roared to live.

"Last one is out," the lieutenant shouted.

The last of the three quads drifted down and landed in the field. The lieutenant raced over with another ranger and started to dismantle the crate. Less than ten minutes later, the parachutes were stowed in bags, the sides of the crates were hidden, and all the quads were running. Two men to a quad, the team started southwest in a sweeping arc.

They watched the power lines closely and avoided direct contact with the population.

• • •

FIVE MINUTES LATER, the loadmaster had pushed the last crate off the rear ramp. Only the three extras remained. He walked forward and flipped the light off, then reached for the telephone on the bulkhead and called the pilot.

"Sir," he said, "we're empty save the reserves."

"Hold one," the pilot ordered.

In the cockpit the copilot was conferring over the radio with the search teams. Once finished, he turned to the pilot.

"We have one damaged on landing at site four."

"Enter the coordinates," the pilot ordered, "and I'll notify the load-master."

The copilot punched the GPS numbers into the navigation computer while the pilot flipped on the ringer on the cargo area telephone.

"Yes, sir," the loadmaster answered.

"We need to drop again," the pilot said. "We had one break."

"I'll be ready, sir," the loadmaster said.

"You've got about fifteen," the pilot said, "until we hit the drop zone."

"Affirm," the loadmaster said, hanging up.

Walking over to a nylon bag carrying his personal items, the loadmaster retrieved a game computer. Turning it on, he began to play solitaire until his watch showed twelve minutes had passed. Then he slipped the machine back into the bag and made sure the crate was free and ready to drop. As the cargo door began to lower and wind filled the rear compartment, the loadmaster stared at the light.

As soon as the light flashed, he ran the crate down the rollers and out the rear. Once the rear door was closed, he walked over to the bag, retrieved the game computer, and resumed his game. Two minutes later the telephone rang.

"That one was good," the pilot said. "We're headed home."

"Sounds good," the loadmaster said.

Sitting on the floor with his back against one of the two remaining crates, the loadmaster listened as the engines of the C-17A grew louder and the pilot increased speed. Then an arcing turn and level flight. The loadmaster began to nod off as the plane headed home.

"THEY INCREASED SPEED," the operator noted. "They are doing just over one-fifty."

"Where's my picture?" the DCI asked.

"I can't get the bird around in time," the operator said quietly. "We'll have tracking but no real-time photo or video."

The DCI stared at the red line flowing down the map of Serbia into Kosovo. "Has anyone figured out what type of aircraft we're dealing with?" he shouted to the room.

No one answered.

"Great," the DCI said. "And how accurate are the locators in the files?"

"We're okay. They are accurate to within a mile, maybe less," someone answered.

ON BOARD THE MIL Mi-17, the pilot lowered the collective and angled the cyclic forward. "We're dropping in the canyon now!" he shouted across the cockpit to the copilot. "We'll maintain five hundred feet until the destination!"

"Sneaky Pete!" the copilot shouted.

"Boss's orders!" the pilot said.

Inside the canyon the locator signals bounced into the walls, then ricocheted, becoming scrambled. In the rear compartment, Mrs. Pestic wrapped her arms around her son as the noise increased and the canyon walls loomed out the windows of the helicopter. She rubbed his hair as he stared up at her with fear in his eyes.

"Soon," she said in Serbo-Croatian, "we'll see Daddy."

BACK AT THE command center, the DCI was staring at the video display on the wall showing the placement of the Special Forces troops.

The ten teams were spread out in an arc twenty or so miles above where the scientists believed the source of the power drain was. Thirty thin tendrils indicating each quad wiggled their way down the map like tiny snakes. The lines would start and stop as each team repositioned. It appeared that the teams were making a slow but methodical search.

"Sir!" the operator shouted across the room.

The DCI swiveled around and stared across the room.

"We just lost the signal from the locators!"

"Mark the last transmission," the DCI said, walking across the room, "then make a circle with that as the top, and the farthest south portion of Kosovo as the bottom."

The operator entered some commands and waited while the computer calculated. Once he had the image, he sent it to one of the video displays on the wall. The DCI walked over and stared at the picture.

The top of the arc was four miles south of Prizren, in a mountainous area. Looking at the map, it appeared as a small slice of Kosovo, with Macedonia to the west and Albania to the east. If one forgot the target circle the entire area was perhaps two hundred square miles. With the circle indicating the highest-probability area it was more like sixty to seventy in total. To an outsider it probably would not seem too difficult.

"We have an area roughly the same size as Washington, D.C., to search, and sixty men on the ground to accomplish that," the DCI said. "How much time do we have?"

"Less than twenty-four hours," someone said.

"Alert the Special Forces teams to move over to the highest-probability area. I want that circle," the DCI said, pointing at the video display, "cut into ten blocks and a team assigned to each block. We are running out of time, so we need this done right the first time."

"Sir," the operator said, "I can do an overlay of the known power lines in the area and send it by satellite to the GP units on the quads. That should speed this up."

"Do it," the DCI said. "And do it now."

• • •

THE MIL MI-17 slowed and lowered into a field near the farm where Pestic was being held. The pilot shut down, the engine and the rotor blade began to slow. He waited a minute, then engaged the rotor brake. The blade slowed, then stopped. Pestic stood to the side as a pair of men dressed in black clothes approached the cargo door. They waited until the copilot opened the hatch; then they helped Pestic's wife and son to the ground and led them over.

Pestic grabbed them and hugged them to his body. Then he led them toward the barn as the pair of men walked back to the helicopter and began to unload the files. Half an hour later the files were inside the barn and the helicopter lifted off. Pestic was having a happy reunion when one of the men entered the barn with a telephone.

"You have what you want now," the voice said. "How soon now until we can activate the unit again?"

"I'll need some time to examine the files," Pestic lied.

"Twenty-four hours," the voice said, "or I order the guards to shoot your son first, then your wife."

"I understand," Pestic said. "I'll have it all fixed by then."

The telephone went dead and Pestic handed it back to the guard, who exited.

"What is it?" his wife asked.

Pestic motioned to his wife to come close and whispered. "We have one day," he said quietly, "to figure out our escape."

"What about that?" she said, motioning to the Tesla device.

"That will be," he said, "what keeps them from following."

"And if we don't escape?" she asked.

"Then we are witnesses and not participants," Pestic said. "And once that does what it is intended to do, they won't want any witnesses."

A tear rolled from her left eye. "I'm scared," she whispered.

"So am I," Pestic agreed.

• • •

IN THE HAGUE, Radko Ilic was standing in his cell with a tailor at his feet.

"Usual break, Commander?" the tailor asked.

"Yes."

"Will you be needing an overcoat as well?" the tailor asked.

"Definitely," Ilic said.

The tailor rose from his feet and slipped the tape measure around his neck. "I'm done here, sir," he said. "If you could remove the pants I'll take them out and sew them."

Ilic unbuttoned the pants and handed them over. His lawyer, who was standing nearby, handed him the pants he had been wearing. The tailor left, and Ilic walked over to a tea set and poured a cup. He glanced over at the lawyer, who nodded no; then he sat down at the small table in the cell.

"Has the plane been arranged?"

"The Netherlands government has it on standby," the lawyer answered.

"And the flight path has been cleared through to Belgrade?"

"Through Germany, Austria, and Hungary, then home," the lawyer agreed.

Ilic slipped a sugar cube into his mouth, then sipped the tea. "Has the president been approached about stepping down?"

"As you requested," the lawyer answered. "His answer is no, just as we thought."

Ilic nodded. "Then we go to war again, until I resume my rightful place as leader. How many loyalists can we muster?"

"Since your incarceration," the lawyer noted, "your popularity has actually grown. The fact that the UN meddled in Serbian affairs has angered a large segment of the population. We think the majority of the citizens will not oppose your efforts."

"What about the army?"

"We've made a great deal of inroads," the lawyer answered. "As you ordered, the commanders of the troops nearest Belgrade were approached first. We think we can field a majority that, if they won't join our efforts, at least will lay down their weapons until the situation sorts itself out."

"So our primary problem will be the KFOR troops in Kosovo."

"The threat of the Tesla device should keep them at bay," the lawyer noted quietly.

"What about our neighbors?" Ilic asked. "Any problems there?"

"Doubtful," the lawyer said easily. "They have problems of their own."

Ilic smiled. The long years of imprisonment were already becoming just a memory. He was picturing himself sweeping into Belgrade at the head of a column of tanks, a victorious leader who had defeated the forces of the UN and returned to claim his rightful place as leader of his people. Only the president stood in the way of a quick and peaceful transition.

"Contact Ratzovik," Ilic said easily, "and have him offer the president fifty million to step down."

The lawyer made a note on his pad. "Before you return? That's a lot of funds to move in a short time."

"Ratzovik can do it," Ilic said. "He's a genius at that sort of thing."

The lawyer nodded slowly. "About Ratzovik," he said, "I find it odd he has made no demands about a place in the new government once you're free."

"Perhaps," Ilic said, "he's stolen enough from me over the years to feather his nest. I would not doubt as much."

"Do you wish me to promise him anything? To ensure this all takes place as planned?"

Ilic sipped some tea, then shook his head. "Not unless he insists. Then promise him anything you want."

"You'd allow him to serve with you?" the lawyer asked in amazement.

"Hardly," Ilic said. "The man is more twisted than a mountain road. Even with all the brutality that has surround our nationalistic movement, Ratzovik has always stood out. I want him nowhere around me."

"So once you're free," the lawyer said, "you'll take him out?"

"As soon as I return," Ilic said quietly, "and have him disclose where all my funds are placed, he will be arrested, sentenced, and executed."

"That's good," the lawyer said, "because I never trusted him a bit."

"Nor did I," Ilic said easily. "Nor did I."

## 19

THE CHIEF OF the Belgrade Police Department sat behind his desk with a cup of coffee, and a cigarette burning in his ashtray. The chief was of medium height and stocky. His neck was hardly visible, and it appeared as if his square head, crowned by thinning white hair, was simply attached to his shoulders. Both the chief, and the uniforms festooned with medals, made for an imposing sight.

Detective Pavic opened his file.

"The unknown party has been identified," he began. "His name is Bozdar Maladric."

"Are you certain?"

"Maladric was formerly in the Serbian Army, and he had his service serial number tattooed on the sole of his foot. Once I had that I simply matched his fingerprints to the records to confirm."

"Have you questioned his family?" the chief asked.

"No known family," Pavic said, consulting his notes, "but we questioned the other residents of his apartment complex. No one seemed to know much—apparently this Maladric spent a great deal of time away."

"Friends from the military?"

"I have men working on that," Pavic admitted. "His commanding officer was a man named Galadin Ratzovik, but we have been unable to locate him, or as yet, any of the men who worked directly with Maladric."

The chief nodded, then puffed on the cigarette for a few moments. "We need motive," he said slowly, "as to why Mr. Bodonavik was killed. What was in the files that were stolen that would be so valuable to assassinate an aide to the president?"

"From what I've been able to determine, the files were the records of Nikola Tesla," Pavic noted, "and they were taken by Bodonavik for safekeeping after a recent fire at the Tesla Museum."

"So someone who knew the location of the files sold Bodonavik out," the chief said.

"They were moved by a Serbian Army detail," Pavic said. "Bodonavik then sent the men on a paid vacation. We've taken the men who moved them into custody, but no one knows anything."

"People who work at the museum?"

"Questioned," Pavic said, glancing at the notes. "They had no idea where the files were being transported. Bodonavik did not disclose that to anyone except those who moved them to his apartment."

The chief nodded and stubbed out his cigarette. He quickly lit another. "Then the leak must have come from the BIA," he said at last, "and that was why their man appeared at the apartment so soon after the killing."

"Those are my thoughts as well."

"We have a few hours until we meet with the president," the chief noted, "and right now we have little to tell him."

"I'm still digging," Pavic said easily.

"Dig harder and deeper," the chief said, "and find the vein of truth here."

"Very good, sir," Pavic said, rising.

Pavic left the office and waited down the hall for the elevator. Once it arrived he rode down and walked out to his squad car. Then he drove toward Maladric's apartment to see if his men had missed anything.


"WHAT IF THE location of the files was leaked from here, from the e-mail Slavja sent, then extracted?" the head of the BIA said to the agent who had gone to Bodonavik's apartment. "Then the agency is responsible for the death of Bodonavik. The president will not like that one bit."

"No, he won't."

"What's Slavja's position on this?" the head of the BIA asked.

"I tried his portable phone twenty minutes ago," the agent said, "and got the recording. I left my name and number and instructed him to call back immediately."

"And he hasn't?"

"No, sir."

"Find him and bring him here to me," the BIA chief ordered.


ZORAN WAS STILL an hour and a half from Belgrade when his telephone had rung. Seeing the number was from the BIA exchange, he'd let the answering machine pick it up. In the past twenty minutes he'd listened to the recording three times. Each time his feeling of dread had grown. His cooperation with Taft had been a mistake—he knew that now. Once his agency caught up with him—and they would—it wouldn't take long for the truth to come out. He had sold out his side for a vague promise, and if the Americans did not come through, he was finished.

Clutching the card Taft had given him, he pulled over to the side of the road and dialed the number. The voice at the other end answered with the extension only.

"2524."

"This is Zoran Slavja. A man named John gave me this number."

"What do you need?"

"I need to speak to him immediately," Zoran said.

"Hold on," the voice said. "I'll patch you through."

• • •

TAFT WAS SIPPING orange juice in the first-class lounge at Ronald Reagan International Airport. Glancing up at the monitor, he noticed his flight was boarding. He finished the drink, then rose from the leather-covered chair. He was halfway across the lounge when his telephone rang once.

"Taft."

"This is Zoran," a crackling voice said. "My people are trying to contact me, and I think I need out."

Taft moved closer to the window to try to improve the reception. "Where are you, Zoran?" he asked.

"A little over an hour from Belgrade in the truck."

"Here's what I want you to do," Taft said. "Call your wife and have her pack one suitcase for her and the baby and one for your father. Instruct Nadia to do the same. Meanwhile, you keep driving toward the city. I'll call my partner and have him make the arrangements. Either he or I will call you back shortly with instructions."

There was a pause. "How do I know this is real," Zoran asked, "that you're not just shining me on?"

"I made you a promise," Taft said, "and those I do not break."

"I'll make the calls right now," Zoran said.

"Then be ready for this to move fast," Taft said. "Once I set it in place, there is no turning back."

"I understand."

The phone went dead. Taft dialed Martinez.

"How come you are not on the plane?" he asked.

"Just boarding now," Taft replied.

"What have you got?"

"Set the plan in motion to pull out the Slavja family."

"Now?" Martinez asked.

"Number one priority."

"You got it," Martinez said.

"I'll call you from the plane," Taft said, disconnecting.

• • •

"IF THE BIA is looking for him," Mather said, "he won't pass through passport check at the airport."

"The plan has two choices," Martinez said. "First is falsified documents and a lift out by commercial or private plane. The second is a drive to the Romanian border—even without fake passports we think we can get them through."

"Which do you like?" Mather asked.

"First, I want you to round up Zoran's father, wife, and their baby," Martinez said. "Then grab the sister. Take them to your office or a safe house. I'll call and check the airports and see if they have been alerted to look from Zoran; if they have, the plane idea is out."

"So you want them all together?"

"Yes," Martinez said, "with Zoran as soon as he reaches the city."

"How long do I have to round them up?"

"Zoran reaches Belgrade in an hour," Martinez said. "Once he reaches the city we have to believe the BIA will be looking for him pretty seriously."

"What if they have already approached the family?"

"You do whatever you need to do to bring them in," Martinez said.

"Even if it blows my cover?" Mather asked.

"Whatever you need to do," Martinez said. "We'll clean up any wreckage later."

"I'm on it," Mather said.


IN THE BARN in Kosovo, Vojislav Pestic was flipping through the documents from the file marked 1901–1910. Pestic was doing this to kill time while he planned his family's escape. More than anything else, he was certain he already had the coil's proper settings. The strange thing was that now, in examining the files, he was beginning to doubt his measurements. Most of the mathematical formulas he was reading appeared different. Reaching for his notes, he compared the two.

The files had definitely been changed.

Just then a guard entered the barn holding out a cell phone. He handed it to Pestic.

"Yes?"

"Do the files solve your problem?" Ratzovik asked without preamble.

Pestic thought for a second. He considered telling Ratzovik about the files, then decided it would serve no useful purpose. "I think they will," he answered.

"And the sheet of paper absolving you?"

Pestic glanced at the paper his wife had brought. It was short and purposefully vague. It mentioned that Pestic was just following orders when testing the Tesla device; it failed to mention that Ratzovik had held his wife and son as hostages to make him comply.

"Adequate."

"Then we can do this tomorrow at 6:00 P.M.?"

"I'll work all night to make sure we're ready," Pestic lied.

"We only have a few hours' leeway," Ratzovik noted. "It has to function by then."

"And if I do," Pestic said, "then my family and I can go free?"

"Absolutely," Ratzovik said quickly.

"I'll make the necessary adjustments soon," Pestic said. "Then all we will need is a sufficient amount of electricity for this to be successful."

"Good," Ratzovik said. "I'm looking forward to watching this work."

Pestic swallowed. "You're coming here?"

"Yes," Ratzovik said quietly, "I'd like to meet your family and watch this in person."

The words cut through Pestic like an icy dagger. Once Ratzovik arrived, their fate would be sealed.

"I'm looking forward to that," Pestic said slowly.

"Tomorrow then," Ratzovik said before the phone went dead.

The guard retrieved the telephone and folded it in half. Then he slid it into his pocket and walked. Pestic's wife was across the barn watching their son, who was taking a nap. She rose and walked to Pestic's side. The scientist's face was a pasty white, and tiny drops of sweat dotted his forehead.

"Vojislav," she said, wiping the sweat with her hand, "what happened?"

"We must leave here tonight," he whispered.

"Who was that on the phone?" she asked.

Pestic paused and stared up at her. "That was death," he said quietly, "and tomorrow he comes calling."

# 20

RAIN FLOWED OFF the windshield as Mather drove into central Belgrade. It was muggy inside the coffee shop van. Mather cracked the side window and stared at the scrap of paper listing the address once again. Zoran's employment with the BIA had yielded at least one perquisite: his apartment was in a good area. The apartment was just down the street from Princess Ljubice's palace and only a block off the Sava River. The area was scenic but had a high population density.

Removing the Slavjas without being detected would be tricky.

Mather turned left off Kneza Markovica onto Kralja Petra, then continued a block until he ran into Kostancicev, where he turned left again. Halfway down the street he slowed and looked for a spot to park while staring up at the eighteen-story apartment complex. A car was pulling away from the curb, and Mather signaled his intention with the turn signal. The cars to his rear pulled around him, and he pulled forward, then backed into the spot. Climbing from the van, with a bag in his hand, he scanned the street for unmarked government cars. Finding it clear, he crossed the street and made his way to the lobby entrance and opened the glass doors.

Like many of the structures built during Tito's reign, the inside of the building lacked style. All the elements were there—marble flooring, a chandelier, a desk where the doorman waited—but the appearance was more sterile than welcoming. Off to one side was a series of couches and overstuffed chairs showing wear. Three older men, most likely former bureaucrats, were reading newspapers in the chairs. The couches, by contrast, were empty. Along the far wall was an alcove containing the mailboxes. The elevators were just past the doorman's desk. Mather walked over and held up the bag.

"Delivery for 1213," he said in Serbo-Croatian.

Then Mather opened the bag and showed the doorman the cup of coffee inside. The doorman grunted and reached for the telephone. After a few whispered words he motioned to the elevators. "Go on up," he said before returning to his crossword puzzle.

Mather walked over to the elevator and pushed the up button, waited until the doors opened, and walked inside. Pushing twelve, he rode up to the floor, exited, walked down the hallway, and knocked on the door. The door was opened a crack, and Nadia's face peered out.

"A friend sent me," Mather said quietly.

Nadia opened the door, and Mather walked inside.

Just off the entryway were a trio of suitcases. On the couch in the living room was a woman with brunette hair holding a baby, and an older man with a shock of white hair. The man rose from the couch and walked toward Mather. The man was short, five and a half feet tall, with a medium build, and a small potbelly that came from age.

"I am Danal, this is my daughter-in-law Adria with Josip," he said, extending his hand to shake. "And, of course, you know Nadia."

Mather shook his hand. "Actually," he said, nodding toward Nadia, "we've never met."

Danal tilted his head toward Nadia. "This is not the American you told me about?"

"No, Daddy," Nadia said, "this is not him."

"The other man was called away," Mather said, "but he asked me to take you to safety."

"Where is my Zoran?" Adria asked, rising from the couch with Josip in her arms.

"He will be meeting us soon," Mather said, "but right now we need to get out of here. Danal, are you familiar with this building?"

"Yes," the old man said. "I live here, two floors below."

"How can we reach street level without using the main elevator?"

"There is a freight elevator on the side of the building used for moving in and out," Danal said. "It leads to a loading dock that exits on the side street."

"Good," Mather started to say. "We are going—"

THE PAIR OF BIA agent walked into the lobby like they owned the building. Dressed in black suits and dress shoes whose heels clicked on the marble, they glanced at the men seated in the chairs as they approached the doorman. Pulling a badge from an outer pocket of his suit coat, one of the men flashed it at the doorman.

"State Security," he said. "We need the Slavja residence."

The doorman looked up at the men.

"Actually, there are—" the doorman began to say.

"Just tell us the number," the second agent barked.

"Ten-twelve," the doorman said as the two men walked toward the elevator, "but the son has—"

But by then the men were already boarding an elevator that had just dropped off passengers. The doors closed, and they started up. The doorman reached for the telephone. No one answered at 1012, so he dialed 1213.

"THANKS," NADIA SAID, hanging up the receiver.

"What is it?" Mather asked, seeing the look on her face.

"There are BIA agents on the way up here," she said. "The doorman sent them to Dad's apartment by mistake."

Mather reached behind his back and withdrew a handgun that was riding in the small of his back. "We need to move now," he said.

"What about the bags?" Adria asked.

Mather thought for a moment. "We need to bring them," he said a second later, "or when the BIA breaks down the door they will know you are planning to flee."

"I'll take these two," Danal said, reaching down. "Nadia, you bring yours, and Adria, you just worry about the baby."

With Mather covering the hallway with the gun in his hand, they quickly walked down the hall to the freight elevator. Once they were in front of the elevator and had pushed the button, Mather turned to them.

"I'm going to go down and get my van and drive it into the loading dock," he said quickly. "I'll meet you there in a few minutes."

"How are you going to go down?" Nadia asked.

"I'll take the passenger elevators," Mather said. "They are not looking for me."


WHEN NO ONE answered the knock on the door of apartment 1012, the BIA agents broke the door down and searched. Finding it empty, they headed back to the elevator, rode down, and approached the doorman's desk again.

"You said 1012 is the Slavja residence?" one of the agents said.

"One of them," the doorman said. "You did not let me finish."

"We need Zoran Slavja's apartment," the second man barked.

"That is 1213," the doorman said.


JUST AS THE doorman finished his sentence, the elevator carrying Mather opened at the lobby floor. Walking out, he headed past the doorman's desk.

"Just a second," the doorman said to the BIA agents heading for the elevator again.

The agents turned.

"This man just made a delivery there," the doorman said.

The BIA agents stared across the lobby at Mathers. "Is anyone home?" one of the agents asked.

"They were a minute ago," Mather said in Serbo-Croatian.

Then he turned and walked out of the lobby as the BIA agents pushed the button for the elevator. While they waited, one of the agents was thinking long and hard. The delivery man looked familiar, but he couldn't quite place him. The elevator doors opened, and the BIA agents entered.


MATHER SPRINTED ACROSS the street, started the van, then drove to the side street and down a ramp leading to the loading dock. Pulling up next to the elevator, he climbed out and opened the passenger doors and rear cargo door. A few seconds later, the freight elevator stopped and the door opened. The Slavjas ran across the short distance, tossed the suitcases in the rear, and climbed inside. Mather closed the doors, put the van in gear, and started up the ramp.


AFTER A FEW knocks on the door, the BIA agents because impatient and forced it open. They quickly walked through the apartment and found it empty. They were back in the hallway again when one of the agents spoke.

"Now I remember," he said. "The coffee shop we've been staking out."

The agents were making their way back to the elevator now. "The one you suspect of being an American Intelligence front?" his partner asked.

"That one," the other agent said as the door to the elevator opened again.

"What about it?"

"That's where I've seen the deliveryman."

"Shit, shit, shit," his partner said.


THE VAN WAS moving so fast when Mather hit the top of the ramp that the front tires left the pavement. Shooting onto the side street, he did a quick left, then a right on Pop Lukina. Another quick left and he was on Brankov Most, where a bridge led over the Sava River.

They were across the river and into New Belgrade before the BIA agents reached the lobby once again. In the next hour more BIA agents would show up and the entire building would be searched from floor to floor.

The would find no trace of the Slavja family.

JOSIP WAS TOO young to recognize the tension in the van. He was gurgling happily and tugging on his mother's nose. Mather had turned left when they crossed the river, down to Drugi Bulevar, then turned right to go west again. Drugi Bulevar would take them to the airport, seventeen kilometers away. At this instant Mather was steering the van with one hand while he dialed on his phone.

"Call the ball," Mather said when Martinez answered.

"Abort the airport," Martinez answered, "even with the false passports. The BIA has already distributed photographs of the family at the airport, train, and bus terminals. You will have to drive them out, Steve."

"Where's Zoran?" he asked.

"Still on I-75 just below Belgrade," Martinez said. "Where are you?"

"Driving west toward the airport."

"Can you make it to I-75?"

"Hold on."

Mather turned to Nadia, who was in the front passenger seat. "Do you know where to catch I-75?"

"About five minutes from here there is a turnoff."

"I'm five minutes away," Mather answered.

"I'll have Zoran skirt the city and start north," Martinez said. "You make your way to Novi Sad, and we'll have you all meet up there."

"What then?" Mather asked.

"I'm not sure yet," Martinez admitted. "Once you are near Novi Sad, find a forested area, pull off the road, and wait. By then I'll have the arrangements made. It'll be either Romania, Hungary, or Croatia for a border crossing."

"Larry," Mather said quietly.

"Yeah, Steve?" Martinez said.

"They almost got us."

"Feels good, huh," Martinez said as he disconnected.


ZORAN WAS SHAKING with tension. Not so much for himself but for his family. Partnering with the American had been risky, and he should never have done it. Still, if it somehow worked out and his family reached safety and Serbia was spared from retribution by the United States for acts of the madman, it would all have been worthwhile. The thought gave him little comfort, however, and he lit another cigarette.

Right then his telephone rang.

"Still on I-75?" Martinez asked.

"Yes."

"Pass Belgrade and continue north to Novi Sad."

"My family—" Zoran began to say.

"So far they are safe and headed in that direction," Martinez said. "You will all meet up there."

"Thank you, Mr. Martinez," Zoran blurted.

"Don't thank me now," Martinez said. "We're not out of the woods yet."

"But my family—" Zoran started.

"Let me worry about them," Martinez said. "You be careful on the drive north. They came for your family, and our man just got away. That means they are looking for you right now. Be careful at any fuel stops, and call me when you're close to Novi Sad."

"I'll be careful."

"I'll be here," Martinez said, hanging up.


TAFT WAS SIPPING a glass of tomato juice in the first-class cabin as the cart containing lunch made its slow way toward him. The movie had already started, but Taft had no interest in watching. It was a half-baked spy tale starring Ben Affleck and Drew Barrymore. Affleck had to save the world from certain destruction while at the same time sorting out his relationship with his spunky partner, played by Barrymore.

Taft figured there would be at least one bomb that ticked down to number one before Affleck cut the red wire. And at least one car chase where the pursuers flipped their car over onto the top. Taft had disabled a few devices in his time—always with more time than seconds until detonation. And in all the chases he'd been involved in, not a single car had flipped over onto its roof nor burst into an explosion when the gas tank ruptured. One had burned—when the leaking fuel hit the hot exhaust—but there was no explosion, just a cloud of black smoke from the burning interior of the vehicle.

Taft, like a cowboy watching a Western, found most spy movies unbelievable.

Instead of the movie, Taft decided to concentrate on the woman across the aisle. The plane was not full, and each of them had their rows to themselves. She was dressed in a blue-striped business suit with a knee-length skirt. Her white silk shirt billowing around the lapels of her suit coat was unbuttoned enough to give a hint of cleavage. Her hair was pinned up, and she was wearing a pair of horn-rimmed glasses that she periodically removed to chew on the side pieces. Periodically typing commands into her laptop sitting on the tray table, she looked like a naughty schoolteacher.

Catching him staring, she glanced up and smiled.

Taft diverted his attention, and reached for his portable telephone, and switched it on.

"What's up?" he said quietly when Martinez answered.

"Mather got the family out of the apartment just in the nick of time," Martinez said. "We intercepted reports from the BIA that their agents were at the building when he made his getaway."

"Stevie is a big, bad secret agent," Taft said. "Give him kudos from me."

"They're not safe yet," Martinez noted. "I have to mate the group up with Zoran, then get them all across the border."

"No flying out, huh?"

"Airports, train, and bus terminals are on alert."

"Which way are you thinking of taking them?" Taft asked.

The woman in the aisle across from him shifted in her seat. Her skirt raised, and Taft caught sight of a waxed thigh and a pair of polished black pumps. The first-class cabin was beginning to turn into some teenager fantasy flick. Taft tried to concentrate.

"They will be in the northern part of the country," Martinez said, "so that gives us Romania, Hungary, or Croatia as choices."

"Remember Chuck Smoot?" Taft asked. "He helped us on the Einstein case."

"Sure."

"I think he's assigned to Bucharest now," Taft noted. "He's a good hand—and he can probably handle the border crossing."

"Good idea," Martinez said, "I'll check it out and get back to you."

"I'm even working when I'm on vacation," Taft joked. "Now, what's the deal with this weather?"

Since crossing over Indiana, the plane had been in light turbulence. Taft had checked out the window and found a thick layer of clouds below.

"Nasty storm brewing," Martinez said. "Denver International is still allowing landings, but as of right now the leg on to Telluride is grounded."

"What about an airport nearby?"

"The nearest other airports are Montrose and Grand Junction," Martinez said, "and both are socked in right now."

"That leaves driving," Taft noted.

"Seven hours on mountain roads," Martinez said, "on top of the three more hours your flight will take. You'll be doing the roads at night—and you're not familiar with them."

"What do you want to do?"

"I'll talk to Driggs and see what he says," Martinez said, "but you may need to spend the night in Denver."

"I'll need a hotel, then," Taft said.

"Brown Palace downtown as usual?"

"My favorite."

"I'll call and make a tentative reservation," Martinez noted. "As your concierge, is there anything else you might require?"

"One more thing," Taft whispered. "Pull up the TSA records for the woman in the seat across from me."

"You horn dog," Martinez said, laughing. "Hold on."

Taft waited. As he did, he glanced across the aisle again. Now the woman had raised the armrest between the seats and had curled one of her legs underneath herself. As he watched, she input another command, then turned the computer off and folded it in half. She was reaching down to slide it into a case when Martinez came back on the line.

"Her name is Catherine Elder," Martinez said, reading from his computer. "She's a frequent traveler, or so I would guess from the fact that she has a fast-pass card for security."

"Hometown?"

"Denver," Martinez said.

"Thanks, old buddy," Taft said. "I'll take it from here."

## 21

AS THE NIGHT grew dark, Vojislav Pestic stared at the sheet of paper he had demanded from Ratzovik outlining his involvement. If he and his family somehow made it to freedom, it might save him from being charged with the destruction of the mine in Spain and the subsequent loss of lives. If it ever became known that the disaster occurred because of the Tesla device and was not simply a freak of nature, Pestic did not want to be the one charged with the deaths. He folded the sheet of paper into a small square, attached it to a strip of duct tape he tore from a roll, then motioned for his wife to come close.

"Turn around," he said.

Pestic's wife turned her back to him. Raising her top up, he taped the note to the small of her back. "Should anything happen," he said quietly, "give this paper to the authorities."

His wife turned around and nodded silently.

Pestic stared at the Tesla device. He had made the final adjustments earlier in the evening in anticipation of Ratzovik's arrival tomorrow. It was now tuned to hit the target Ratzovik had specified. If Pestic and his family were unable to escape, their last and final chance was a successful strike and Ratzovik's promise to allow them to go free.

It was a long shot—but Pestic needed every chance he had to save his family.

Walking to the window on the side of the barn, he stared out. It was one day before full moon, and the glow from above lit the grounds with pale yellow light. One guard dressed in black was patrolling the perimeter near the tree line. The second was closer to the house, and Pestic watched as the man struck a match to light a cigarette. Pestic watched as the flash of light settled down, illuminating the man's face, followed by the red glow as the end of the cigarette was ignited. The match was blown out and only the red glow remained, dancing through the night like some strange firefly.

Escaping would not be easy.


EACH OF THE ten U.S. Special Forces teams was each assigned a letter designation, from A to J. The A Team was the farthest east near the Macedonian border, with the remaining teams forming an arc toward where the J Team was stationed, near the border with Albania. Swiftly heading south on the muffled quads, each team inspected the surrounding area and reported back to the U.S. Navy ship offshore in the Adriatic Sea.

So far nothing of interest had been found.

Riding down the main power line rights-of-way, they periodically diverted off, following the smaller power lines to individual homes and ranches, which were searched one by one. It was a slow and tedious process, but no team had yet to be detected.

Warrant Officer Mike Davis made a slashing motion with his arm across his neck, and the other two quads in his group shut down their engines. Suddenly the forest was silent.

"I need to report in," Davis said quietly.

The six men climbed off of the quads. Two men walked a short distance away to urinate in the bushes, one reached for a bottle of water to drink, the others just stretched while Davis stepped away and flicked on his radio.

"Team Indio to support."

"Support."

"Eight miles south and report negative contact."

"Affirmative."

"How close are Hilo and Jake?"

"Hilo is approximately three miles east," the radio operator on board the ship said. "Jake is closer to two miles west and skirting the border."

"Affirm," Davis said.

"Indio," the operator said, "command would like a condition report."

"Mountainous and forested but access along the lines is reasonable," Davis reported. "We've had to dismount to physically walk a few of the smaller lines to their terminus, but we have been able to access everything within the grid assigned."

"Hold on," the radio operator ordered as he conferred with his commander.

Davis leaned back and stretched his back as he waited. The quads' jarring ride over the rough terrain was making everyone sore.

"Indio, support here."

"Go ahead," Davis said.

"Continue south as scheduled," the radio operator said. "Watch for slow-flying plane flying north to south sometime in the next two hours. It's one of ours."

"Affirm, airborne next two hours."

"Support out."

"Indio out."

Davis's team was back in place clustered around the quads. Davis slid the radio back into the holster built onto the gas tank of his machine. "Men," he said, "watch for a north-to-south flyover sometime in the next two hours—it's one of ours."

"They doing an electronic sweep?" one of Davis's sergeants asked.

"That's my guess," Davis said.

"Maybe they will find us a target," the only corporal on his team noted.

"Let's hope," Davis said, "but in the meantime let's head out and continue along the lines. Is everyone doing okay?"

The men nodded and began to climb aboard the machines again.

Davis pushed the starter on his quad. The drivers of the other two machines started up as well. Davis's team roared south until coming to the first line heading from the main high-voltage power line. Then they slowed and followed it to the end and searched.

From Macedonia to Albania the other teams were doing the exact same procedure.

The gap between them narrowing, the net was slowly closing.


PESTIC WAS RACKING his brain trying to come up with an escape plan. The barn was just south of the house the guards used, with the main door facing north. There was a large side door on the east side, but that was also in view from the house. Their only chance was the west side, which had no doors or windows. That side was dimly lit and there was a line of trees less than ten feet distant.

Outside, a wind was kicking up, and the boards of the old barn creaked.

The west side was their only hope, but they would need to make it through the wall of planks that formed the side, then make it across to the safety of the trees without being seen. In the days he'd been held inside the barn, Pestic had heard the guards walking along the west wall from time to time as they did their rounds.

The guards weren't stupid—they knew their weak point.

"I'll be right back," Pestic whispered to his wife.

On the south end of the barn, comprising a third of the length, was a hayloft. The extra floor was supported by six-by-six posts, which were framed with four-by-eights running the width of the barn and covered in planks to form the floor the hay sat upon. A ladder to gain access was built onto the framing alongside the west wall.

Pestic climbed up the ladder and surveyed the loft. Half of the hay had been used before Ratzovik had acquired the farm. The rest had sat for more than a year and was drying into straw. Walking back along the west wall, Pestic picked a spot and started to move the bales away from the wall. Moving them forward, he built a tunnel through the bales until he had access to the west wall, with a space large enough for a person to fit.

Once that was completed, he removed a hand drill with a hole bit on the end from where he had slid it into his belt. Cranking the drill, he bored a peephole. Once through, he removed the piece of wood from the end and peered out. The trees nearby were a little small for what he had planned, so Pestic plugged the hole back up, moved south another eight feet, and repeated the procedure.

Peering from the hole, Pestic could see the large oak tree just a little farther south, surrounded by the spruce and pines. From where he was in the loft, Pestic was almost twenty feet off the ground. The oak tree had a thick limb at about fifteen feet that looked like it might be able to support their weight. Behind the oak was only forest.

If he and his family could make it across the gap, they had a chance.

Pestic stared at the roof of the loft. There was a pulley system with hay hooks and ropes for moving the bales; he figured he could rework it to do what he needed. Now the only problem was how to make an opening in the wall without being detected.

The framing of the barn was on six-foot centers, with the planks that formed the outside nine feet in length and laid in an overlapping fashion for strength. Between the main posts were two-by-four supports where the exterior planks were nailed when they did not end on a main beam. The main posts were too thick to hand-saw, but Pestic figured he could make it through the two-by-fours and exterior planks.

Reaching into his pocket, he removed a razor knife and scraped away on both sides some of the exterior planking from where it attached to the two-by-fours. He did this on the top and bottom so he could fit a saw through the planks to cut the two-by-fours. If Pestic could cut straight down along the main supports and then through the exterior planking, he could then sever the two-by-fours at the top and bottom and pull the entire piece inside the loft.

He would then have a nice door to the outside. Unless a guard noticed the sawdust on the ground or happened to look up and see the opening, Pestic figured the wind outside would dissipate most of the sawdust. As for a guard glancing up, there was little he could do about that. Pestic walked through the hay tunnel to the ladder, then climbed down and whispered to his wife.

"I think I have found an escape route," he whispered. "Have you and our boy ready to leave in an hour or so."

"What should we bring?" she asked.

"Only the bare essentials," Pestic said. "We have to take a rope from the hayloft across to a tree and then down to the ground. From there we will try to make our way to the nearest farmhouse and ask for help."

"We will be ready, my love," she said.

Pestic nodded and walked over to the tool bench. Finding a couple of wood saws in different sizes, one with a pointed end and one whose end was flat, he grabbed them and peered out the window. The guards were still out there. With the saws in his hand he walked over to the west wall and set the saws on the ground. Removing the drill from his belt, he bored a peephole.

"Alert me if one of the guards starts down this wall," he said to his wife.

Then, saws in one hand, he climbed the ladder into the loft and started his project.

"BARN IS CLEAR," one of Davis's sergeants said.

Davis nodded and stared down at his parabolic microphone. The dish was pointed at the house. Other than a clock that had chimed a few minutes ago, he had heard no signs of life.

"This was on the door," the corporal said, handing Davis a sheet of paper with tape along the top edge.

"First Sergeant Gibbons," Davis said, "what does this read?"

Gibbons, the only one in the team who could read Serbo-Croatian, glanced at the note for a second and handed it back. "Bardan, if you come by, please check the animals—we have gone to the hospital in Prizren."

"Note to a neighbor?" Davis asked.

"Neighbor or relative who lives nearby is my guess," Gibbons said.

"Corporal," Davis said, "tape this note back on the door. Sergeant, if you could please check to see if the animals in the barn have food and water, we'll be on our way."

The two men headed off while Davis broke down the parabolic microphone and placed it back in its box. He was just attaching the box to the back of the quad when the two men returned.

"The note is reattached," the corporal said.

"They must have just left tonight," Gibbons said. "The troughs are full of water and grain."

"I'll call in and report," Davis said. "Then we'll be on our way."

PESTIC WAS THROUGH one side of the planks and halfway through the second side when his wife whistled a warning that a guard was approaching. Racing back to the stairs, he climbed down and waited, faking sleep. One guard slid the door open and shined a flashlight toward them. Seeing them all lying together with their eyes closed, he shut the door quietly.

Pestic waited as he heard a second guard walk along the west wall. He followed the sound, which did not pause as the guard walked along the west wall, then around the south end of the barn and along the east wall. When the sounds died down, Pestic crept over to the windows on the east wall near the tool bench and peered out.

The guards were back in position near the house. So far, so good.

Climbing back up into the loft, Pestic finished sawing through the exterior boards. Then he took the saw with the pointed end and severed the two-by-four on the bottom. Now all he had to do was cut the top two-by-four and drag the entire panel inside.

Glancing up at the simple pulley system, Pestic cut the rope with his knife and estimated the length of the rope at about twenty-five feet—more than enough for what he needed. Removing the pulley that rested on a hook from a circular metal support screwed into the roof beam, he threaded one of the cut ends of the rope through the circle and tied it off. Making sure the hay hook was firmly attached to the other end by tugging on it, Pestic walked back through the tunnel and climbed down.

Walking over to the tool bench, he retrieved a can of grease used to lubricate metal, and he cut some work rags into several strips. Then he walked over to his wife.

"Wake up our boy," he whispered, "then climb up into the loft. I have just a few more things to do; then we can try our escape."

His wife nodded and walked over to where their nine-year-old was sleeping.

Pestic climbed back up the ladder, made his way through the hay to the rope, and began to grease it halfway down the length. He was sawing away the last two-by-four when his wife and son appeared in the open space inside the hay bales.

"Be very quiet and listen," Pestic said. "First I want you to each take these rags and gag yourself. If you scream in fear, we will be caught."

His son and wife took the rags and helped each other attach them around their heads.

"Good," Pestic said, smiling. "Now I'm going to cut through the last board, remove the panel so we have an opening, and toss this line across to a tree outside. Once that is done, I will slide across. You go next," he said to his son, "and your mom will follow."

Pestic demonstrated how to place the other strips of cloth over the rope. "Make sure you hold firmly to the ends. I'll catch you on the other side."

His wife and son nodded, but they both looked scared.

"Okay," Pestic said, "just a few more minutes."

Walking over to the wall, he sawed through the last two-by-four. Carefully holding the panel by the middle two-by-four, he turned it out and dragged it inside. There was now a large opening to the outside.

Taking the rope with the hook on the end, Pestic swung it back and forth to gain momentum and tossed it across the distance. The hook went over the limb a few feet lower in height, then fell down toward the ground. Snagging the hook on a lower limb, Pestic tested, found it held, then tightened the line by retying the end of the circular fitting on the roof's main beam.

There was now a lifeline to the tree. Pestic took a strip of cloth in his hand and slid it over the top of the greased rope. Then he peered out the opening toward the house and, finding no one watching, held tight and slid across the distance. When planning the escape, Pestic had feared he might slide too fast and slam into the tree, but even with the grease on the rope, he moved relatively slowly, about the speed of a slow walk.

Once he reached the limb the rope was dangling over, he climbed up and sat on the limb. Then he motioned for his son to come across. His son slid slowly over, and Pestic helped him around the trunk of the tree to another limb, where he motioned him to quietly sit. Then he waved at his wife to come across. She hesitated for a second but then strung her cloth over the rope and started across. Pestic grabbed her and yanked her up to the limb. Then he kissed her on her gagged mouth.

One by one they made their way down the tree trunk to the ground.

Then as quietly as possible, they made their way into the forest. Within half an hour they were almost a mile away from the barn and headed north-northwest.

# 22

IN THE COMMAND center for the CIA, time was running out.

"The Compass Call flight is over the area!" a technician shouted across the room to the assistant DCI.

Compass Call was the popular name for the USAF EC-130-H electronics warfare airplane. Based on the popular Lockheed Martin C-130 turboprop, the four-engine, propeller-driven plane had a cargo compartment stuffed with electronic early warning and detection gear.

The assistant DCI stared up at the map displayed on the floor-to-ceiling monitor attached to the wall. The EC-130-H was almost at the end of the first east-to-west line. He watched as the plane made a sweeping turn over the Albanian border, then line back up for the next pass, which was west to east and slightly to the south. The grid they had established was like a lawn mower cutting the grass, back and forth in straight lines until the entire area of southern Kosovo would be covered.

It was a tedious task—but it should yield a signal from the locators inside the files.

"How long until the grid is completed?" the assistant DCI shouted.

"One hour, twenty minutes," the technician answered.

"It'll be just about daylight by then," the assistant DCI noted.

"Yes, sir," the technician said.

"As soon as they are finished with the grid," the assistant DCI said, "pull them out."

"What if they haven't captured the signal?" the technician asked.

"Have them retreat," the assistant DCI ordered. "I don't want the Russians catching wind of our presence."

"Yes, sir," the technician said.


PESTIC STOPPED NEXT to his wife, who was bent over at the waist, panting.

"Love," he said, "we have to keep moving."

Reaching over to his son, who stood next to his mother, he patted his back. "How are you holding up?"

The son raised his hand and gave a thumbs-up signal.

Pestic glanced ahead. There was a rise ahead, with a fifteen-hundred-foot elevation increase to the top. Once they created the rise, he'd feel better about their chances.

"We make it over that hill," he said to his wife, "and we can take a break."

Sucking in mouthfuls of air, she rose upright and nodded. "Let's do it," she said gamely.

The three made their way forward as the sky in the east began to lighten.


ON THE OTHER side of the rise, Warrant Officer Mike Davis and the Indio team finished searching an abandoned barn. The quads were line up alongside the wall, out of sight.

"Doesn't look like this has been used in a few years," First Sergeant Gibbons said.

Davis nodded and glanced north. There was a droning sound from far away and he listened, then removed the parabolic microphone and pointed it airborne. The sound quickly became defined, and Davis could hear the noise of the four engines and the slapping sound made by the propellers.

"Sounds like the eyes in the sky are north of here," Davis said to the team. "They should be over our area shortly."

Davis decided to rotate the dish around in a circle before placing it back in the case. He was pointing it south toward the rise when he picked up the sound of wood cracking.

"Shush," he said.

The team stood silently. Davis trained the dish toward the top of the hill. He could just make out the sound of muffled footsteps. Two, maybe three people, and they sounded like they were running.

"We have unknowns in the area," Davis said quickly, "just over that rise. Sergeant, take the corporal and do a reconnaissance. You two go east," Davis said, pointing at two of his men. "Sergeant Earhart and I will take the west flank. Use night vision and do not fire unless fired upon."

The men quickly spread out and starting making their way through the brush and trees. Other than Davis, who was carrying the parabolic microphone and had his rifle slung over his shoulder, the men had their weapons unlocked and facing forward. The slightest pull on their triggers and a field of lead would rain through the trees.

"WE'RE ALMOST THERE," Pestic said to his wife and son.

The three were standing below a rock outcropping near the crest of the hill. Pestic motioned them to skirt the rocks so they could travel through a treed glade to the right. Exiting from the bottom of the outcropping, they started through the trees. A few more minutes and they would be over the rise and could rest.

DAVIS WHISTLED, AND his team stopped in place. Gibbons and the corporal were just below the crest—they crouched down and aimed their weapons at an opening in the trees. Davis and Earhart were just to the left, the other two members of the team to the right of Gibbons and slightly lower.

Whoever was coming was walking into a trap.

"WHEW," PESTIC SAID, "that was a haul. We have some downhill for a bit; let's take it slow and easy for a few minutes."

Reaching over, Pestic took his wife and his son's hands. Three abreast, they started down the hill and into an open meadow.

GIBBONS SAW THE three first. He raised his hand and swept it back and forth like he was waving. The others saw his motion and took their fingers off their triggers. Gibbons watched the three walk past, and once they were slightly below his position, he slid from the trees, followed by the corporal.

"Stop," he said in Serbo-Croatian.

Pestic and his family froze. From out of the trees to both sides, four men in camouflage suddenly appeared with rifles trained on them. Pestic heard the sound of men above them walking slowly down the hill.

In most people's life there come a time when all hope seems lost. Perhaps it comes from an investment gone bad that wipes out all one has amassed. Sometimes it appears when diagnosed with a disease. Often it simply comes from the wear and tear of ordinary life when dreams are dashed and reality hooks its claws into you.

Pestic felt it right now.

They had tried, but he had failed. And Pestic knew the final outcome would be death to him and his family. Ratzovik's men had caught them—and there would be no further chance to escape. Tomorrow at this time they would be lying in shallow graves. Pestic's shoulders drooped as the reality set upon him like the icy kiss of a fist. A tear ran from his eye down his cheek.

"Raise your hands in the air," Gibbons said in Serbo-Croatian.

Pestic, his wife, and his son complied.

From behind and out of sight a pair of hands quickly patted down their bodies, searching for weapons. Finding nothing, the corporal spoke.

"They're clean, boss," he said.

Davis walked closer. "I'm Warrant Office Mike Davis, United States Army," he said. "Do you speak English?"

The words hit Pestic with a wave of joy. Only seconds before, his fate had been sealed. Now salvation was upon them, and he could barely control his emotions.

"Yes, I do," Pestic blubbered as his emotions overwhelmed him. "I do."

Davis walked closer, placed his hands on Pestic's raised arms, and lowered them. "Get these people some food and water," Davis said to Gibbons, who quickly reached into his pack, brought out a bottle of water and a few meal replacement bars, and handed them over.

"Stand down," Davis ordered his men, who were now surrounding the Pestic family in a half circle.

The team lowered their weapons and stood waiting.

"Now, sir," Davis said, "could you tell me your name and what you are doing out here so early in the morning?

It took Pestic a few minutes to get his emotions under control.

Then he told Davis everything.


INSIDE THE EC-130-H, USAF specialist Landon White stared at a blip on the screen, reached over, and adjusted a dial on the console. White was sitting sideways in the fuselage on a metal chair covered in black leather. The entire inside of the EC-130-H was covered in electronic panels, and three other specialists, two men and one woman, were staring at the displays. White swiveled around and spoke to the woman, who was one of the two monitoring the wall of instruments on the other side of the plane.

"Mel," White said, "what do you think about this?"

Specialist Melody "Mel" Adams had the knack. It was something you could not train into a person—you either had it or you did not.

Electronic signals were always out there; it was how they were interpreted by a human that made most of the difference.

Mel stood up and reached over to White's panel. Adjusting a few dials, she watched the squiggly lines on the graph. Then she reached over and opened a folder that listed the amplitudes the NIA had supplied the air force for the mission.

Staring at the graph, she adjusted the dials once again and stared at the results on the monitor.

"You got it, Landon," she said quietly. "Call it in."

White reached for the intercom button and alerted the pilot.

He was just sitting back in his chair when he felt the plane speed up. The fuselage tilted as the pilot made a turn.

"Mel, it feels like we're headed back to Italy," White said. "Buy you a drink out by the base pool?"

"I do all the hard work?" Mel said easily, "and you offer me one lousy drink?"

"How about a burger and a beer?"

"Now you're talking," Mel said.


"COMPASS CALL REPORTS they got the hit!" the technician shouted across the room to the assistant DCI. "They are beaming the data to a satellite and down to us momentarily!"

"What's the status on the teams?"

"They have all reported in within the past fifteen minutes except for Indio," the technician reported.

"Call him and find out status," the assistant DCI said. "Then alert them all we'll be sending new orders soon."


"YOU CAN LEAD us back there?" Davis was asking Pestic.

"Sir," one of the sergeants said, interrupting, "we have control on the radio requesting a status report."

Davis took the radio.

"Control, this is Indio team leader."

"We need a status report," the CIA technician said, "and then stand by for new orders."

"Status is," Davis said, "that we know the location of the device."

The assistant DCI took the radio microphone from the technician. "Indio leader," he said quickly, "explain."

Davis started to explain.

## 23

"COME IN," BENSON said.

"I just received this from the CIA," Allbright said, walking into the office and sliding a file onto Benson's desk.

Benson opened the file and read the contents.

"The electrical engineer had a confession taped to his wife's back?" Benson said.

"Right," Allbright said. "It implicates a man named Galadin Ratzovik as the ringleader."

"What do we have on him?"

Allbright took another file from under his arm. "He's wanted by the UN War Crimes Tribunal for atrocities he committed in Kosovo. He was tied to Bozdar Maladric, who the Belgrade police found dead at the apartment of Zarko Bodonavik, the Serbian presidential adviser killed in the theft of the Tesla files."

"So," Benson said, "Ratzovik is Ilic's man in Serbia."

Allbright slid into a chair in front of the desk and placed his arms on the edge with palms apart. "That's the problem, General," he said. "Our research indicates that Ratzovik and Ilic were not that close—at least recently. Taps placed near the conference area used by Ilic and his lawyers reveal that as recently as a few days ago Ilic was trying to find Ratzovik himself. Apparently Ratzovik was in charge of the former commander's ill-gotten gains, and Ilic was concerned he had stolen the funds."

Benson was quiet for a moment. "Perhaps he was using the money to fund this scheme," Benson suggested, "and couldn't tell Ilic because of the need for secrecy."

Allbright nodded. "Those were my thoughts as well. So when I found this out from the CIA a few moments ago I called our Currency and Funds Department to see if they could track the movement of the money."

"What did they find?" Benson asked.

"They are still working on it," Allbright admitted, "but they have already turned up large-scale funds transfers to a trading account in Geneva, Switzerland."

"So Ratzovik invested in stocks and bonds for Ilic," Benson said. "Nothing unusual there."

"The accounts were in Ratzovik's name only," Allbright said, "and they were massive positions in gold as well as a recent large short position in dollars."

Benson sat quietly for a moment. "That doesn't make any sense," he said at last.

"That's what I thought, too," Allbright noted.

"We might have the culprit, but there is another complication," Benson said. "The guards we sent to watch over the European power station have been reporting back. The electrical system in Europe is so interconnected there is no way to shut down segments to cut southern Serbia off. The way they explain it, if they take out just one of the trunk lines, it has a trigger effect. Cut some of the power to Serbia and you also impact the sardine factories in Italy, or the tramways in Austria, or the factories in France."

"Damn," Allbright said.

"The way it was explained to me," Benson said, "is that the grid is so overlaid among the countries that it is like if a fuse went out in your house and then your neighbor's refrigerator stopped working."

"So we cannot cut the power to Serbia?"

"No," Benson said quietly. "The threat must be stopped at the source."

"Damn glad we're no longer in charge of this," Allbright said.

"Me, too," Benson said. "Me, too."

THE SERBIAN PRESIDENT sat in his office in Belgrade. With his key adviser Bodonavik dead, the advice he was receiving from the other men farther down the line was mixed and without strong positions.

"Did none of you learn anything from Zarko?" he thundered. "I don't need possibilities—I know what those are. I need gut instincts. You're not scientists, you're advisers—give me some advice. First, as I asked before, what are the citizens going to do when Ilic returns?"

One of the junior men started double-talking again, but the president cut him off.

"All of you," he said, motioning to the door, "get out. You're all useless."

As the men started filing out, the president reached down and activated his intercom. "Did Milorand arrive yet?" he asked his receptionist.

"He's here in the lobby, sir," the receptionist said.

"By all means send him in immediately, then bring in tea."

Dragoslav Milorand was sitting in a chair outside the office watching the men file out of the president's inner sanctum. He was the far side of eighty, with a shock white, thinning hair and a neatly groomed white mustache. His liver-spotted hands held the end of a gold-plated eagle-head cane.

"Sir," the receptionist said, "you've been asked to go inside. Can I help you get up?"

Milorand was wearing an expensive pair of French-made slacks and a tailored shirt, silk tie, and silk sport coat. Propping the cane against the floor he levered himself to his feet. "I have it, thank you," he said, smiling.

Milorand was somewhat of a legend in Serbia. He had first begun working for former President Tito in the 1960s, and had remained a key adviser until Tito's death in 1980. Once Tito was gone, Milorand had gone into private practice, was behind the scenes as communism was denounced in 1990, and remained a behind-the-scenes political player until Ilic became commander. Once Ilic was in charge, Milorand fell from favor. However, the fortune he had amassed as well as the political connections he had built throughout the world kept him away from any political persecution or retaliation. During Ilic's reign, Milorand had spent most of his time in France.

Once Ilic was extradited, Milorand began to return more and more often to his mansion in Belgrade. For all intents and purposes it seemed that Milorand was retired and had been for years, but the truth was a little more complex. Most countries in the world have at least a few men like Milorand—they operate as a sort of quasi-diplomatic department. Using contacts and friendships built over decades, they work behind the scenes to keep their country on track. Milorand was old, but he was far from finished.

"Mr. Milorand," the president said, rising from behind his desk and walking forward, "I want to thank you for agreeing to visit today."

Milorand switched the cane to his other hand, then reached out to shake with the president. "The honor is mine, Mr. President."

The president motioned Milorand over to a seating area near the fireplace, where there was a couch and a pair of wing chairs. The fireplace was dormant for the summer, but the area was comfortable enough without it.

Milorand took a seat in one of the wing chairs, the president on the couch.

"It's been nearly a year," Milorand said, "since we have visited."

"The reception for the Japanese conglomerate," the president agreed.

Milorand had arranged for a Japanese concern to open a manufacturing plant near Smederevo, and the president had assisted the process with tax abatements.

"How is your family, sir?" Milorand asked politely. "Your daughter must be in her second year of university now."

"She is," the president said, "and doing fine."

"Your brother?"

"Still working with a group of investors to build up the ski area tourism at Zlatibor," the president said. "It's his passion."

"He's good at it, sir," Milorand said. "You should be proud."

The president nodded as the door to the office opened and the receptionist entered carrying a silver platter with a teapot, sugar, cream, and various cookies. She set it on the table in front of the couch and retreated. The president poured two cupfuls, then made a motion toward the sugar and cream. Milorand shook his head no, and the president handed him the cup.

"I need your advice," the president said directly.

"Whatever I can do, sir," Milorand said, taking a sip from the cup.

"Former commander Ilic is scheduled to return to Serbia today," the president said.

"I think," Milorand said, "you'd better explain."


THE DCI BLEW into the control room like a Texas tornado.

"What have we got?" he asked the assistant DCI directly.

"Less than an hour ago one of our Special Forces teams intercepted the scientist in charge of the Tesla device as he was trying to escape from the captors. He's given us the name of the man behind the scheme, Galadin Ratzovik, and agreed to lead the teams back to the site."

"Excellent," the DCI said. "Now let's cut the power lines to the site and be done with this threat once and for all."

"If only it were so simple," the assistant DCI said. "The scientist—actually, he's an electrical engineer—claims Ratzovik had the power lines laid underground."

"So chances are we would never had located the facility if this man had not gotten free and been captured by our forces."

"Probably not."

"You're moving the rest of the teams into place?" the DCI asked.

The assistant DCI pointed to a map displayed on one of the monitors. The ten teams were converging on Team Indio's location. The green squiggly lines the quads made as they traveled looked like spiderwebs make from Silly String.

"Air strike?" the DCI inquired.

"We could have that done in a few hours from either a navy ship in the Med or heavy bombers out of Turkey," the assistant DCI noted. "I've asked the military to form plans and stand by."

"But then we wouldn't have the device."

"Exactly," the assistant DCI said.

"How long until Ilic is due to be released?"

The assistant DCI stared at a digital clock on the wall that was counting the time. "Two hours, twenty minutes; then a flight time of three hours to Belgrade."

"So we have five hours to recover the device?" the DCI said.

"Four hours, twenty minutes," the assistant DCI said, "if we want to preserve the bombing option. Once we order the strike it will take forty minutes before the fastest jet can be over the target area."

"At this time I want you to coordinate with the ground teams like you're doing," the DCI said, "for an assault on the location and possible recovery. Preserve the air strike as a future option for now."

"Got it," the assistant DCI said.

"I'm going to see the president," the DCI said, "and try to get something signed off on this."

"Bag of worms," the assistant DCI noted.

"Someone else needs to call this," the DCI agreed.

"SO THAT'S ABOUT the score," the Serbian president finished.

Milorand nodded slowly. "I assume, Mr. President, that you asked me here for my opinion and advice, not pandering and double-talk."

"Precisely."

"Though you are the duly elected president, once Ilic returns, the populace will call for your ouster as a retaliation against Western influence in Serbian national affairs vis-à-vis the UN tribunal. I would give your presidency a matter of days, not weeks, before it folds to the pressure. At first there may be support inside your cabinet, but once the popular support shows for Ilic, your insiders will start to defect one by one to his side. If you lose the military it would accelerate the process and then you and your family could be threatened. Without a military presence to command order, the crowds could become inflamed and make a move to capture you themselves. You and your family could be held as prisoners or worse."

"A Russian imperial family scenario?"

"More like Mussolini," Milorand said directly.

"What about the world community if Ilic returns?" the president asked. "How will they react?"

"Immediate sanctions, condemnation, possible military action, occupation," Milorand said. "Serbia would be set back several decades, at the least. At the worse, some other country might be an occupying force."

"Fifty million to ruin my country," the president said.

"Excuse me, sir?" Milorand said.

"Ilic's minions offered me fifty million if I stepped down upon his return."

Milorand was silent for a moment. "Sounds like they do not know you too well, Mr. President," he said slowly.

The Serbian president smiled. "Thanks for the support," he said, "but I'd be lying if I said the thought did not cross my mind once."

"Everyone has thought, Mr. President," Milorand said. "It's how we act that is the measure of character."

"What can we do?" the president asked plainly.

"Here's a few ideas."

Milorand began to slowly talk through the situation.


GALADIN RATZOVIK STEPPED from the helicopter and immediately knew something was wrong. He began to walk toward the farmhouse and met the head of the guard detachment halfway. It was early afternoon, and though he did not know it, in the woods nearby were sixty U.S. Special Forces troops awaiting an order to attack.

"What's the problem?" he asked the leader of the guards.

"Pestic and his family escaped last night," the man said. "We have teams out searching, but they have yet to turn up anything."

"He escaped?" Ratzovik shouted, "How?"

"Cut through the wall of the hayloft in the barn and ran a rope to a nearby tree."

"And your men have yet to capture him?"

"We have not, sir," the head guard admitted.

Ratzovik reached into his jacket, removed a handgun from the holster under his armpit, and shot the leader of the guards directly in the forehead. A spray of brain matter spewed through the air, and the man dropped to the ground in a heap, with a pool of blood quickly staining the ground.

"Now," Ratzovik said, "who has some good news for me?"

"SIR," THE DCI said, "I'm sorry we had to meet so early, but there have been a series of developments in the Tesla affair that require your attention."

"I awoke at five," the president said. "It's almost seven now. I've already had a plate of bacon and eggs and four cups of coffee. You have my full attention."

The DCI quickly explained the situation.

"What time is it now in Serbia?" the president asked.

"Almost 1:00 P.M." the DCI noted.

"And when is Mr. Ilic due to be released?"

"Less than an hour from now."

"So," the president said, "if he is released on time there will be no reason for his people to strike at The Netherlands."

"That's our read on the situation," the DCI agreed.

"And it will take him a few hours of flight time to reach Serbia?"

"Correct, sir."

"Do we have anybody inside The Netherlands who can screw up the radios in the jet that is carrying him home? Some way to ensure that he is not in communication with his people on the ground?"

"We can jam them through satellites," the DCI noted, "or have his flight followed by an electronics jamming jet."

"So that gives us a couple more hours to act," the president noted.

"Almost three until he touches down," the DCI said, "plus time on the ground in Belgrade until he is detected by the citizens."

"I'm sure his people are smart enough to send press releases to the local media as soon as he lifts off," the president said.

"We can dispatch men to the radio and television stations and suppress the news," the DCI said.

"Do that and make sure the newspapers are covered as well."

"So you agree we should let him leave The Netherlands?" the DCI asked.

"Yes," the president said, "but if we don't force him down and he reaches the ground in Belgrade, I want him dealt with immediately."

"How so, sir?"

The president looked over at his national security adviser, who until now had remained silent. He stared into his eyes but said nothing. The man nodded.

"Go with the planned recovery for now with the option in place for bombing. He'll fill you in on the rest," the president said, rising and walking from the Oval Office.

Once the president was safely out of the office, the national security adviser motioned for the DCI to follow him into a small secure room nearby that was not wired with voice recorders.

"We'll sign a finding for the planned assault with the bombing option retained," the national security adviser said quietly. "As for the second matter, we want nothing traced back to us. Use Serbs if you can find them or off-the-record operatives if need be, but in no way does Ilic walk away from the airport at Belgrade."

"I'll do it, sir," the DCI noted.

"That's what we like to hear."

# 24

AS SOON AS Martinez had explained the situation with the grounded flights, Malcolm Driggs had quickly decided to drive east himself. Even if it had cleared up in the morning and Taft had been able to fly to Telluride, by the time he arrived, learned the information, and left again, it might have been too late. Fortified by gas station coffee and Dixieland jazz, Driggs had made the journey in less than seven hours.

It was 5:00 A.M., with the sun starting to light the horizon on the Eastern Plains outside Denver, when Malcolm Driggs reached the Brown Palace Hotel. He was exhausted and sore. Removing his bags from the rear of the SUV, he handed the car over to the valet.

"Could you have it washed and fueled?" he asked. "I won't need it again until tonight at the earliest."

"Yes, sir," the valet said. "And your name, please?"

"Driggs," he said.

The valet handed him a ticket, then climbed inside. Driggs watched as he wheeled the car from the front into a nearby garage. Then Driggs waited as a bellman took the bags. The doorman opened the door, and Driggs walked into the lobby.

The Brown Palace Hotel was built in the 1800s during the height of the Colorado mining boom. For years she was acknowledged as the finest hotel between Kansas City and San Francisco, and she has witnessed a host of rich and famous people through the years. Lovingly restored numerous times, the hotel possesses the type of timeless elegance that newer hotels are unable to duplicate.

"Good morning, sir," the front desk clerk said. "How may I help you?"

"I have a reservation. My name is Driggs."

The clerk tapped a few commands into the keyboard. "Yes, Mr. Driggs," he said a few seconds later, "we have you all taken care of."

Then he reached behind to a wall with old-fashioned mail slots, removed an envelope, and handed it across the desk. "This was left for you."

Driggs opened the envelope and quickly read the contents while the clerk motioned for the bellman to come closer. The clerk quietly gave the bellman Driggs's room number.

"Is there a house phone nearby?" Driggs asked.

The clerk pointed to an ornate carved wooden table in the foyer where an antique brass telephone resided. Driggs walked over and dialed a room number. Surprisingly enough, the room answered on the first ring.

"John Taft," a husky voice said.

"This is Driggs. I'm down in the lobby."

"Do you want to take a shower and freshen up before we meet?" Taft asked.

"Hold on," Driggs said, placing his hand over the receiver. "When does the restaurant open?" he asked the clerk.

"Five-thirty A.M. sir," the clerk said, "about twenty minutes from now."

Driggs removed his hand from the receiver. "The restaurant opens in twenty minutes," he said. "I'll clean up and meet you down there then."

"Five-thirty in the downstairs restaurant," Taft agreed.

Driggs motioned to the bellman, who was standing a discreet distance away. Pushing the cart containing the few bags Driggs had brought toward the elevator, the bellman pushed the button, and the two men stood waiting.

One of the bags on the cart was a satchel partially opened and stuffed with maps and atlases. The elevator doors opened, and the bellman slid the cart inside, Driggs followed behind, and the doors shut.

Downtown Denver, where the Brown Palace is located, is home to nearly a thousand oil companies big and small. The doorman stared down at the satchel of maps. "Are you a geologist, sir?" he asked as the elevator ascended.

"No," Driggs said. "I write books."

The bellman stared closely.

"Hey," he said a second later, "you're that Malcolm Driggs fellow."

"Guilty as charged," Driggs said.

The elevator was almost at the floor. "I've always wanted to ask you something," the bellman asked. "You have all those old cars, right?"

The elevator slowed, and the doors slid open. The bellman wheeled the cart out as he continued talking. Driggs smiled and nodded at the bellman's question.

"What's your favorite?" the bellman asked as he wheeled the cart down the hall toward the room.

"That's a tough one," Driggs said. "They're all great. However, if I had to pick a favorite right now, it would be the 1959 Mercury station wagon."

The bellman reached the room and was opening the door. "That seems an odd choice," he said as he wheeled the cart inside and started to unload the bags.

"It was my wife's," Driggs said, smiling, "and she passed away a few years ago. Sometimes when I drive it I remember all the good times we had."

The bellman simply nodded. There was nothing that needed to be said. Taking the ten-dollar bill Driggs held out, he started for the door.

"Whatever you need, Mr. Driggs," he said when he reached the door and opened it again, "just call down and ask for me—my name is Derek."

"Thanks, Derek," Driggs said as the door closed.

Placing his suitcase on the bed, Driggs opened it and removed his shaving kit and fresh clothes. Then he walked into the bathroom and showered and shaved. Eighteen minutes later he was riding down in the elevator.

"I LEFT MY number on the notepad," Catherine Elder said as she finished dressing. "Don't be an ass and not call."

"Put your address down, too," Taft said as he popped out of the bathroom after splashing his cheeks with aftershave. Taft had a towel wrapped around his waist and he removed it and started to dress.

"Why?" Elder asked.

"I like to send flowers," Taft said, slipping into his underwear and then a pair of slacks.

Elder walked over and placed her hand on Taft's chest, then tilted her head up and kissed him on the lips. "*I* should send *you* the flowers," she said.

Taft was sliding a shirt over his shoulder; he lined up the buttons and started to fasten them, starting at the bottom. He grinned. "Okay," he said, "but no candy—I'm watching my figure."

Elder shook her head back and forth and walked for the door. "Number is on the pad," she said, walking out of the room.

THE ELEVATOR CARRYING Driggs descended only two floors, then stopped, and the door opened. A woman dressed in a blue-striped business suit with a knee-length skirt and a silk blouse walked inside. Her hair was tousled, as if it had been pinned up earlier, and her face was showing equal parts tiredness and glow. The signs were obvious.

"Good morning," Driggs said quietly.

"Yes, it is," the woman said, smiling.

The elevator door opened at the lobby, and Driggs chivalrously held it open so the woman could pass through first. She headed straight for the front door. Driggs turned and started for the restaurant.

"Good morning, sir," the hostess said. "How many will there be?"

At the same time, Taft was sliding on a pair of loafers. He opened the door of his room and headed down the hall for the elevator.

"There will be two," Driggs said, "and we need a private area so we can talk."

The hostess nodded and removed a pair of menus. Smiling, she led Driggs toward a banquette that sat alone and was built into the wall.

"This will be quiet," she said easily, "even if we fill up later."

"Thanks," Driggs said, sliding into the booth. "If you could bring us a pot of coffee now, we'll wait and order when my other party arrives."

"Right away, sir," the hostess said.

Driggs sat and glanced around the room. Red brick walls rose from dark wood floors, and numerous light fixtures cast the room in a pale glow. The room had the feeling of a ski lodge sans skiers. The waiter brought a silver pot containing the coffee just as a tall, blond-haired man slowed at the hostess station.

"I'm meeting someone," Taft said, sweeping past the entry, "I think that's him there."

Taft walked over to the table and extended his hand. "I'm John Taft," he said, reaching down and shaking hands. "You must be the world-famous Malcolm Driggs."

Driggs motioned for Taft to sit. "I don't know if I'm famous," Driggs said, "or just damn lucky."

Taft reached over and filled his cup from the silver pot. "Now what do you have that is so important that you would drive all night to meet a poor civil servant like me?"


"YOU HAVE THE arrest warrant," the chief of the Belgrade Police Department said to Detective Pavic. "Now go find Ratzovik and bring him in."

Detective Pavic rose from his chair, clutching the warrant. "We've got several locations to search," he said. "I'll need at least a dozen men."

"Take whoever you need," the chief said. "Just find Ratzovik."

Detective Pavic nodded and walked from the office. Twenty minutes later he had assembled his teams and sent them on their way. And although in the next few hours the police would search throughout Belgrade, Ratzovik would prove impossible to find.


DRIGGS AND TAFT had both ordered eggs Benedict from the waiter. While the food was cooking, Driggs opened his satchel and started to remove various files.

"Here's the thing," he said quietly. "Remember in the Tesla reports Karl Esbenson said there was a mention of Ames?"

"Yes," Taft said. "We checked that out. There were no records of Tesla having ever visited Iowa. At least any we could find."

"Ames was also the name of a mining town just above Telluride," Driggs said, pointing to a map. "Since Tesla was involved in the electrification of Telluride, it's most probably what he was referring to—Colorado, not Iowa."

"Damn," Taft said, "we missed that completely."

"I did some more digging through my files and found out Tesla had in fact been involved in the construction of an electrical plant at Ames, Colorado, that was built to supply electricity to the mines nearby. I found records that he was there during the construction in 1901 before he ran into financial trouble with the Wardenclyffe facility. Now move forward a few years. In the Esbenson records I located a mention of Iver Esbenson secretly purchasing some electrical equipment that had been owed by Tesla when the equipment went up for sale at a sheriff's sale in Colorado Springs in 1906. I have reason to believe this was the same equipment he used in his earlier experiments trying to deliver electricity underground to Cripple Creek, Colorado. Then, in the archives of the Telluride newspaper, I found a two-line mention that Tesla was back in Telluride in the spring of 1906—April, to be exact."

"So he was using his old equipment somehow in conjunction with the power plant he had designed. Nothing criminal there," Taft noted.

The waiter arrived and slid the plates of eggs Benedict onto the table.

"Anything else right now?" the waiter asked.

"No," both men said.

The waiter retreated, and they were alone again.

"Let's eat it while it's hot," Driggs said. "We can talk while we eat."
The two men started eating.

"Here's the thing," Driggs said, opening an atlas to the Colorado page. "Notice where Cripple Creek is in relation to Colorado Springs."

Taft stared at the map. "A little west, twenty miles or so."

"And remember that Tesla's laboratory was slightly south of Colorado Springs proper, in the prairie."

"Got it," Taft said.

"I ran the longitude lines one to the other," Driggs said, finishing his bite. "It's almost a straight line west along the latitude line."

"So," Taft said, "there are not many other towns nearby. Tesla probably needed to be near civilization to prove his point."

"Fast forward to 1906 with what we now know—that Tesla was in Ames in April."

"Okay," Taft said, forking some hash browns into his mouth.

"And remember that when Tesla was doing the Colorado Springs to Cripple Creek tests there was talk of the ground shaking and other physical disturbances."

"Got it," Taft said, finishing his bite and pushing the plate away.

"Now," Driggs said, "what major event happened in the United States in April of 1906?"

Taft was racking his brain for the answer, but Driggs supplied it next.

"The San Francisco earthquake," he said quietly. "And the Esbenson records show that Iver had receipts from a trip there at that time."

Taft's eyes widened.

Driggs flipped the pages of the atlas to a map of the United States, then removed a ruler from his satchel and laid it on the line from Ames to San Francisco. The line was straight along the latitude line. Both Colorado Springs to Cripple Creek and Ames to San Francisco were within hundredths of degrees of the same latitudes.

Pushing his plate away, Driggs removed another map and opened it to Europe and the Mediterranean. He laid the ruler across Kosovo and out to the west. Italy and Spain were halved. Taft reached for the map and stared at it closely.

"Magnifying glass?" Driggs asked.

Taft took it and stared at the cities along the line. The line led through Avezzano and Palencia, near the forty-second-degree latitude line. "Son of a bitch," Taft spit out.

"It appears," Driggs said quietly, "that Tesla discovered a way to transmit electricity through the Earth, all right—I figure it must follow the magnetic belts inside the Earth. The problem for him was that it travels in almost straight lines across the globe. Well," Driggs finished, "that and it causes earthquakes."

Taft was sitting in shocked horror. Driggs opened another atlas and spun it around.

"I went ahead and followed the same line across the Atlantic," he said. "It enters the United States between Boston and New York City, goes below Detroit, above Chicago, through the middle of Iowa, across the top third of Nebraska, southern Wyoming, and then forms the southern border of Idaho and Oregon above Utah, Nevada, and California."

Taft stared at the line.

"Now," Driggs said, "I'm not privy to all of what you know. But if it was me, and I was in your shoes, I figure if they amp up the power on the next test I'd be thinking the next event would be somewhere along that line."

Taft nodded and reached in his pocket for his telephone. "Can you go to Washington if we need you to?" he asked Driggs as he dialed.

"In for a penny," Driggs said, "in for a pound."

## 25

"I NEED TO get Driggs to Washington now," Taft said as soon as Martinez answered. "Space suit stuff."

"Hold on," Martinez said, shouting for his secretary to enter the office while at the same time punching commands in his computer to locate airfields. "I'm working on it—now explain what happened."

Taft started talking at the same time the secretary entered the office. "Get me Mr. Allbright here immediately—in person, not on the phone," Martinez said placing his hand over the mouthpiece, "and contact the air force and request the schedule of today's high-altitude recon flights. Tell them we're going to need a single-person high-speed transport from Buckley Air Force Base outside Denver to D.C. ASAP. You got it?"

"Yes, sir," the secretary said, leaving the office.

"So you see The Netherlands was never a possible target," Taft continued, "even if they wanted to. Whoever is behind this cannot strike it from Kosovo."

Taft quickly rambled off Driggs's theories. As he was talking, Richard

"Dick" Allbright burst into the office. "Hold on," Martinez said. "Mr. Allbright is in the room. I'm putting you on the speakerphone."

Martinez hit the button, and Taft's voice floated through the air. Taft quickly recapped what he had explained to Martinez.

"We're going to need Driggs here," Allbright said, "at a National Security Council meeting."

"I've already got my secretary coordinating with the air force to put him on a high flier," Martinez said.

"Where are you right now?" Allbright asked.

"Mr. Driggs and I are at the Brown Palace Hotel in Denver," Taft answered.

The secretary entered. "The air force chief of staff is on the phone," she said.

Allbright stood up and walked over to another phone, which was sitting on a sideboard in Martinez's office. He punched the flashing light. "This is Dick Allbright, sir," he said.

"Morning, Dick."

The two men had known and worked with each other for years.

"I need to get a man from Denver to D.C. right away," Allbright said. "Can you help us out?"

"What's the priority rating?"

"Direct from the commander-in-chief in conjunction with the Kosovo incident you were already briefed on," Allbright said.

"Fair enough," the air force chief of staff said, "I've got a Dark Star currently over the Pacific ocean, near California, flying an east-to-west course. If I call him right now, he can set down at a base east of Denver in about twenty minutes. Once he takes off again your party will be here in about fifteen more."

"I need it, John," Allbright said, calling the chief of staff by his first name.

"You got it, but have your man there ASAP," the chief of staff said. "We don't like this bird in the open for long."

"Yes, sir," Allbright said.

While Allbright had been talking, Martinez was on the line with the head of the Secret Service detail in Denver. He had explained the problem already.

"Lights and sirens," he finished.

"My people will be at the hotel in under five," the Secret Service man said. "There should be only limited traffic, so at high speed through the city they should be at the base in under fifteen minutes from pickup."

Allbright was talking into the speakerphone to Taft as Martinez finished. "We have it arranged, John," he said. "Leave your stuff and go to the front door. Someone is coming for you directly."

"Should I go along, sir?" Taft asked.

"Yes," Allbright said. "Once we get Driggs airborne, we'll figure out your assignment."

"Okay, sir," Taft said. "I'm hanging up."

Taft disconnected and motioned to Driggs. "Sir," he said, "if you would follow me, please."

Taft walked quickly out of the restaurant and through the lobby. He flashed a badge at the front desk clerk. "I'm with the National Intelligence Agency," he said quickly, "working on direct assignment for the president of the United States. Mr. Driggs is helping me as well. I want the bags in our rooms packed and held here at the front desk."

"I have a car here, too," Driggs added.

"And Mr. Driggs's car needs to be secured as well," Taft said. "You will be called with further instructions later. Do not discuss our visit here or any subsequent actions you take with anyone. Do you understand?"

The sound of a siren grew louder out on the street.

"All bills for this stay go to this address," Taft said, handing the clerk a card. "We weren't here, and none of this happened."

"I understand," the clerk said.

At just that instant a black Chevrolet Suburban screeched to a stop in front of the door. An agent jumped from the passenger seat and with handgun held in front, he walked around the front of the truck and approached the door while speaking into a lapel microphone.

"Come on, Mr. Driggs," Taft said. "Our ride is here."

• • •

"I WANT EVERYTHING on that line!" Benson shouted over the phone. "Put as many men as you need on it! We're back in now!"

Allbright burst into Benson's office just as he was disconnecting.

"Taft and Driggs have been picked up by the Secret Service," Allbright said. "Driggs will be here within the hour."

"I called the president and arranged a National Security meeting for one hour, twenty minutes from now," Benson said. "I've got Science and Technology searching for sites on the forty-second-degree latitude line for possible targets. Hopefully we'll have at least a few options for the president by then."

"I was thinking about what we were talking about the other day," Allbright said, "about Ratzovik having the large positions in gold and the dollar shorting."

"Go ahead," Benson ordered.

"The line skirts New York City and most of the major metropolitan areas, so even if we receive an earthquake in the U.S. it probably won't be severe enough to destabilize markets enough to cause a massive run-up in gold and a massive downturn in dollar value. It'll have an effect—but it will be short-lived."

"So you don't think this has anything to do whatever with Ilic being released?" Benson asked. "That this is strictly a grab for the cash?"

"I think Ilic and his freedom was merely a ruse Ratzovik was using to foster a far larger plan," Allbright said, "so the question is: What is he trying to destroy? What would make the price of gold rise through the roof and the dollar plummet like a rock?"

THE BLACK SECRET Service Suburban was racing east on Colfax Avenue at speeds of more than ninety miles an hour. Along the cross streets, Denver and Aurora police cars were situated blocking any traffic, and the computer jamming device under the hood of the Suburban was changing all the lights to green.

"You men all right?" the agent in the passenger seat asked.

"Peachy," Driggs said. "You don't know how many times I wished I could drive Colfax Avenue like this myself."

"Cuts through the traffic headache," the driver agreed.

The Suburban blasted past the old Fitzsimmons Army Hospital grounds and under Interstate 225. Driggs peered out of the window as a shadow passed ahead of the racing Suburban like the world's fastest cloud was racing east and blocking the sun. Then he caught sight of the light gray swept-wing Dark Star as it lowered to land.

"Hold on," the driver said. "We're turning on Tower Road."

Slamming on the brakes, the driver spun the wheel, and the Suburban skidded into a right-hand turn, then started south, toward the base. As they approached, the guard waved them through the gate and they began following an air force blue pickup truck that was already moving in the direction of the hangar area. The truck drove toward a hangar where the doors quickly slid open. The Suburban followed and slammed on the brakes. Then the hangar doors closed.

The Secret Service agent in the passenger seat jumped out and opened the rear door. "Mr. Driggs," he said, "follow that man."

An air force lieutenant motioned to Driggs. "What is your height and weight, sir?" he asked.

"Six-four," Driggs said, "and about one-eighty."

"Airman Randall," the lieutenant shouted ahead to a man standing in front of an office, "looks like we need a number one."

The airman retreated inside the room and returned a second later with a gray suit. "Come here, sir," the airman said to Driggs.

"Down to skivvies, please, sir," the lieutenant said.

Taft had followed them over and was watching. Driggs kicked off his shoes, stripped off his clothes, and stood in his underwear. The airman unzipped the suit and helped him inside. Once Driggs was inside and the suit was zipped up, the airman connected a portable canister to a fitting and sucked out the air until the suit fit like a second skin.

"Roger Ramjet," Taft said as the airman retreated into the office and returned with a helmet.

"The pilot will help you secure your helmet and hook you up to the systems, sir," the airman said.

Driggs rotated around to where the Dark Star was sitting across the hangar. It was light gray with a flowing top like a stealth bomber; the underside was also molded to slip through the air. There were numerous small openings for air intake and dispersal and a pair of small stabilizer wings top and bottom. A ramp with a stairway was extended almost to the ground.

"Come on, sir," the lieutenant said. "I'll help you inside."

With his helmet under his arm like an astronaut, Driggs walked toward the craft.

"I'll be in touch!" Taft shouted after him.

But Driggs was silent, in awe of the magnificent airplane. He walked over to the stairway and climbed inside.

A few moments later a horn sounded from Dark Star and a series of lights on the fuselage flashed from the front to the back.

"Sirs," the lieutenant said to Taft and the Secret Service men, "you need to move the truck and clear the hangar. If you wish to watch the takeoff you'll need to be outside the hangar."

The doors to the hangar slid open. Taft walked through as the Secret Service men drove the Suburban outside and to one side. Taft leaned against the hood of the Suburban and waited. A few seconds later he heard a high-pitched whine, then felt a rumble through the air.

Dark Star was moving more than sixty miles an hour as she exited the hangar. Heading straight down the runway directly in front of the hangar, the plane accelerated so fast the sweep of Taft's head could barely keep up.

Halfway down the runway, the pilot rotated, and the light gray craft headed almost straight up into the sky and disappeared from sight in only a few seconds. The lieutenant walked over to where Taft was standing.

"I've been ordered to give you an office to use," he said.

Taft motioned to the driver of the Suburban to roll down his window. After thanking the men for the ride, the Suburban pulled away.

Taft started to follow the lieutenant, who was holding a stopwatch in his hand. "Where's she right now?"

The lieutenant stared down at the stopwatch. "Kansas," he said quietly.

# 26

"THE CIA ASKED us to handle it," Allbright said, "and Benson told them we would."

Larry Martinez was sitting in Allbright's office. The tension Martinez was feeling was obvious—he was rocking back and forth, and his feet were tapping the floor. "The Certain we're not Involved Agency," Martinez blurted. "Those puss boys have a good record of running from any dirty work, don't they?"

Allbright nodded slowly.

"I don't know how the hell we can pull that off," Martinez said. "All we have is Steve Mather—and he's up north in Novi Sad, coordinating the Slavja family extraction."

"Can we send him south?"

"Chuck Smoot is coming in from Hungary," Martinez admitted, "to do the actual border crossing with the family. But even if Mather heads south, we'd only have a single man to make the shot on Ilic. Policy dictates three minimum to ensure success."

"Or two," Allbright said, "if absolutely necessary."

"That still leaves us one short."

Allbright opened a file on the desk. "Zoran Slavja has a marksman rating from his time in the Serbian Army before he entered BIA service. He could be the backup shooter."

"From the fire to the frying pan," Martinez said. "That should go over big."

TAFT WAS SITTING in an office at Buckley Air Force Base, studying an atlas of the United States, when his portable phone rang.

"What have you got?" he asks.

Martinez explained his and Allbright's conversation.

"That's a lot to ask," Taft said quietly. "I'm sure the BIA is scouring the country for Zoran as we speak. We ask him to return to Belgrade now to assist Mather—we're not only endangering him more, we're also asking him to commit murder on his own soil."

"I don't think it will come to that," Martinez said. "I think Ilic's jet will be forced down somewhere along the route."

"Well," Taft said, "the powers that be aren't too sure, or they wouldn't be formulating a backup plan with only two shooters."

"Your call," Martinez said, "but they will send in Mather anyway—you know that."

Taft was silent for a moment. "I'll make the call," he said at last.

CHUCK SMOOT HAD arrived at the safe house in Novi Sad just over twenty minutes ago. He and Mather were studying maps, planning the escape route. Zoran had found the safe house just over an hour before, and after an emotional reunion with his family he was guarding the door and watching the grounds of the house from outside. He had just finished a sweep of the perimeter when his portable phone rang. Checking the caller ID and finding that the call was from outside Serbia, he answered.

"This is Taft."

"Zoran."

"Did you make the safe house?"

"I'm here."

"Has our friend from across the border arrived?"

"He's here," Zoran said. "Thank you."

"We've run into a snag," Taft said.

Then he explained, finishing with, "If Ilic makes it into Belgrade and assumes command again," Taft said quietly, "your country will be torn apart."

Zoran was silent. The decision was a tough one—personal safety versus the possible fate of his country. In the end there was only one choice to make.

"Mr. Taft," Zoran said quietly, "you have been honorable so far. If I agree to do this—I want you to assure me that if something happens to me my family will be provided for."

"You already have that," Taft said quietly.

"True," Zoran said, "but I spoke to my family when I arrived here. All things being equal, they would rather not leave Serbia behind."

Taft thought for a moment before answering. "You want your old job back with the BIA?"

"No, Mr. Taft," Zoran said slowly. "I want to be in charge."

"I'll need to call you back," Taft said. "I can pull strings, but I'm not the puppetmaster."


INSIDE THE COMMAND center of the CIA, a threat assessment team was scouring through piles of data trying to find Ratzovik's target area along the forty-second-degree latitude line. After adjusting the parameters to ten miles to each side of the line they were still finding that most of the land along the line was sparsely populated.

"Sir," the assistant DCI said, "other than part of Massachusetts just south of Boston, where the line enters the United States, the only other major city along the route is Cedar Rapids, Iowa."

The DCI stared at the map of the United States displayed on the full-screen monitor. Ratzovik could have picked almost any other latitude within Serbia to launch the assault and he would have had more destruction. If his aim *was* to destroy a city and wreak economic havoc on the United States, he'd chosen poorly.

"Run the Boston metro area and Cedar Rapids," he said, "and project a six-point earthquake onto both."

"We did that, sir," the assistant DCI noted, "and determined that neither area had any fault lines whatsoever. Both Italy and Spain had active fault lines—our scientists believe that the electricity on its own does not make the quakes. It shakes the ground, to be sure, but the earthquakes were triggered on existing faults."

"Then run all known fault lines in the United States."

"That's what we're working on now, sir."

"I CONFERRED WITH my boss. The best I can do," Taft said to Zoran after talking to Allbright, "is to tell you we will try. As you know, the appointment as BIA chief would need to come from the Serbian president. Right now there is not the time to have our president broach the subject with your president. Everyone is juggling monkeys right now."

Zoran was quiet. "You could have lied, and told me it was a done deal."

"I don't lie," Taft said quietly. "I've learned over the years that in the end, when all is said and done, I still have to live with myself and my actions. We'll do our best—but that's the only promise I can give you."

Zoran was silent.

"You in?" Taft asked directly.

"I'll do it," Zoran said at last.

"Tell Mather," Taft said. "Martinez already briefed him."

Zoran relayed the information to Mather.

"Then we stay here for now?" Smoot asked. "Until this all shakes out?"

"Sounds logical," Mather said.

Zoran walked over and kissed his family good-bye.

"Let's do it," he said a second later.

• • •

AT NIA HEADQUARTERS, General Benson was reading through a list of possible threats along the forty-second degree of latitude when Martinez entered.

"The author is on the ground. He's being transported here as we speak."

Benson stared at his watch. "I'll take him over to the White House for the briefing. In the meantime, what should we do with Taft?"

"He's on vacation, sir," Martinez said.

"Bullshit," Benson said. "Put him in an air force plane or helicopter and have them fly the forty-second degree of latitude. If the scientists come up with a plausible target, I want him be available to lead ground operations."

"Okay, sir," Martinez said. "I'll get it done."

Benson waved Martinez from the office, then pushed the intercom button as he was exiting. "Get me Sandra Miles," he said loudly.

SANDRA MILES WAS sitting in her office alternately staring at a map of the United States on her desk and her computer monitor, which displayed water supplies. Her brown hair was pinned up, and a pair of cat's-eye glasses rested on her chest on a silver chain. She was dressed in a skirt with a jacket draped over the chair. The sleeves of her blouse were rolled up. She traced the line across the map with her finger.

As one of the key agents in the NIA's Science and Technology Division, Miles was used to thinking outside the box. She was doing that right now. The telephone rang.

"Miles," she said.

"General Benson," the voice boomed over the line. "Do you have anything yet, Sandy—anything at all?"

"I'm still working on it, boss," Miles answered. "I'm looking at infrastructure right now."

"I'm going in to the briefing soon," Benson said.

"As soon as I know something," Miles said, "you'll know something. Do you want me to interrupt you in the briefing if I come up with it?"

"Absolutely," Benson said.

"Then I will," Miles said.

The phone went dead, and she turned back to the computer. Saving the water data, Miles pulled up the U.S. telephone grid. After studying that for a few minutes she entered the commands to show the U.S. rail-road grid.

Her plan was to examine, one by one, those things that make the United States hum.

RADKO ILIC WAS dressing in his new suit, brushing his hair in front of the mirror in his cell. He was antsy but trying not to let it show. Placing the brush back on the small shelf near the sink, he glanced in the mirror, saw a strand out of place, and reached for the brush once again.

"So the president won't take the offer?" he asked his lawyer.

"No," the lawyer said, "and he claims that as soon as you touch down he will have you arrested and imprisoned. Even if he had taken the bribe, none of your people would have been able to reach Ratzovik in the past twenty-four hours. Ratzovik is the only one with access to that amount of funds, and he seems to have disappeared again."

"I'll deal with Ratzovik as soon as I'm in Belgrade," Milosevic said quietly. "For now the more pressing problem is what to do about the presidential threat."

"I had some of your supporters in Serbia make inquiries inside the Serbian military, like you asked. It appears that the president would have a hard time carrying through on his plans. While they wouldn't all support your return, neither will they be the henchmen for the president. Most of the highest-ranking officers want to wait and see what the people choose to do—if the majority wants you back in power they will help that process. If popular support is not so strong, they figure your fate is a matter for the Serbian Supreme Court to decide," the lawyer said.

"What about the local police?"

"The last word we received from our sources," the lawyer said, "is that they had an arrest warrant for Galadin Ratzovik, charging him with complicity in the killing of Bodonavik. The farther and faster you separate yourself from him the better."

Ilic nodded. "BIA?" he asked.

"Since their leader is an old crony of yours," the lawyer said, "that helps you and hurts the standing president. The problem then arises that the president knows that and may seek to mitigate their powers before you arrive back in Belgrade."

"How?" Ilic asked. "We're due to leave here in half an hour. He'd have to clean the ranks in the BIA while we're in the air—what, four hours tops?"

"He's still in charge," the lawyer noted. "There's a lot he could do."

"Nonsense," Ilic said. "Everything is in our favor."


THE PRESIDENT OF the United States and his national security adviser were meeting in the Oval Office before the main briefing was to begin.

"Take it from the top again," the president said.

"Ilic has not departed The Netherlands yet, but is due to within the hour. Once he's in the air we have four hours of time before he reaches Belgrade."

"And our Special Forces have surrounded the location where we believe the device is located?" the president asked.

"Yes, sir," the national security adviser noted.

"And the Serbian president?" the president asked. "We have not yet spoken to him?"

"No, sir; you wanted to reserve that for yourself."

"What's the intelligence inside Belgrade? Do the citizens know Ilic is returning?"

"No, sir. We've been monitoring the newspapers, radio, and television, and there has been no mention of his return. Intelligence believes the supporters of Ilic are waiting to leak the information when he is closer to Belgrade as a sort of surprise-and-shock campaign. Apparently Ilic has attempted to bribe the president to stand down. If that happened, it's better for Ilic to arrive unannounced and simply take over the government of Serbia quietly and quickly. Then any opposition doesn't have time to formulate a plan, while at the same time he can strengthen his ties with his support by removing any anti-Ilic factions inside the government."

"Who in the government is for his return," the president asked, "and who is opposed?"

"Opposed is obviously the president," the national security adviser noted, "and he has elicited help from Dragoslav Milorand."

"Milorand has the money people and the higher classes, right?"

"Correct, sir. I think the president can also count on support from the Belgrade Police Department, at least until there is a legal ruling on Ilic's status as returning hero or war criminal."

"The military?" the president asked.

"Neither strongly for nor against one side or the other," the national security adviser said, reading from a summary from the intelligence services. "Most of our analysts believe the military will follow the people's wishes. They won't kill their own to support Ilic, nor will they rise up against the population on the standing president's orders."

"What about their spy agencies?"

"The primary intelligence service is called the BIA," the national security adviser said, reading, "and the head is an old friend of Ilic's."

"For Ilic," the president said, "and against the duly elected president."

"Correct, sir."

The president was silent for a moment. "This is a bag of worms," he said finally.

"More like snakes, sir," the national security adviser said.

"I guess it is time," the president said, "to call the president of Serbia."

"Yes, sir."

## 27

"SIR," THE LIEUTENANT said after knocking on the office door and entering, "your transportation has arrived. They are touching down now."

Taft stood up and followed the lieutenant onto the tarmac. To the south, a strange-looking gray airplane was approaching. As Taft watched, the propellers started to rotate upright as the craft slowed. Then it hovered and started to set down.

"Osprey, huh," Taft said quietly.

"CV-22 out of Kirtland in New Mexico."

The lieutenant motioned to a pickup truck a few feet away. Taft climbed in the passenger seat. The lieutenant climbed behind the wheel, started the engine, then adjusted the portable radio attached to the ceiling. He started driving slowly toward the runway, then stopped a short distance away.

"They'll call when it's clear to approach."

Taft nodded. He watched while the Osprey blades slowed, then stopped. A door on the side started to drop at the same time as a voice came over the radio.

"You're clear, lieutenant," a voice said.

Placing the truck back in gear, the lieutenant drove closer, then stopped. "Sir," he said to Taft, "they're ready for you."

Taft reached over and shook the lieutenant's hand. "Thanks for your help," he said, climbing from the cab of the truck.

"That's what I'm here for," the lieutenant said as Taft walked toward the Osprey.

An air force captain was standing just inside the Osprey near the open door. Guiding Taft inside and into a seat, he motioned to the front. "Major Schilling is the aircraft commander. I'm Captain Hobbs."

Taft looked forward and saw Schilling waving his hand, holding a clipboard, in greeting. Taft smiled and returned the wave. "I'm John Taft, special agent, National Intelligence Agency."

"Secret agent?" Hobbs said easily.

"Afraid so," Taft said.

"Mr. Taft," Schilling shouted from the pilot's seat, "we were not given any information as to flight plans. Could you fill us in as to our ultimate destination?"

"I'm awaiting orders," Taft said, "as to our actual final destination. For now we need to fly straight north into Wyoming until we reach forty-second degrees latitude. By then I should know if we will be patrolling west or east along that line."

"Can you fill us in as to what we should be looking for?" Hobbs asked.

"Not at this time," Taft admitted.

"Straight north to the forty-second degree of latitude," Schilling shouted.

"Yes, sir," Taft said.

"You got it," Schilling said as he reached down and started the engines again.

Hobbs made sure Taft was belted into the seat; then he walked forward and climbed in the copilot's seat. A few minutes later the Osprey lifted off, rotated the nose around, pointing north, then started forward flight. Taft watched out the window as the rotor blades started downward until they locked in place. The Osprey accelerated.

Taft stared out the window at the sprawl of Denver and the suburbs below. Off to his right was the massive Denver International Airport. For now it sat almost alone on the prairie, but Taft could see building taking place nearby. What looked like several hotels were under construction, and to the west was the beginning of a massive housing development. Taft settled in for the ride.


DRIGGS WAS IN the rear of an armored SUV. The driver approached a building with a sign that read Capco Mining and called his location in on the radio. Pulling in front of the modern-looking structure, he slid to a stop and turned around in his seat.

"Just a minute," the driver said. "The head of our agency in coming down."

A few seconds later the front doors opened and two men walked out. One was dressed in a suit and looked to be an aide. The other was wearing a uniform festooned with ribbons and a single star on each shoulder. The aide opened the rear door, and the general smiled at Driggs and climbed inside.

"General Earl Benson," he said, extending his hand. "I want to thank you for coming here on such short notice."

The aide closed the door, and the driver placed the SUV in gear.

"No problem," Driggs said.

"You know we're going to the White House?" Benson said to the driver.

"Yes, sir," the driver replied.

"So," Benson said, "Mr. Martinez filled me in on your theory—you're certain that the underground electricity beams travel only in a straight line."

"Well," Driggs said, "at least within a short distance of a straight line."

"So," Benson said, "if that is true and the device is now situated at the forty-second degree of latitude in Kosovo, that cuts a wide strip across the United States."

"Yes, sir," Driggs said.

The driver accelerated and entered a highway near the NIA headquarters.

"Let me ask you something," Benson said. "You're a pretty creative guy—what with the novels you've written and all—if you were the bad guy in this story, what would you be looking to destroy?"

"What's the ultimate reason?" Driggs asked. "What does the bad guy want to achieve?"

"We think now," Benson said, "it has to do with money. Gold and bonds."

Driggs nodded. "Let me mull this over while we drive."

Benson nodded.


GALADIN RATZOVIK WAS fuming. The guards who had gone out searching for Pestic and his family had yet to return, and they were not answering calls on their radios. He stood in the barn, staring at the Tesla device. It appeared like the device was ready for use. All he needed to do was add power; still, he was stuck. He knew that if he activated it now, the people he had sinking the receiver shaft at the exit point would not be finished, and nothing would happen. His second problem was the time on the London gold exchange and at the bond trading desks. For him to profit, the time of the destruction had been carefully planned; there was no changing that.

He stared at his watch. Ilic would be leaving the jail soon, and the flight to Belgrade would take several hours. He was safe at least until Ilic arrived. By then his men on the other end would have the receiver set in place.

There was nothing he could do but wait—and Ratzovik hated when he was not in complete control of a situation. Once his guards returned with Pestic and his family, he would have something to occupy his time. The thought of the slow torture of them made him start to become aroused.

He would slowly peel the skin off their bodies until they begged him to die.

That would make the time pass nicely.

WARRANT OFFICER MIKE Davis stared down at the Serbian bound at the wrists and ankles with plastic ties.

"You recognize him?" he asked Vojislav Pestic.

"He is one of the guards at the facility."

"How many of you are in the search party?" Davis asked.

The Serb was silent.

"Ask him in his language," Davis ordered Gibbons, who bent down and began talking to the man.

Just then Davis's radio squawked.

"Sir," the corporal said, "we captured two more men."

"Any injuries?" Davis asked.

"We had to butt one of the men with the end of a rifle," the corporal admitted, "but he just has a nasty lump on his head."

"No noise or anything that would tip off the principals?"

The corporal and his partner had been working closer to the barn than the other teams.

"No," the corporal said. "We were reasonably quiet."

"Bring them in," Davis ordered.

Pestic had stepped back away from the guard. Even contained by the plastic cuffs, he still scared the engineer.

"That's three," Davis said to Pestic. "How many were there total?"

"Nine," Pestic answered.

"That's a third of them," Davis said. "I kind of doubt there are any more out here."

In the past couple of hours Teams A through J had all moved closer to the barn and now formed a loose circle just over a mile away from the location. The teams had remained hidden in the brush and forest and had been ordered to be as silent as possible to avoid detection. Davis pushed the button on his radio.

"Team leader," he said, "this is Davis. Start closing the net."

• • •

THE PRESIDENT OF the United States sat in the Oval Office with the telephone on speaker. In a chair in front of his desk his national security adviser sat waiting.

"I have Dragoslav Milorand here with me," the Serbian president said. "He has agreed to advise me."

"Hello, Mr. Milorand."

"Good afternoon, Mr. President," Milorand offered.

"Mr. President," the U.S. president said, "the situation is this: My country believes that a weapon of mass destruction is located in Kosovo and is threatening The Netherlands. To protect their country The Netherlands has agreed to release Radko Ilic from imprisonment and return him to Belgrade. Our intelligence sources indicate that you are aware of this and have been asked to step down as president."

The Serbian president stared at Milorand before answering. Milorand nodded.

"That is correct."

"But you have chosen not to do this."

"Correct."

"I would like to offer help from the United States in this matter. Is this of interest to you at this time?"

Milorand nodded again, and the Serbian president answered. "Yes, it is."

"All right then," the president said. "First off, we believe your intelligence service, the BIA, is infiltrated with Ilic supporters, so I will ask that this conversation be kept only between you and me and our advisers."

"I understand."

"The United States believes that we have located the device and have set in place plans to disable or destroy the device. Right now, however, we are still assembling the necessary personnel and cannot effect this plan until after Ilic is due to be released."

"I understand," the Serbian president said in a shaky voice.

"Do not worry about Ilic at this time," the president said. "We have instituted a variety of plans to deal with him, both in transit and if he reaches Belgrade. Is there anyone in the military or police leadership in your country who you are absolutely sure you can trust?"

"The military, no," the Serbian president said. "The chief of the Belgrade Police Department I believe supports me."

"Ask him to come to your office," the U.S. president said. "We may need his help later."

"I will do that, sir."

"Mr. Milorand?"

"Yes, sir."

"I understand you are an influential man in your country?"

"Some say that, sir," Milorand answered.

"Do you have contacts in the print and broadcast media?"

"Many, sir."

"You should attempt to ensure that news of Ilic's release does not make it out."

"What about from The Netherlands?" Milorand asked. "With the Internet and the twenty-four-hour news services, if the news is reported, we will be unable to stop it from reaching Serbia; it will leak through."

"The Netherlands is keeping this all hush-hush," the president said, "and our intelligence has indicated that the Ilic camp is as well—at least until he reaches Belgrade."

"Then I should be able to lean on my friends for a blackout on any coverage," Milorand agreed.

"Good," the president said. "Now as to the matter of U.S. personnel operating in Serbia, we have dispatched both military and intelligence operatives already. I would like a letter from you stating that they were invited by you, as the Serbian president, and they are performing their duties within your country with your full approval."

"I will draft it and have it sent to you immediately," the Serbian president agreed.

"Excellent," the U.S. president said. "That might save me some grief later."

"What of the device itself?" the Serbian president asked. "How are you planning to defuse it?"

"Hopefully without the need for bombing," the president said.

"However, if it comes to that, we have prepared. The area where we believe the device is located is sparsely populated, so I can assure you that if we have to bomb the target, the only loss of Serbian life will be those who are behind the threat."

"I understand."

"As for you and your personal security at this time," the U.S. president said, "we would like to offer the services of some of our intelligence operatives as a kind of executive security force. If we combine some of our men with the Belgrade Police Department, we think we can guarantee your safety until this is over."

The Serbian president glanced over at Milorand, who nodded.

"Thank you, sir. I accept the offer."

"In addition, the BIA will need to be dismantled and rebuilt after this," the president said. "We have had one of their officers assisting us from early on. When the time comes, we would ask that you consider him for a leadership post."

"We will look at that when the time comes."

"The last order of business is Mr. Ilic himself," the U.S. president said. "Do you believe he would receive a fair trial in a Belgrade court pertaining to his activities with ethnic cleansing?"

Milorand shook his head no.

"I don't think so, Mr. President."

"Then, if you do not feel comfortable with him being tried in your country for his crimes," the U.S. president said, "I ask that you leave it up to us as to his deposition."

"Agreed."

The U.S. president paused for a moment and glanced over at his national security adviser, who nodded that everything had been covered.

"All right, then," the U.S. president said. "I want to thank you for your cooperation and assure you that a protective force will be placed around you immediately. Let's both hope and pray that this situation can be ended quickly and without bloodshed."

"That is," the Serbian president said, "my dream."

# 28

SANDRA MILES HAD her desk covered with books and maps. The overflow was sitting on the floor of her office, and she was walking among the data, checking one thing and then another. Stepping over to an easel where a large white tablet was hanging, she crossed off a line. Stepping a few feet away to where a cork billboard was attached to the wall, she made a notation, then returned to the desk.

What economic disaster would cause gold to rise and the dollar to fall?

That was the question she continually asked herself as she worked.

Her first train of thought had been involved with water. What would happen if an earthquake hit Lake Erie or Lake Michigan, both of which the forty-second-degree latitude line passed through? Cleveland and Chicago might be swamped with tsunamis and suffer widespread destruction, but both cities, while important, were not the economic linchpin of the entire country. She sensed she was missing something.

Boston? An attack there might bring about widespread loss of life; however, Boston was also not an economic linchpin like New York City. There was high tech in Boston and some major corporations made their home there, but destruction in Boston in the overall scheme of things would not stop the economy in its tracks.

Detroit was just north of the line. Years ago, when all the car manufacturers were clustered nearby, wiping out Detroit might have brought the United States to its economic knees. Now, however, the factories were located throughout the country, from Alabama to California. Hit Detroit and there would be repercussions, but the effect would be nowhere as great as in years past. Economically bad, yes—but nothing that would bring about a depression.

That left the wide-open spaces of the Midwest and the West. The farm states of Iowa and Nebraska, the ranching state of Wyoming. An attack here might affect the food supply of the country, but any loss could be supplemented from stock already stored as well as importation from outside the country. The line along the top of Utah, Nevada, and California was sparsely populated and economically deserted.

Maybe the intent was to trigger the fault lines already in California by a strike along the northern border. Miles downloaded the fault lines and inspected them carefully. A strong enough shake to the north might shake the plates loose and start tremors to the south. California was an economic powerhouse as far as states went. If California faced widespread destruction, the results could prove devastating.

Miles walked over and made a note on the pad on the easel.

Planes and trains and automobiles were next. The goods of the United States relied on transportation, and other than Boston, there were no major seaports along the path. Major highways along the forty-second degree of latitude were also few and far between. The railroads were a different matter, however. Numerous lines cross that latitude, and if the rails were severed, transportation could be affected. Miles made a note.

As for airports, other than O'Hare, there were no major ones along the route.

Water again. For drinking and bathing—the stuff of life. People can survive weeks without food, but only days without water. Miles thought about that but again came up short. Each municipal area had their own water treatment and supply facilities. There were tens if not hundreds of thousands across the country; hitting one of the many would affect only a tiny area. This would have no effect on gold prices.

Miles thought about communications next. Decades ago, before the breakup of AT&T, a well-placed strike on a telephone exchange might have slowed the economy. Hit the right area, and it might have even brought business to its knees for a few days. Now, however, with cell phones in this country as common as erasers on chalkboards, knocking out one area of telephone service, even the entire land line system, people could still communicate.

Water and specific cities were dismissed by Miles, as was transportation infrastructure and telephone traffic. What do we use every day? Miles thought aloud as she walked over to her computer. The Internet? Sure; some do.

And then it hit her like a slap across the face.

She punched in commands into the computer and watched as a map appeared. Lines ran like spiderwebs throughout the country, intersecting like a fine lace cloth. Electricity. The very thing that lights our lights and cools our food and makes it all come together into a modern society. Turn off the lights and chaos would ensue.

But where along the forty-second latitude was there a target?

INSIDE PINKIE'S SMOKIN' Lounge in Norfolk, Nebraska, the air was living up to the sign out front. A blue haze from cigarette smoke hung in the air at the five-foot level, and the smell mixed nicely with the aroma of stale draft beer and pickled eggs.

Tommy Belwood raised his empty beer bottle by the neck and waved it back and forth like a pendulum. The female bartender, who went by the initials CJ, scurried down to Belwood's end of the bar. She slid open the cooler, grabbed another cold one, and popped off the top, using the opener built into the cooler side. Placing a fresh cardboard coaster on the bar, she sat the bottle on the top.

"Hey, big spender," she said sweetly, "how come you're not out plowing?"

Belwood was just under sixty years of age and had spent his entire life farming. His hair, once brown, but now given to flecks of gray in the sides and back, was slicked back and combed. Belwood was dressed in a pair of clean denim overalls and was wearing a clean and pressed button-down shirt with pearl buttons. In this part of the world he was a dandy—at least at midday.

Reaching out with his massive scarred left hand, Belwood took the bottle and took a swig. "This year I hired some boys," he said proudly.

CJ took the empty and tossed it into the trash can. "Prices up that much?"

Belwood snubbed out his cigarette and reached for the pack on the bar again. As he was tapping one out, CJ reached over and grabbed a book of matches, pulled one out, and lit it. She waited until Belwood had the filter in his mouth, then reached over and lit the end. Over to the side, a couple of younger men were shooting pool. Scattered throughout the lounge were retired men in groups holding court.

"Got a new truck, too," Belwood said.

"What are you growing out there?" CJ asked with a laugh.

Belwood like flirting with the bubbly bartender. Around these parts she passed for the local hottie. Ever since his wife had passed away last year, Belwood had been lonely. Flirting with a pretty girl seemed okay right now. Belwood just wished his wife was here to share in his recent good fortune. Even if she had been, she wouldn't have minded him making harmless banter with a pretty girl.

She'd always known that in the end he'd come back to her.

"Oil lease money," Belwood said. "An outfit came by the place a couple weeks ago and offered me money up front to drill a test well."

While Belwood and CJ had been talking, an older man had slid up to the bar alongside them. He stood there with a empty glass in his hand.

"Another 7&7?" CJ asked him.

The man nodded and set the glass on the bar. Bart Kendall had retired from farming more than a decade before. He sold his farmland and bought a house in town. Now he hung around Pinkie's and the local grocery store, offering unwanted advice and strong opinions.

"Ain't no oil out there," Kendall said. "Not any in this entire county. Out in western Nebraska, Kansas for sure, but none around here."

CJ set his fresh drink on the bar, and Kendall placed the correct change down and retrieved the drink. He thought tipping was something you did to a cow late at night.

"You a geologist now?" Belwood said.

"Nope," Kendall said, turning and retreating to the corner where he held court to anyone who would listen. This afternoon, as on most afternoons, there were few takers.

"Diesel with the leather interior," Belwood continued, "and that satellite radio thingy."

"I'll try and slip outside in a bit," CJ said, "and take a gander."

Belwood nodded. "Before you do that," he said grandly, "why don't you put in an order for a steak sandwich for me."

"You keep this up," CJ said, "we're gonna need to bring in extra help tonight to count the money."

"Medium rare," Belwood added, "with crispy fries."

CJ made a notation on the order pad then walked toward the ordering window.


IF ANYONE HAD checked around a bit they would have quickly learned that this was the first well Jackalope Oil & Gas had ever attempted to drill. Like the mythical western creature from which the company derived its name, Jackalope was fake as well.

Their rig was old and decrepit and the team of men operating it spoke with a Serbo-Croatian accent. A real oil company driller would have looked aghast at the hole they were boring—it was about as straight as a politician's morals. The fact that they had not gotten the pipe string stuck down the hole was simply luck. Had there been any oil, and even if they had hit the reservoir directly, they would never have made any production. The well, like the rig they used, was crap.

The foreman stared across the field where a man was running a tractor down the rows. In the distance, not a mile away, was a large complex where thousands of electrical lines converged. The forest of wires looked like a net from where the foreman stood.

But the net was not designed to catch things—it was designed to send them on their way.


"HOW YOU DOING back there, Mr. Taft?" Captain Hobbs asked.

"Okay," Taft replied.

"That's Greeley we just passed to the right," Hobbs noted. "We'll be crossing the Colorado and Wyoming border in the next half hour."

Taft had been watching out the windows since they left the Denver area. Having grown up in the Denver area, he was used to the contrast. Colorado is like two states. There are the high mountains everyone pictures when they think of Colorado. However, the area to the east is more like Kansas.

"I know," Taft said. "I grew up here."

Hobbs glanced back and smiled. "You sure you're allowed to tell us that?"

Taft nodded and smiled. Whatever the military officers he dealt with might say, he had always found them somewhat in awe of a spy. "It's okay."

Major Schilling turned his head. "You got us a target yet, sir?"

Taft just swung his head back and forth.


"WHOA," MILES SAID aloud.

She reached for the telephone and quickly dialed.

"Technology," the voice that answered said.

"John, this is Sandra," Miles said quickly.

"What can the CIA do for the NIA?" he asked.

"You familiar with the U.S. power grid?"

"Intimately."

Miles had spoken to John on the numerous occasions when their operations intersected. She'd even had the occasion to meet him in person once, when they were both attending a conference. He was that rarest of people, devoid of attractiveness but with an ego that raged out of control. He was thin and with a hatchet face; his shoulders were littered with flecks of dandruff that somehow escaped the helmet of greasy hair on his head.

She had been as much shocked as horrified when he had asked her out as they sat at the bar in the hotel where the conference was being held. She had begged off, citing a pounding headache, but he had persisted. Head to my room with me, he had said, and you'll be hurting in two places. The thought had brought shivers down her spine.

"Can you give me a quick overview?"

"Sure," John said. "Will you take me up on that offer I made?"

"Maybe," Miles lied, "but right now I'm working, and this is important. I don't want to call your higher-ups, but I need some info now."

John backed down—the only thing he had ever accomplished in life was his job with the CIA, and they kept him locked in a back room, writing reports. Another mark on his record would not help him any.

"Sorry," he said quickly. "The United States is comprised of three main power grids; they are the Eastern Interconnect, the Western Interconnect, and the Texas Interconnect. Within that there are numerous reliability councils. The system is also tied to Canada and Mexico at various points. The various lines intersect, distributing the electricity to where it is needed most. If there are shortages in one area, the power can be redistributed to another to make up for shortages."

"So if one area goes down, another can help out?"

"That's the idea," John said. "But as the New York City blackouts a few years ago proved, that doesn't always work."

"What if there was a widespread failure somewhere on the line?" Miles asked.

"Depends on where it was located," John said. "Texas is kind of its own little world, but the East and West trade a lot back and forth."

"Where are the critical areas?"

"Midwest mainly," John said. "A lot comes together there."

"Specifically," Miles said quickly.

"If I had to point out one spot," John said slowly, "probably Nebraska. Because of the fact that their senator in the old days was against control of anything by big corporations, the entire state is a hodgepodge of rural electric associations and smaller companies. That wouldn't be so much of a problem except a lot of the main lines intersect there."

"Anyplace exactly in Nebraska where problems might arise?"

"Oh, hell, yeah," John said. "Norfolk. There's a giant intersect station there as well as a step-down facility to balance frequency between grids."

Miles was staring at a map that showed the United States. Norfolk, Nebraska, was almost exactly on the forty-second latitude line.

"What would happen if Norfolk fried somehow?" she asked.

"I wager a guess it would shut down the power to most of the United States except for parts of Texas. Well, Texas, and, of course Alaska and Hawaii—they have their own deal. You know—" John started to say.

But the phone went dead as Miles slammed down her receiver.

"Mr. Allbright," she said a second later, "I need a car to take me to the White House, and I need you to meet me in the hall so we can talk on my way down."

"Have you got it, Sandra?"

"I do, sir," she said quickly.

"I'm on my way," Allbright said.

A few minutes later the door to the elevator on Miles's floor opened and Richard Allbright stood inside.

"Car's coming," he said as Miles stepped in and the door closed. "What have you got going?"

"The U.S. power grids intersect in Nebraska on the forty-second degree of latitude line."

"You think Ratzovik will try to trigger an earthquake there," Allbright said, "and destroy the area?"

"No, sir," Miles said. "There are really not any fault lines in the area. I think the threat of an earthquake turned us away from the true idea behind his plans. I think we've been looking at this all wrong. He's not trying to create earthquakes, that's just been the end result. What he's attempting to do is electrify the Earth and short out the power lines, like if you touch the end of battery jumper cables together."

The elevator had reached the ground floor, and the two stepped off.

They started walking to the front door. Through the glass wall Miles could see a car pulling in front.

"What are we talking about if this happens?"

"The loss of power in 80 percent of the United States for an indeterminate period of time," Miles said.

"General Benson will already be in the briefing," Allbright said, glancing at his watch. "You send in a message you need to see him immediately. I'll get Taft over there."

"Very good, sir," Miles said as she opened the door to the car.

As she slid into the seat, Allbright bent over and addressed the driver. "Sirens and lights," he said.

"Yes, sir," the driver said.

Miles shut the passenger door, and the car roared away.

Allbright reached for his portable telephone and dialed. "Tell Taft, Norfolk, Nebraska," he said as soon as Martinez answered.

"I'll do it," Martinez said.

"I'll be right there," Allbright said.

"I'm here," Martinez said as the phone went dead.

## 29

THE BRIEFING ROOM inside the White House was filled to capacity.

Benson and Driggs sat on the far side of the table from the entrance, almost as far away as one could sit from the president. The director of Central Intelligence, various military leaders, key advisers, and government officials were seated and waiting. A marine guard opened the door, and the president and his national security adviser walked into the room. The president headed for the head of the table, the national security adviser the first seat to his right.

"Good morning, people," the president said. "Let's begin."

"Sir," the DCI said, "if I may go first."

The president nodded, and the DCI quickly explained the situation in Kosovo. As the president listened, he continually glanced down to the end of the table, where Benson and Driggs were seated.

"Thank you," the president said when the DCI had concluded. "I see we have a new person in the room," he said, pointing to the end of the table. "Excuse me, but aren't you that author Malcolm Driggs?"

"Malcolm Driggs, sir."

"Unreal," the president said. "What brings you here this morning? Are you trying to swap the world of fiction for even a more false world?"

"Mr. President," Benson said, "Mr. Driggs has been assisting us on the Tesla case. He has come across some interesting observations that need airing."

"Well," the President said, smiling, "then by all means go ahead."

Driggs looked around the table before speaking. There were enough ribbons on the uniforms of the military men and women to decorate the hair of all the females in a small Pacific island nation. The others at the table were all instantly recognizable from television and magazine political coverage. It might be easy to be intimidated or nervous, but Driggs was simply too old and had seen too much to let it bother him.

"Thank you, Mr. President." Sipping from a glass of water to wet his throat, he resumed speaking. "Recently while visiting my old car warehouse in Colorado, I was contacted by an agent of the NIA seeking information about Nikola Tesla. Further contacts with this agent gave me impetus to research Tesla thoroughly. First, I'd like to give a little background. Nikola Tesla was the man who discovered alternating current and was a major inventor of numerous electrical devices as well as an experimenter in alternative methods of electrical delivery. One of his primary focuses was attempting to transmit electrical energy through the Earth wirelessly. Had he accomplished this, he would have became rich beyond his wildest dreams. Most of his experiments in this field were conducted in Colorado, my adopted state, so I have had an interest in his work for a number of years. Since the incidents in Serbia were revealed to me I dug a little deeper and here is what I have learned."

Driggs sipped from the glass of water again.

"The original experiments in Colorado Springs in the late 1800s were followed up a few years later—in 1906, to be exact—with another test designed to transmit electricity underground from Ames, Colorado, near Telluride, to San Francisco, California. I believe this test triggered the San Francisco earthquake."

Driggs looked around the room. "Could someone please place a map of the United States on the monitor?"

An aide punched commands into a computer, and the map came up.

"Now highlight Colorado Springs, Colorado, and Cripple Creek, Colorado, as well as Ames, Colorado, or Telluride and San Francisco."

Dots appeared on the massive screen denoting the places.

"May I approach, sir?" Driggs asked the president.

The president waved him up to the head of the table.

As Driggs was walking forward, a marine guard entered the room. He walked over to General Benson and whispered in his ear. Benson motioned to the president that he needed to step out, and the president nodded his approval.

Driggs reached the monitor and pointed to the dots. "Could you now run a line between the points and overlay the longitude and latitude lines."

The aide entered the commands, and the map was redrawn. The president and the rest of the room stared at the marks.

"As you can now see," Driggs said, "both of Tesla's tests—at least if we believe my theory as to the cause of the San Francisco quake—transmitted the electricity in an almost straight line, following along that latitude from creation to termination."

The room perked up. Several people shifted in their chairs, but the room quickly grew silent again. Driggs smiled at the aide.

"Now if you would please bring up a world map and show the earthquakes in Italy and Spain as well as the possible delivery point as southern Kosovo."

The map slowly filled the screen.

Driggs began to point to locations.


OUT IN THE hallway, Sandra Miles was talking a mile a minute.

"Sir," she said breathlessly, "I think I have identified the target as an electrical switching station in Nebraska."

"But Nebraska is hardly earthquake-prone," Benson said.

"I don't think Ratzovik is attempting to create an earthquake," Miles said quickly. "I think he's trying to fry the main U.S. electrical grid and plunge the country into chaos."

"That would make the price of gold skyrocket," Benson admitted.

"To the moon," Miles said.

"Have you researched the implications if this happens?"

"Some sir," Miles said.

"Enough to go in front of the briefing with your findings?"

"I can wing it," Miles said.

"Follow me inside," Benson said, motioning for the guard to open the door.

"I DON'T KNOW why," Driggs was concluding, "but it is my strong opinion that electrical energy transmitted underground follows belts in the Earth that form straight lines. If the point of initiation is in fact southern Kosovo, The Netherlands cannot be effectively targeted."

The president was staring at the world map with interest.

"But the United States can," Driggs finished. Turning, he walked back to his chair.

"This is not good," the president said. "Since this was discovered we have been preparing for an outcome that is impossible to achieve while at the same time almost ignoring the threat to our own country."

Benson motioned to the president.

"Yes, General Benson," the president said, "what *else* have you got?"

"Mr. President," Benson said, "this is Sandra Miles. She is one of the lead agents in the NIA's Science and Technology Division. She has come across some disturbing information."

The president was pouring coffee from a silver thermos on the table. "Well, go ahead," he said. "It can't get much worse."

"I'm afraid it does, Mr. President," Miles said, standing off to the side of the room. "Once Mr. Driggs disclosed his theory to the NIA I was tasked with researching threats along the forty-second degree of latitude. As you see from the map, there are few major cities along the line. Our intelligence indicates that the man we believe is behind this scheme, one Galadin Ratzovik, has taken large positions in gold and dollar shorts. What would cause maximum disruption in the United States, thus causing the value of gold to skyrocket while depressing the dollar? I think I have located that target."

"Go on," the president said.

"As we all know from the blackouts of the past few years, the electrical system in the United States is for the most part linked among states and regions to regulate peak demand periods. One of the primary switching stations is near Norfolk, Nebraska, almost directly on the forty-second degree of latitude line. This area is not prone to earthquakes and has few faults. However, I have come to believe that Ratzovik's intention is not to trigger a quake, but in fact to use a surge of electricity to destroy the delicate interior workings of the switching station."

"Good Lord," the president blurted. "Give me some idea of the impact to the United States if this is successful."

"Mr. President," Miles said, "it would be absolute chaos. Most everything in the United States is controlled by computers and powered by electricity. Water pumps that supply drinking water would fail, food storage lockers would heat up, and food would spoil. The citizens of the United States would not have food and water for starters. Streetlights would not operate, hospitals would be unable to treat the sick and injured, gas pumps would fail. Land-based telephones would be affected. Air traffic control systems would go down, affecting air travel. The switching stations for the railroads would be unable to function. Almost immediately people in the United States would be unable to eat, drink, travel, or care for their sick. Pharmacies would be unable to receive restocking, and medicines that need refrigeration would spoil. Any outbreak of disease would run rampant, and without fresh water and the ability to flush toilets, some outbreak of disease is almost a certainty. People would not have access to funds as banks would be shuttered and ATM machines rendered useless, so even if there was anything to purchase, there would be no funds available to buy anything needed. Police, military units such as National Guard, and security forces such as the Department of Homeland Security and the Border Patrol would be rendered ineffective as well as being outnumbered by a crazed population." Miles paused. "Should I go on, sir?"

The president slowly shook his head no. He paused before speaking.

"The United States would be plunged back into the Stone Age."

"It would be somewhat worse, sir," Miles said. "In the Stone Age people had the skills of hunting and gathering—I'm afraid those skills are lost nowadays."

"Where are we at on the assault on the location of the Tesla device?" the president asked the chief of staff of the army.

"It is due to begin right about now," he said, glancing at his watch.

"How long until we can have bombers over the site?" the president asked the air force chief of staff.

"If I give the order right now," he said, "an hour to an hour and a half."

"Navy?" the president asked.

"Scrambling jets from a carrier we have in the Indian Ocean," the chief of naval operations said, "the same or a few minutes less."

"Do we have any agents near Nebraska now?" the president asked.

Miles bent down and whispered in Benson's ear.

"Sir," Benson said, "Ms. Miles informs me that my second-in-command was ordering Agent Taft to the area as she left our headquarters."

"Taft," the president said. "What have we got here—a one-man army?"

# 30

ALLBRIGHT WAS SITTING in Martinez's office in a chair next to the desk. They were both staring at the computer monitor, which displayed a real-time satellite image of the area around Norfolk, Nebraska.

"Zoom in," Allbright ordered.

Martinez entered the command, and a rectangular area forested with electrical lines came into sharper focus.

"That's the switching station," Allbright said, pointing to several acres with a forest of poles and wires strung overhead.

Martinez was staring at the screen intently. "What's that?" he asked, pointing to an area to the side.

"Looks like an oil drilling rig," Allbright said dismissively.

Martinez punched commands into the computer and zoomed in on the rig. A crudely lettered sign said: Jackalope Oil & Gas.

"Forget that," Allbright said. "Zoom out and let's look around the switching station again."

"Wait a second, sir," Martinez said. "This may be the key. You take a look. I need to make a couple of telephone calls."

Martinez stood up, and Allbright slid into his chair and started searching the area around the drilling rig. Martinez grabbed a number from his Rolodex, then walked to the telephone on a side table. First he hit his intercom.

"Run down a company for me," he said to his assistant, "Jackalope Oil & Gas. It might be Nebraska-based, but search nationwide anyway."

"Yes, sir," she said.

Then he dialed a number in Texas.

"This is Larry Martinez," he said when the phone was answered. "I need to speak to Duke Rawlings."

"Duke's out at a rig," the sweet tea voice of the receptionist said. "Hold on and I'll switch you over to his portable."

Martinez waited while the telephone transferred. Rawlings was a contact Martinez had made when working on a case a few years prior. Martinez had placed him on his Christmas list, as well as sending him some autographed photographs of the president for his help. Martinez was a master at nurturing contacts, and he spent a quarter of his time on the pursuit. In times like this, the personal massaging always paid off.

"Rawlings," a baritone voice said.

Martinez could hear noise in the background.

"Duke," Martinez said loudly, "this is Larry Martinez."

"Mr. M," Rawlings said. "How's my favorite secret agent?"

"Doing good, Duke," Martinez said, "but I need some help. Some information from your area of expertise."

"Shoot, whatever you need."

"Oil drilling in Nebraska?"

"What county?" Rawlings asked.

"Madison."

"Prospects are shitty," Rawlings said immediately. "Probably more oil in the eye-talian salad I had last night than Madison County. You'd be better off drilling in D.C.—with all the greasy politicians up there you probably hit something."

"Jackalope Oil & Gas?"

"Never heard of the outfit," Rawlings said, "and I've been around so long, I know almost all the players."

This was it—Martinez could feel it in his bones.

"Thanks for your help," Martinez said quickly. "I've got to go now."

"Ain't no problem," Rawlings said, "Give me a call sometime when you've got more time to chat."

"I'll do it," Martinez said, disconnecting.

Martinez glanced over at Allbright and shook his head. Just then his intercom buzzed.

"Yep," Martinez said.

"I found no corporate records with the name Jackalope Oil & Gas, Nebraska or nationwide," his receptionist said. "No, wait, hold on—I got something."

Martinez stood there for a second.

"Just downloading the state of Nebraska oil and gas regulatory agency records. Jackalope Oil & Gas posted a bond for drilling a site less than a month ago. The bond was written by a Swiss company based in Geneva.

"Good work," Martinez said, hanging up.

"Well?" Allbright said, staring up.

"We got them, boss," Martinez said.

"THE DRILLING PIPE must be the receiving unit," Martinez said to Taft a few seconds later. "They must be planning to electrify the Earth around the switching station.

"How long do we have?" Taft asked.

"Not long, old buddy," Martinez said.

"Isn't that always the case," Taft said quietly. "You need to find me the sporting goods store in Norfolk."

Martinez entered commands into his computer. "What do you need?"

"Guns, man," Taft said. "Some hunting rifles and shotguns."

"Here we go," Martinez said reading the name off the screen.

"Map it," Taft ordered.

"Done," Martinez said a second later.

"Is it in the city?"

"Kind of," Martinez said, "but there's a town park nearby."

"Send the map to my phone, then call the local police," Taft said. "Explain that the Osprey will be setting down in the park. Have them clear out any people. Next, ask them to try and round up some dynamite or some kind of explosives. Third, ask them to give me a deputy to ride shotgun."

"What's the plan?" Allbright shouted at the speakerphone.

"I'm going to remove the threat," Taft said quickly, "however I can."

"You're going to blast your way in there," Allbright said, "and try and dynamite the rig?"

"You got a better idea?" Taft asked.

"Not this late in the game," Allbright admitted.

"All right, then," Taft said, "let's get it on."

MATHER AND ZORAN were on the top of a series of hangars at the Belgrade airport.

"Okay," Mather said, "I'm going to move down about fifty yards and take up position. That will give us a triangular field of fire if the jet carrying Ilic makes it here."

Zoran was holding an evil-looking .50-caliber sniper rifle Mather had retrieved from the weapons locker in the coffee shop. The scope attached to the top of the rifle looked like a pair of field binoculars.

"I understand," Zoran said.

"Laser-tag the target if he appears," Mather said. "Then go for a kill shot. Keep firing until the clip is depleted. I'll do the same."

Mather started to walk across the roof.

"What is the chance of this not working?" Zoran asked.

Mather turned on his heels. "About zero," he said. "Ilic's feet touched Serbian soil and he's ours. I need to know now: Do you have a problem with that?"

"No," Zoran said.

What they were preparing for was nothing less than an assassination. Still, there didn't seem to be any other choice. If Ilic made it away from the airport and linked up with his supporters, there would be few other chances to stop him. The ethnic cleansing would begin anew. And

Zoran had a feeling that this time the world community would be quick to act. War would break out again in Serbia. And this time, he knew, there would be an occupying force sent to ensure that it never happened again.

"Then don't you miss," Mather said, "and neither will I."

Zoran bent down and peered through the scope. The magnification was amazing. Panning down to the tarmac, he could read the lettering on a gum wrapper that someone had tossed to the ground. If Ilic came into his sights, Zoran would be able to see the hair growing from his nose. And that's what he would aim at.

# 31

THE DOOR TO Radko Ilic's cell slid open.

After so many years imprisoned inside with the door always closed, having the door open seemed strange. Ilic made a few tentative steps toward the door, as if he were afraid it would slam shut again. Seeing it remained in place, he poked his head out and then walked into the hallway in front of the cell. Two Dutch guards stood off to the left, while to the right his lawyer stood, waiting.

Ilic turned and walked toward his lawyer.

"The warden will meet us just outside the cell block," the lawyer said, starting toward the metal door at the end of the hall. "He'll lead us to the courtyard parking lot in the center of the prison. That's where the convoy that will takes us to the airport is waiting."

Ilic nodded but said nothing—the strange sensation of freedom after being cooped up for so many years had yet to fully register. Somehow none of this seemed real.

The lawyer approached the metal door, stared up at a remote camera, and waved. The door slid open, and he walked through to the hallway on the other side. As soon as Ilic, followed by the pair of guards, had exited, the cell block door slid shut again. The prison warden, who was standing off to the side, motioned for them to follow. The warden walked fast, leading them through the Byzantine maze of hallways to a set of stairs. Ilic was following the warden, with the lawyer a few feet behind. The two guards, walking side by side, brought up the rear.

Once they reached the lower level of the prison complex, the warden opened the door, and Ilic could smell fresh air for the first time in a long time. Just like air blown into a balloon, the fresh air caused Ilic to inflate. Sucking in breaths as he walked closer to the door leading outside, the former commander seemed to rise in size and stature. Squaring his shoulders, he stepped through the door the warden held open.

Ilic stepped into the sunlight.

Four vehicles sat in the courtyard with their noses pointed toward the exit gate. The first was an armored personnel carrier, gray with the markings of the Dutch Army. A soldier poked his head from the main turret and the engine revved as soon as he shouted down to the driver that Ilic was in the courtyard. The second two vehicles were an identical set of black armored Mercedes-Benz sedans. The fourth vehicle was a two-ton truck with a canvas cover over the rear. Ilic couldn't see inside— but Dutch troops armed with assault rifles were huddled behind the cover.

The warden walked toward the sedans. Ilic and the lawyer followed close behind. The sound of a helicopter in the air nearby grew louder, and Ilic stared up to try to catch a glimpse of the craft. The helicopter was just out of sight—but by the sound Ilic guessed it was flying in an oval pattern over the prison grounds.

"Take your pick," the warden said when they reached the sedans.

Ilic hesitated for a second, then chose the one first in line. He motioned to it with his hand. The warden opened the rear door, and Ilic, followed by the lawyer, climbed inside. The warden shut the door.

"Clear!" the warden shouted toward the guard shack near the gate.

The gate slid open and the armored personnel carrier rolled through the opening and then turned right. The pair of sedans started driving toward the gate, with the two-ton truck following. As they drove up to the gate, Ilic swiveled around in his seat to stare at the prison courtyard through the rear window. He kept watching until the Mercedes-Benz was safely through the gate and onto the street. Then he turned to the lawyer.

"So far, so good," Ilic said quietly.

GALADIN RATZOVIK WAS smelling a rat. The guards who had been dispatched to recapture the Pestic family had not returned, nor could they be reached by radio. The men had not simply disappeared—someone was out there, and it was someone sent to stop his plan.

Walking toward the barn, he opened the door and walked inside. He stared for a second at the Tesla device; then he reached for his cell phone and flipped it open.

"Run calculations," he said as soon as Bernal answered, "with gold at $800 an ounce and the Euro at two to one to the dollar. Then give me the total value of my holdings."

Ratzovik could hear Bernal typing the factors into his computer. "The gold holdings and options would be worth $2.8 billion," Bernal said. "The dollar shorts roughly the same—give or take."

"So five billion plus?" Ratzovik asked.

"There will be commission subtracted," Bernal said, "but it is safe to say the value of your portfolio would be over five and a half."

"How long would it take to unload all my positions," Ratzovik said, "if the prices I just mentioned are reached?"

"A little over an hour," Bernal said, "for that size of sales."

Ratzovik stared at his watch. "The London market is open for four more hours?"

"Correct," Bernal said. "Then the overseas markets open when London closes."

"I'm issuing a sell order to liquidate all my positions beginning when gold reaches $800 an ounce or above. Do a staggered ladder approach over an hour's period of time," Ratzovik said, "no longer."

Bernal stared at his computer screen. "Sir," he said, "gold is at $514.20 right now."

"Just enter the order," Ratzovik said. "I have a feeling gold is going up."

Ratzovik disconnected and dialed another number. The connection took almost a minute to make. Then the phone on the other end started ringing.

"Here, sir," the voice that answered said.

There were clanging and grinding sounds in the background.

"How far down are you?"

"We just went past 150 feet," the voice said, "and pulled the pipe and added another section. We should be at total depth in the next hour or so."

"Once you are at total depth," Ratzovik said, "leave the pipe in the hole and pull the men off the rig. Then retreat using the escape route I outlined."

"South Dakota, North Dakota, and into Winnipeg?"

"Exactly. A plane will be there in Winnipeg, waiting," Ratzovik said.

"Can I tell the men where we will be going, sir?"

Ratzovik considered if he should answer this question, then decided it was okay.

"You'll meet up with me," Ratzovik said, "in South America."

Ratzovik flipped the telephone shut.

Only one more hour to wait. Then he would send the stream of electricity to the United States, destroying their electrical infrastructure. By the time he made his escape from Serbia, his positions would have been closed out and he'd be sitting on a fortune. By tomorrow this time, he'd be in South America, a new man with a new identity.


ILIC STARED OUT the window as the convoy entered the A-4 roadway. "We're headed to Schiphol?" he said, referring to Amsterdam's international airport. "There isn't an airport closer to The Hague?"

"Not for the size jet The Netherlands assigned us," the lawyer noted.

"How far is it to the airport?"

"About forty miles," the lawyer said.

"An hour's drive?" Ilic said warily.

"It won't take that long," the lawyer said, staring out the window. "The police are blocking the on-ramps entering the roadway."

Ilic stared out the window. At the sides of the roadway, police cars with flashing lights were blocking access to A-4. And although he could not see it, to the rear of the two-ton truck a pair of police cars were forming a rolling barricade. The Netherlands was taking no chances in getting rid of Ilic.

It was almost like Ilic was commander again. Police escorts, limousines, and private jets. His heart swelled with pride and ego. In a few hours he'd be back on top.

The lawyer noted Ilic's smile. "The jet is a Falcon 2000EX," he said quietly. "Top of the line."

Ilic smiled, showing all his upper teeth. By nightfall he'd be taking his rightful place at the head of his country once again. Only a few more hours.


THE HIGHEST-RANKING MEMBER of the Special Forces teams was a captain who was in charge of Echo Team. Born into a military family and groomed for leadership since birth, the captain knew instinctively how the command game was played. As soon as the teams were assembled, he made a command decision and placed Davis in charge of the operation. Sometimes leadership was simply knowing who to let lead.

"Thank you, sir," Warrant Officer Davis said after the captain transferred command.

The sixty men who made up the strike force were clustered around Davis. The barn and house where Ratzovik and his men were hiding were just down the hill. The complex was barely in sight through the thick forest of trees.

"Men," Davis said, "time is of the essence. Command has informed us that bombers are being readied to leave the ground. That will place them over the area somewhere between an hour and an hour and a half from now. We must be in and out before the bombers arrive. Here's our mission: Inside the barn is an experimental weapon the United States would like to see recovered if possible. If not, it *must* be destroyed. If we cannot subdue the enemy and capture the weapon intact, then the bombers have been ordered to turn this area into a wasteland. One way or another, this threat *must* be neutralized. Do you all understand?"

He looked around at the men. They were nodding in assent.

"Excellent," Davis said. "But I want to be very clear on this: If I give an order to retreat, I do not want you to hesitate. If the time comes and we are not finished, we're pulling out and letting the air force take over the problem."

All the men nodded.

"I want to deploy in the following manner," Davis continued. "From here on the high ground we will form an upside-down V-shaped or pincher formation, leaving the rear or lower end of the barn open. A distance below the end of the barn, Teams D and E will lie in wait, out of the field of fire. They will be awaiting anyone who tries to escape in that direction. Teams D and E, make sure that you are down on the ground or behind natural cover in case rounds from the other teams deflect into your direction."

The D and E team leaders voiced their agreement.

"The remaining teams that make up the assault force should position themselves with their weapons pointing toward the wide area of the upside-down V. Do not position yourself so that you might fire across the inverted V, only down toward the barn. Is that clear?"

There was a rumble of agreement.

"If we align properly, we will be firing down toward the target and not near each other's positions. Be sure you watch your targets carefully," Davis continued. "If you are unsure what you have in your sights, do not fire. The force we are going up against is less than a dozen men, so we stand no chance of being overrun. Work carefully and pick your targets. I do not want a single casualty from friendly fire. Understood?"

The men agreed quietly.

"Good," Davis said. "Now for the team leaders, here's where I want each of you positioned."

Davis sketched each team's position on the ground. He looked up to make sure that all the team leaders knew their place and that the plan was agreed upon. Once he saw that everyone knew their place, Davis turned to the captain.

"We're ready, sir," he said.

"Commence when ready," the captain said.

"Okay men," Davis said, "Move into your positions. I'll make the first shot. After that, you may all fire when ready."

It would take Davis and the teams about twenty minutes to move into place.

Then the fun could start.


"COMMANDER-IN-CHIEF IN THE room," the DCI said loudly.

The president, followed by the national security adviser, entered the command center.

"Give me an update, please," the president said.

"The first of the three bombers has left the ground," the DCI said, pointing to a monitor. As they watched, another red dot appeared on the map. "That's number two up now. Three should be away in the next few minutes."

"The assault teams?"

"They just radioed they are moving into position and should commence the assault on the barn in the next twenty minutes. Their intelligence suggests they will meet with limited resistance—ten to a dozen men in total. They expect to secure the barn and the contents with a short but definitive fight."

"Where's Ilic?" the national security adviser asked.

"He has left The Hague," the DCI said, "and is expected at Schiphol International Airport in less than ten minutes. The Netherlands has the plane waiting, and it is due to take off the minute he arrives."

"So," the president said, "he will be out of The Netherlands and in the air before we have this resolved."

"I'm afraid so, sir," the DCI said.

"What about on the other end," the national security adviser asked, "in Nebraska?"

"We assembled a team as soon as we received notification about the target," the DCI said, "but they have not left the ground yet. Once they do, the flight west will take several hours."

"We may not have several hours. What about air force fighters?" the president asked.

"The military is stretched to the limit currently," the DCI said. "The quickest they can launch a flight is more than an hour from now. We have them working on it—but by then the Kosovo barn should have been secured by the assault teams."

"What about the NIA agent?" the president asked.

The DCI reached for a telephone. "I'll call General Benson and get an update."

# 32

"THAT'S THE ELKHORN River in the distance!" Taft shouted forward to Major Schilling.

Taft handed Captain Hobbs his cell phone with the map. "We need to land there," he said, pointing. "It's a park. The police should already be there, waiting."

Hobbs pointed the direction to Schilling, who adjusted the CV-22 controls. In a few seconds they were over Interstate 275, at the west end of Norfolk. Schilling started to lower the Osprey and flew east, toward Johnson Park.

IN THE PARKING lot of Johnson Park, Deputy Clifford Rogers watched the gray airplane approach. It slowed and rotated the propellers upright, then started to descend. The park had been nearly clear of people when Rogers had arrived. Two old men had been sitting at a picnic table playing chess, but they were at the far end of the six-acre park, under a canopy and away from the landing zone. Rogers had asked them not to approach the craft. Once they'd agreed, he'd told them they could stay. People living in a small town needed every thrill they could find.

As the Osprey lowered onto the grassy park, Taft shouted forward again: "I'm going to meet the deputy, secure some weapons, then I'll meet back here in a few minutes!"

Schilling was concentrating on the descent so Hobbs answered. "Affirmative."

As soon as the Osprey touched down, Hobbs unbuckled, walked back, and lowered the door. Taft climbed down and ran across the grass to the police car. Rogers was standing next to the cruiser and staring at the plane.

"John Taft, National Intelligence Agency," Taft said, running over and flashing his badge. "Take me to the nearest gun store."

Rogers could have made a joke or asked questions, but he did neither. He simply opened his door, climbed behind the wheel, and waited until Taft got inside.

"It's just up the street," he said, placing the cruiser in gear.

Driving a block down First Street, Rogers turned right on Norfolk Avenue, which is also Interstate 275, and slid into a spot on the street. Jamming the cruiser into park, he quickly climbed out. "Walt's Guns and Ammo," he said.

Taft headed for the door, with Rogers right behind. Taft opened the door and walked inside. The inside of the small brick building smelled like gun oil and leather. The proprietor was behind the counter with a handgun disassembled on a cloth in front of him. He glanced up.

"Afternoon, Cliff," he said to Rogers.

"This is a government agent," Rogers said. "He needs to purchase some weapons."

The man nodded as if this were an everyday occurrence. "What exactly do you need?"

"Deer rifles, shotguns," Taft said, "and lots of ammunition. I hate it when I run out of ammo."

Walt nodded and smiled, then reached down to his beltline, where a cluster of keys was attached to a chain, and unlocked the gun racks. "Take your pick," he said.

"The twelve-gauge autoload," Taft said in a voice like the Terminator in the movies, "that scoped rifle . . ."

"The two-seventy Winchester," Walt asked, "or the .300 Weatherby Magnum?"

"The Weatherby," Taft said.

Walt grabbed the rifle and a box of shells and set them on the counter, then reached for the shotgun and a box of ammo and did the same. "Next?"

"What are you bringing?" Taft asked Rogers.

"Shotgun and my service revolver."

Taft caught sight of a semiautomatic rifle. "What's that?"

"Two-twenty-three Swift with scope."

"Throw that in as well," Taft said. "Now handguns—what have you got?"

"Anything you want," Walt said. "Close in or farther away?"

"Close in."

Walt unlocked the case under the counter when the handguns were displayed. "Ruger .357. It's a good weapon."

"Got two?" Taft asked.

"One blue," Walt said, retrieving the weapons from the case, "one nickel."

Reaching over, Walt removed a paper box of ammunition and set that on the counter as well. Taft reached into his pocket, removed his wallet, and started to slide out a credit card. Walt waved his hand back and forth in a no.

"We can settle up later," he said.

Taft slid the boxes of ammunition into his pockets, then gathered up the rifles and shotgun. "Grab the handguns, please," he said, motioning with his head to Rogers.

Taft pushed open the door making the cowbell attached to the slide ring.

"Thanks for stopping by, Cliff," Walt said as Rogers followed him out the door.

Rogers ran forward and opened the rear door, and Taft placed the weapons in the rear seat. Once the handguns were stowed, Rogers climbed behind the wheel and started the cruiser. Pulling a U-turn in the road, he accelerated back toward First Street.

"You mind," Rogers asked when they were in sight of the park again, "telling me what you have planned?"

"You and I," Taft said as they drove closer to the Osprey, "are going to attack an oil well."

"Damn," Rogers said as they slowed to a stop, "it's about time someone did something about these crazy gas prices."

They parked, and Rogers opened the trunk and removed a bag. "Your partner mentioned explosives. We confiscated this dynamite a few years ago from some kids who were using it to fish," he said. "It should still be good."

Grabbing the weapons and the bag, the two men ran toward the plane.

Three minutes later Taft and Rogers were inside the Osprey. Schilling started the engines. As the CV-22 slowly raised from the grassy park, Taft turned to Rogers, who was seated next to him, and started to explain.

"No shit," Rogers said when Taft had finished.

"Real as rain, my friend," Taft said slowly. "Real as rain."

"So I take it," Rogers said, "the plan is to shoot first and ask questions later."

"Precisely," Taft said.


RADKO ILIC STEPPED from the Mercedes-Benz and walked a few feet to the ramp of the Falcon jet. His lawyer followed behind. Quickly climbing up the ramp and inside the fuselage, Ilic made his way to a seat and sat down. Outside, on the tarmac, the convoy that had brought them from the prison was pulling away from the jet. It drove a safe distance away and parked to wait.

As soon as Ilic and the lawyer were seated, the pilot in the cockpit of the Falcon radioed the tower. When the convoy had approached the airport, the aviation traffic in the area had been asked to begin holding patterns, so the pilot received immediate clearance. The Falcon started taxiing to the runway. Once at the north end it turned and lined up on the runway itself. The pilot radioed he was ready to take off, and clearance came through immediately. Pushing the throttles all the way forward, the pilot steered the Falcon down the runway. Halfway down the tarmac and at the proper speed, he rotated. Like a shot from a cannon, the Falcon left the ground and headed into the air.

Back at Schiphol, the head of the convoy reached for his phone and dialed a number. "They're off safe," he said.

"I'll notify the queen," the voice said.

"THEY'RE OFF!" ONE of the command center operators shouted.

"Report tracking," the DCI ordered.

"We have an AWACS over Germany that has them on scope," the operator said. "Two F-15s on cover are flying in formation over Switzerland. They will wait there for them to pass. In addition, there are two Austrian Eurofighter Typhoons protecting Austrian airspace. We expect Hungary will send up a jet, but they haven't yet."

"Keep everyone close," the DCI said, "but out of sight. If we give the word to intercept, it needs to be done quickly."

"Close tracking," the operator said, "with intercept at your command."

RADKO ILIC STARED out the window at the German countryside far below. As each second passed he was feeling more and more alive. Turning to his lawyer, he spoke:

"I assume they placed food and drink aboard?"

The lawyer understood the implication. He was the hired help. Making his way back to the galley, the lawyer opened the cupboards and found the liquor supply. Then he opened the refrigerator and found a plate arranged with cold cuts and cheese. Below that on another shelf was a plate of bread, crackers, and condiments. Removing the two plates, he carried them forward and set them on the table.

"What would you like to drink, sir?" the lawyer asked.

"Any champagne?"

"Maybe," the lawyer said. "They stocked wine."

"If not," Ilic said, "I'll have a Scotch neat."

The lawyer, not used to his role as waiter, merely nodded.

"I found some champagne," the lawyer said from the rear. A few seconds later, a pop was heard from the direction of the galley. The lawyer heard some rustling from the wall behind, where the rest room was located; then it was quiet again. Noises from the aircraft, the lawyer thought.

Radko Ilic licked his lips and placed some meat and cheese on a cracker.


AT THE DRILLING site the wind was blowing from west to east. The drilling supervisor stared at the depth gauge carefully. They had finally reached total depth. Whistling over the noise, he made a motion with his arm, slicing across his neck to the man operating the engine powering the rig. The man nodded and shut it down. The engine wheezed for a few seconds, then grew silent. After listening to the roar from the machine for the past several days, their hearing was not very sensitive. If they had strained their ears they might have heard the thumping of the propellers on the Osprey, which was approaching just to the east.

Beads of sweat were forming on Major Schilling's forehead. He was flying the Osprey at fifty feet above ground level to avoid detection. If they had an engine or system failure now, the craft would be lost. Without sufficient altitude to correct any problems, chances were the Osprey would crash, and with it would go Schilling's career.

He concentrated and stared at the gauges again.

They had left Norfolk and flown a little to the east, then up along the river and through some low hills. No one on board could see the top of the drilling rig, but Taft knew that the drilling rig, and the switching plant, were just over the rise.

"You can land it, sir!" Taft shouted.

Schilling went through the procedure to bring the propellers up-right, then dropped the Osprey to the ground.

"What do you want us to do?" Captain Hobbs asked.

"I'm going to leave you this rifle," he said, pointing to the .223. Give me and Rogers about five minutes, then lift off and fly over near the rig. Provide cover if we need it."

"You want us to try and take shots from in here?" Schilling said in amazement.

"I'm not sure what you can do," Taft said, "but I'll leave the rifle just in case."

"You got a radio?" Hobbs asked Rogers.

Rogers unclipped his radio from his belt and held it up.

"Use 750 mhz if you need to reach us," Hobbs said as he stepped over to open the door.

The door to the Osprey opened, and Taft reached over and patted Rogers's leg. "Okay, man. Let's go do this," he said quietly.

Rogers followed Taft out the door.

As they climbed up the rise, Rogers spoke. "What are the rules?"

"If it isn't me," Taft said quietly, "and it resists—kill it."

## 33

A LIGHT WIND blew across southern Kosovo, carrying the smell of pine, gun oil, and fear. The few smokers in the Special Forces teams were chewing snuff so as not to taint the air with smoke. The mint scent mixed with the salty tang of their sweat. An electricity was in the air, but not the type that Ratzovik was seeking to harness; this was the electricity caused by a group of humans all prepping to kill.

Fifty soldiers, with the rest guarding the Pestic family or preparing to provide medical support, communications, and backup, lined the area around the barn in the formation. In the past few minutes the teams had crept closer to the house and barn. They hid in the trees and behind rocks, with their rifles at the ready.

Davis was not a butcher, but neither would he risk his teams' lives to save the opponents. His mission was clear: secure the area and recover the device. Anyone who chose to fight would be dealt with mercilessly. Davis keyed his microphone.

"This is the United States Army," he said. "Throw down your weapons and come out into the clearing with hands raised."

He handed the microphone to Sergeant Gibbons, who repeated the order in Serbo-Croatian.

RATZOVIK WAS STILL in the barn with two of his guards. The guards were off to the side, and they peered out the window but could see nothing. Ratzovik reached for his radio and called the house.

"Do you see anything?" he asked the man who answered.

"No, sir," the man said.

"You men!" he shouted to the guards peering out the window. "See anyone?"

"No, sir," one replied.

"Surrender now," Davis said over the bullhorn. "There will be no more warnings."

A minute passed.

Davis sighted down his rifle and fired rounds into the house. Almost instantly, a volley of shots rang out from the other soldiers, and the wall of the barn closest to the house was peppered with rounds.

"Men!" Ratzovik shouted into the radio. "Return fire!"

From the upper floor of the house two men started firing at the woods.

Forty yards away and hidden behind a rock outcropping, Davis turned to his first sergeant. "Sergeant," he shouted, "take out the upper floor!"

From order to action took only seconds. Two *whooshes* were heard as rocket-propelled incendiary grenades left their tubes. Less than a second later, the sound of breaking glass was heard, then the muffled thumps of explosions.

"Teams," Davis said over the radio, "fire at will."

The forest on both sides of the house and barn erupted in a rain of lead. Slivers flew from the walls of the house as the automatic-weapons fire raked across the building. The barn did not fare any better. On the left side of the inverted V, one of the teams was creeping forward. A soldier's foot touched a plate buried in the forest floor, and a second later, an explosion rocked the area. Thousands of ball bearings flew through the air, tearing into the soldiers nearby.

A scream rang out through the forest.

"They laid mines!" Davis shouted over his radio. "Remain in place!"

As the gunfire ceased, a soldier crept through the trees to his fallen comrade. The soldier's left foot was missing at the ankle. He was screaming in pain. Quickly attaching a tourniquet, the soldier injected his teammate with morphine, then reached for his radio.

"Team Delta needs a medic," the soldier said.

Just over a hundred yards away, Warrant Officer Davis was standing in place. "Sergeant!" he shouted.

"Sir."

"Suggestions?"

"I'd have the men fire at the ground and trigger the devices," the sergeant said.

"All teams," Davis said, "fire at the ground in front of you and set off the mines. Once you have a clear path, enter the area through the breach."

A few seconds later the teams began to rake the earth with gunfire.

The land around the house and barn erupted with explosions. Dust, pine needles, and ball bearings flew skyward. The dust had not yet settled when Davis gave his next order.

"Sergeant," he shouted, "level the house!"


GALADIN RATZOVIK WAS not ready to concede defeat. He was furiously flipping switches to deliver power to the Tesla device as he read Pestic's notes. First the tertiary power to warm up the coils. Secondary power would come next, a few minutes after warmup. Once the coils were glowing, Ratzovik could flip the primary power supply lever and dump the main line into the device. That would send the bolt toward the United States and wipe out their electrical grid.

Then he'd figure a way to escape and collect his money.

Ratzovik was nothing if not a dreamer.


A VOLLEY OF mortar shells headed toward the house in an arc. They slammed into the structure, opening holes in the exterior walls and exploding inside. The fire on the upper level caused by the incendiary grenades was burning nicely now. Through the numerous openings in the walls, Davis could see men scurrying about.

"RPGs!" he shouted.

A volley of rocket-propelled grenades left rifle tubes and tore into the house. Explosions rang out as exterior boards flew off the structure and landed in broken heaps on the ground. Automatic-weapons fire continued to rake the building.

Little by little, the walls were coming down.

Father down the upside-down V, teams were firing assault rifles at the barn. Over the past few minutes, they had cleared a path through the mines that allowed them to creep closer. They were only awaiting the signal to attack and secure.

RATZOVIK STARED AT the notes again. Secondary power was now being sent to the Tesla device. Ratzovik stared at the glowing coils.

"Sir," one of his guards said, "we need to retreat. I estimate there are several dozen men out there at least. We are way outnumbered."

The man was standing at the window, watching the maelstrom around the house. His handgun was in his hand, with his arm down at his side. Ratzovik pulled his pistol from his holster, raised it to chest level, and shot the man in the back three times. He flopped down to his knees and tumbled forward.

"How about you?" Ratzovik asked the other guard. "You ready to surrender, too?"

The man stared down at the body of the other guard. Blood was flowing out onto the straw to each side of the body. The inside of the barn smelled like a wet penny.

"No, sir," the man said quickly.

THE HOUSE WAS beginning to look like fishnet. Entire sections of the exterior walls were broken and punched through with holes. The fire raging on the top floor was growing stronger by the second, and tendrils of flames were poking from the numerous openings. No shots had come from inside the house for the past few minutes.

"Start to move on the barn," Davis said over the radio. "I'm coming down."

The teams closer to the barn started creeping forward under a hail of covering fire. From inside, only the single remaining guard was answering.

Davis shouted, "Sergeant, handle the mop-up! I'm going for the weapon!"

Then he started sprinting along the right-hand flank, down toward the barn.

As soon as Davis drew closer he saw the first few men reach the back exterior wall of the barn. They were bending down and attaching wires to explosive packs.

They were planning to blow off a section of wall to see who was inside.


RATZOVIK HEARD THE sound of a thump as one of the soldiers bumped into the wall outside. Pointing his handgun at the direction of the sound, he fired off a few rounds and heard a scream. Ratzovik continued to fire until his clip was exhausted, then popped it out and slid in another. He had just installed the fresh clip as a round shattered the glass window in the barn, striking his remaining guard directly in the forehead. The guard went down like a sack of rice tossed onto a dock. The top half of his head landed a few feet from his body, with the eyes already turning cloudy.

Ratzovik stood for a second and weighed the odds. Escape now seemed but a vague dream. A sane man might have considered surrender—but Ratzovik was far from sane. If he was going to be taken, he would make those who killed him pay.

He started across the floor of the barn toward the primary switch just as the far wall of the barn erupted in a massive explosion. Boards flew through the air like matchsticks dropped from a paper box. Ratzovik was blasted with a spray of a thousand splintered fragments, like someone had exploded a toothpick bomb.

Blood dripped down his face and torso where the slivers of wood had penetrated his body like a thousand spears. Ratzovik tried to pop his ears, but his eardrums had burst. He could not hear the firing outside over the ringing in his head, but his nose caught the scent of gunpowder and almonds.

In his left leg, just above the knee, a spear of wood the width of a soda can went through his muscle and poked out the rear. Blood flowed from the wound like water from a pitcher. Dragging his wounded leg along behind him, Ratzovik made his way a few feet toward where the body of the guard he had shot lay. Reaching down, he took the man's handgun from the ground and checked the clip. Tucking the guard's gun into his front pocket, Ratzovik quickly checked the clip in his again, then held it in his hand. Satisfied both were full of cartridges, he removed the guard's from his pocket again.

Now he had a weapon in each hand.

He started back to the primary switch, dragging his bad leg behind.

When closer to the switch, Ratzovik peered over at the hole in the rear wall of the barn. The outline of a soldier crossed across the hole and Ratzovik fired. He missed.

Ratzovik was almost at the switch.

Outside the barn, eighteen soldiers were lined up at the far wall, near where the hole had been blown in the side. Davis was in the middle, nearest the hole.

Davis shouted, "Let's do it!"

A split second later a thousand pops like that of a bag of popcorn on heat rang out, and the inside of the barn was crisscrossed with bullets. A dozen hit Ratzovik in his lower extremities, and blood flew through the air in a mist.

A second after the covering fire rang out, Davis jumped through the opening in the wall and rolled onto the ground. Twelve feet away, a strange device was glowing like the heating element on a stove. Several feet from that, where a support beam holding up the roof of the barn reached the ground, a man who looked like he'd been shot with wooden bullets was standing with a pair of handguns and both arms in the air like the cartoon character Yosemite Sam. Bleeding profusely, the gravely wounded Ratzovik flipped a switch on the post down at the same time he started to lower the handguns to fire.

Davis raised his rifle and stitched the man's chest with a burst of automatic-weapons fire. The man jerked like a marionette controlled by a nervous master as the high-powered round slammed into his upper body. He fell to one knee, then toppled over like a tree under the onslaught of a chain saw. Davis continued to fire until his clip was empty.

"Hold your fire!" Davis shouted over the radio.

The woods in southern Kosovo grew quiet.

Davis raced over to the wall and shut off the power. Then he stepped over to Ratzovik's body. The man was dead, and his body looked like freshly ground hamburger.

"Secure the weapon!" he shouted to the members of his team who were now entering the barn, "I'll report in."

## 34

AT ALMOST THE same instant as the assault on the barn commenced, Taft and Deputy Rogers reached the summit of the small hill above the drilling rig. Flopping down on the dirt, they peered down at the rig. It was quiet and serene, and the light wind blowing across the prairie grass carried no noises of work being performed. As Taft and Rogers watched, a man climbed into the rear of a pickup truck and sat down in the bed. The truck started rolling forward down a dirt road. A cloud of dust formed to the rear as the truck left the drilling site. A few moments later, as they watched, the pickup reached the main road and turned onto the asphalt.

"Come on," Taft said, rising from the ground, "we caught a break."

With the rifle on a sling behind his back and the shotgun in his hand, Taft ran down the hill, with Rogers close behind. It took the two men almost five minutes to cover the distance to the drilling rig, and when they did, both were winded. Rogers was bent over at the waist to catch his breath. Taft was panting, but he climbed up the steps on the platform and opened the door to the driller's shack. No one was inside. Taft walked back outside and felt the engine that powered the rig—it was still warm.

Rogers had recovered his wind and climbed up the steps. He stood next to Taft.

"Looks like these boys are gone, Mr. Taft."

"Have Captain Hobbs call the Osprey and ask them to follow the truck," Taft said quietly.

FOUR MILES FROM the drilling rig and now doing sixty miles an hour, the man in the bed of the pickup banged on the roof. The truck pulled to the side of the road.

"I left my passport back at the rig in my backpack," the man said, leaning over and speaking into the driver's window.

"Shit," the driver said, pulling a U-turn in the road. "We'll need that."

Accelerating back up to speed, the truck raced back in the direction of the drilling rig. It would take them a couple of minutes to retrieve the passport, but it would make their border crossing a lot easier.

"IT'S A WHITE pickup," Rogers said to Hobbs. "Taft wants it followed."

Rogers heard a whine over the radio as the engines of the Osprey began spooling.

"Acknowledged," Hobbs said a second later. "Follow the white truck."

Taft was staring at the rig. The collars were still attached to the drilling pipe. It looked as if the men had just walked away midway through the job. Either the drillers had hit a snag, or they had reached the depth they were shooting for.

"You know how to run a drilling rig?" Taft asked.

"Nope," Rogers said. "How about you?"

"I'm afraid I do," Taft said, smiling. "That's how I paid my way through college."

"So what's the deal?" Rogers asked.

"They either pinched off in the hole," Taft said, "or she's set up the way they want it. The pipe must be the intended receiver. If I can get it out of the hole, then we know the switching station is safe."

"Makes sense," Rogers said.

"You start setting dynamite charges around the base of the rig just in case," Taft said, pointing down to where the pipe led into the ground. "But I think I can yank this string of pipe out of here and we'll be in the clear."

Walking over to the engine house, Taft pushed the buttons and started the diesel motor. She started hard, but a few seconds later the old engine was rumbling. Walking back outside, Taft slid some gloves he'd found over his hands, then hooked a chain to the first section of pipe and yanked it skyward with the engine.

"THERE'S THE TRUCK!" Hobbs shouted to Major Schilling. "They're going in the direction of the drilling rig!"

"Call and report that to Rogers," Schilling ordered.

Hobbs tried to reach Rogers, but the deputy was under the drilling platform, placing the dynamite. Over the noise of the rig operating he could not hear his radio.

"He's not responding, sir!" Hobbs shouted.

"They are turning onto the dirt road leading up to the rig," Schilling said, staring down from the Osprey.

"What do you want to do, sir?" Hobbs asked quickly.

"There is only one thing to do," Schilling said. "Grab that rifle; we're going to fly the first Osprey into battle."

"Yee haw," Hobbs said.

Schilling turned the Osprey in the direction of the truck, then shouted over to Hobbs.

"I'll override the system and lower the side door!" he said. "You go back there and give that truck a proper greeting!"

THE MEN IN the white pickup truck caught sight of the Osprey's shadow before they viewed the plane itself. They were almost back to the drilling rig when the man in the rear bed looked up and saw the strange craft overhead. The door to the plane was open, and a man in a uniform was poking out with a rifle in his hands. The man in the bed began beating on the roof of the cab. When the driver looked back, the man in the bed pointed skyward.

As Schilling slowed the Osprey and began rotating the propeller upright, Hobbs fired the .223 on semiauto. He was aiming at the tires of the truck. His aim was good. Hobbs peppered the left rear tire and sent a few rounds through the left front fenders of the truck, into the engine.

Steam began seeping from the engine compartment.

The truck veered off to the side of the dirt road.

At the same time Hobbs was firing on the truck, Rogers had finished laying the dynamite around the base of the rig. He twisted off the fuses, so the charges would fire together, but he did not have any extra fuse line so they could light the charges from a distance. Rogers thought for a second, then took a few shotgun shells out of his bandolier. Opening the crimped tops of the shotgun shells, Rogers poured out the pellets, then made a crude trail of gunpowder out from underneath. He was just finishing with the trail of gunpowder and was raising himself up to his full height when he saw the pickup truck. The Osprey was in the distance. Sprinting up the platform steps, he shouted to Taft, who was attaching tongs onto the pipe string to remove a section.

"We have company."

Taft glanced over at the truck; the doors were opening, and men were climbing out.

"I'm kind of busy right now," Taft said, pointing to where he placed the rifle. "Why don't you take that rifle and shake them up a bit."

Rogers grabbed the rifle and walked a few steps toward where the railing outlined the drilling platform. Laying the rifle on the top rung, Rogers crouched down and sighted through the scope. Then he fired a round through the grille of the pickup. The hood cracked open, and the men stepping away from the truck flopped onto the ground.

"I'm calling my department," Rogers shouted, "for backup!"

Switching his radio over to the Norfolk Police Department channel, Rogers placed the call. One patrol car was less than five minutes away and said they would respond immediately. The other car was in Norfolk. It would take them ten minutes to reach the site.

THE BOLT OF electricity surged from southern Kosovo across the Mediterranean Sea, through Spain and into the Atlantic Ocean. It bolted across the great distance west and touched the United States exactly at Marblehead, Massachusetts. The electrical stream had no agenda, no enemies, no purpose save one. It was trying to find a receiver—and it would not stop until it ran out of power or reached something that would accept it.

"I DON'T REMEMBER," Major Schilling said. "Do we have a PA on this bird?"

Hobbs pointed to a switch near the radio. Schilling nodded. The men from inside the truck had started to spread out in the weeds alongside. Schilling didn't know if they were armed, but one thing was sure: He did not want them any closer to Taft and Rogers. "This is the United States Air Force," Schilling said over the PA system. "Put your hands in the air and walk back to the truck."

"What do you want to do?" one of the men from the truck asked their leader.

The man stared up at the Osprey now hovering overhead. Then he glanced toward the rig where the outline of Rogers peering into the scope was visible.

"Let's give it up, men," he said quietly.

THE MEN RAISED their hands and walked back in the direction of the truck.

"They're giving up!" Rogers shouted to Taft.

"Keep them covered!" Taft shouted over the noise from the rig.

"I've got the charges set!" Rogers shouted again. "There is a trail of gunpowder leading to the base of the stairs!"

"Good job," Taft said, attaching the chain to twist another section of pipe out of the ground, "but I think I have this covered. A couple more sections and we should be safe."

The words had no more than left his mouth, when the ground started to shake. Dust rose in the air like grass shaken from a carpet. Rogers felt the vibration in the platform and raced for the steps.

He was halfway down the steps when he heard Taft yell, "Blow it!"

Rogers was on his knees on the ground with a book of matches in his hands. He struck the first one and it sputtered out. The second one ignited, and Rogers tossed it onto the trail of gunpowder. The line of powder sputtered, then began burning in a trail toward the base of the rig.

Taft was still holding the chain attached to the tongs holding the drilling pipe. If he let go now, the chain, powered by the diesel motor, would flail about and rip him to shreds. One or two more seconds and he could release the pipe.

The dynamite exploded milliseconds before the bolt of electricity from Kosovo surged from the ground. The pipe string was severed just as the electricity surged from below. Without a complete circuit, the force of the electricity was diminished enough to save the switching station from all but limited damage; however, the remaining pent-up electricity arced across the gap in the broken drilling pipe. The bolt reached the pipe remaining on the drilling rig just as the rig started to topple over to the side from the force of the explosion.

Like lightning flung by a god, a massive bolt shot from the top of the derrick. The beam passed within fifty yards of the Osprey, then headed out into space. As the rig toppled over, Taft was still holding onto the chain with the tongs.

As he flew through the air, the massive voltage coursed through his body.

Rogers jumped out of the way of the falling rig, but Taft, the last of the electricity still running through his body, lay crumpled underneath a piece of the shredded upper derrick.

"I need an ambulance now!" Rogers shouted to his dispatcher over the radio.

# 35

WARRANT OFFICER DAVIS stepped over the body of Galadin Ratzovik and reached for the switch on the post. He wanted to make sure the power supply to the coils was shut off.

"Guard this!" he shouted to one of his men.

The coils were still red hot and glowing, with waves of heat radiating outward. As Davis watched, the intensity of the glow began to diminish slowly, like a burner turned off on an electric stove. Whatever had happened, it was over now.

He reached for his radio. "Sergeant," he said, "give me a status report."

"The threat from the house has been neutralized," the sergeant reported, "but the fire is burning out of control. We located a water supply between the house and the barn and have hooked up a hose. We think we can keep the fire from spreading to the forest, but that's about all."

"We secured the barn," Davis reported, "and the device inside. Call for the helicopters and make sure the bomb run is aborted."

Davis could hear the sergeant shouting to the radio operator. Davis waited until the sergeant was finished, then continued. "Give me an injury report."

"We have one soldier who stepped on a mine," the sergeant said. "He's serious, but he should live if we can medevac him out. Four others were hit by small-weapons fire, none critical. They are being treated now."

"That's good news," Davis said.

"How about on your end, sir?"

Two heads poked into the hole in the wall of the barn. Seeing Davis speaking into the radio, they entered.

Davis shouted. "How many injured outside?"

"Looked like three men were hit, sir," one of the men said, "but their body armor stopped the rounds. One man was hit from a round that came through the wall, but it passed through the fleshy part of his butt cheek and out the other side. He's being treated now, but he is ambulatory."

"Excellent," Davis said.

He keyed his radio to report.

"Three hit," Davis said to the sergeant, "none critical."

"Good, sir," the sergeant said. "Do you need any of my men down there?"

"I think we're okay," Davis said.

"I'll have the men keep working the fire then," the sergeant said.

The soldier who had been ordered to guard the power switch walked a few steps away and stared at the Tesla device. "Just what the hell is this, sir?" he asked.

"I don't know," Davis said, reaching for his satellite telephone, "but I think it did whatever it was going to do before I could shut it down."


"MR. PRESIDENT," THE DCI said, "the weapon in Kosovo has been neutralized, but the warrant officer in charge thinks is was operating before he shut it down."

The president was sitting in the Oval Office. He turned to the national security adviser. "What's the status on the power grid?"

The national security adviser was sitting with a laptop computer in front of him. He stared at the screen. "Norfolk reports they lost two panels from electrical discharges, but since we had redirected most of the electricity to other stations prior to the assault, there are only limited shortages being reported. Omaha and eastern Nebraska are having sporadic outages. Chicago lost a portion of the western suburbs before they could get the power shifted to other lines. Chicago is back operating now. As far as Omaha and the rest of Nebraska, the experts are not sure how long it will take to have them back online."

"How long until the panels at Norfolk can be repaired?"

"I'll call and get some estimates, sir."

"Damn," the president said, "that could have been a lot worse. We just barely dodged the bullet this time."

"Yes, sir."

"Get Taft on the phone," the president ordered an aide standing nearby. "I want to congratulate him myself."

"Very good, sir," the aide said.

"What else, sir?" the national security adviser asked.

"Let's call the president of Serbia," the president said quietly.


"WHAT'S HAPPENING?" GENERAL Benson asked.

Benson and Allbright were standing in Martinez's office.

"His phone just rings," Martinez said quietly.

After the collapse of the drilling rig and the near miss by the bolt of electricity, Schilling set the Osprey down. Once the Osprey was secured, Hobbs and Schilling cautiously approached the men clustered around the white pickup truck.

"Sir, could you cover them with the .223?" Hobbs asked.

Schilling nodded and pointed the weapon toward the men's chests.

Hobbs dug around in the toolbox of the truck and located a roll of duct tape. Taping the men's hands together behind their backs first, Hobbs then bound their legs. When that was done, he ordered them onto their stomachs in the dirt. Pulling their hands up and their legs bent at the knees, he hog-tied them.

"I don't think they are going anywhere," he said when he was finished.

From the distance the sound of sirens grew louder.

A Norfolk Police cruiser arrived first. Hobbs stayed by the pickup to help the officer place the men in the back of the squad car, while Schilling raced over to where Rogers was tearing away the twisted wreckage of the rig that was lying on top of Taft.

He had finally cleared enough away to see Taft when Schilling reached him.

"What do you need me to do?" Schilling shouted.

Taft looked like he had been beaten with a lead pipe—which he had. His face was black and swollen, and his limbs were twitching with involuntary muscle spasms. White foam flecked with blood was around the corners of his mouth as well as blood coming from his nose and ears. The hair on his head as well as that visible on his arms was standing straight out, like a forest of tiny, limbless trees. One leg was twisted around and over to one side, and both of his shoes had been blown off his feet.

Rogers bent down. "He's not breathing!" he shouted to Schilling.

"I'll take the chest," Schilling said.

Rogers bent down and started to blow into Taft's mouth.

They continued the CPR for several seconds until Taft wheezed. Schilling bent down and placed his head on Taft's chest. "We have a heartbeat," he said, "but it's faint."

The entire time Rogers had been working to free Taft, his telephone had been ringing.

"Could you please answer that phone?" Rogers said to Schilling, "I'm going to continue the chest compressions."

Schilling reached down and took the phone from Taft's pocket. He flipped it open.

"This is Major Schilling."

"I'm trying to reach John Taft," Martinez said quickly.

"Mr. Taft is busy right now," Schilling said, not being able on the spur of the moment to think of anything else to say.

"This is General Earl Benson," Benson said, bending down closer to the speakerphone. "Mr. Taft works for me—I need to know if he disabled the receiving unit."

Schilling stared down at the crumpled body on the ground. "He did that, sir," he said quietly, "but he paid a heavy price."

"What do you mean?" Martinez fairly shouted.

"It looks like he took the brunt of the electricity through his body," Schilling said. "Then the rig fell on top of him."

"Is he—" Martinez choked.

"He's alive," Schilling said quietly, "but just barely."

A second police car rolled over by the pickup, followed by an ambulance. Schilling waved to direct them over.

"We're losing him again!" Rogers shouted.

"There is an ambulance here now," Schilling said, "and I have to go."

The phone went dead.

Martinez stared at Benson.

"Go," Benson said. "I'll have an air force jet at Andrews waiting when you arrive."

Martinez bolted from his chair and ran out of the office.


"THE THREAT HAS been neutralized," the president said. "Now we need to decide how would you like to deal with Mr. Ilic."

"Where is he now?" the Serbian president asked.

The president looked at his aide before answering. The aide wrote a word on a pad and held it up. "He's still over Hungary."

"Will The Netherlands take him back?"

"I'll find out," the president said.


THE CH-53E SUPER Stallion helicopter dispatched from the ship in the Adriatic Sea hovered over the meadow near the barn, then touched down. Four Navy SEALs climbed out and ran over to the barn.

"Ensign Crowe," their leader said to Davis.

"Warrant Officer Davis."

"We're here for the device," Crowe said.

"My men disassembled as much as we could before you arrived," Davis noted.

"Can your men assist with the loading?" Crowe asked.

Davis shouted orders, and several of his team started lifting pieces of the Tesla device. The SEALs did the same, and men began carrying the parts out to the helicopter. Crowe glanced around the barn. The setting sun was filtering through the numerous bullet holes in the exterior walls, and the light made a display like a disco ball.

"I noticed the building ablaze on the way in," Crowe said, looking around again. "Looks like you all had a little party here today."

"No cake and ice cream," Davis said wearily.

"But you achieved your mission?"

"That we did," Davis said quietly.

"Casualties?" Crowe asked. "I have a few men trained as medics."

"One man stepped on a mine." Davis replied.

"Render aid." Crowe said to a medic.

Davis bent down and picked up a cardboard box. "I'll carry this out," he said.

"What is it?" Crowe said as he bent down to retrieve some parts from the device.

"I think," Davis said, "it's the instructions."

Crowe nodded and followed Davis out the door.

Six minutes later, the device was stowed in the Super Stallion and it lifted off.

Four minutes after that, additional helicopters came for the army teams. As they lifted off, Davis stared down. The quads were arranged in a line behind the barn, and the house was but a smoldering pile of rubble. Davis turned to his first sergeant.

"That was a day's work," he said quietly.

The first sergeant simply nodded; there was really nothing to be said.

"Whatever those men were trying to achieve, they paid a high price," Davis said quietly. "No one got out alive."

"Whatever it was," the first sergeant said wearily, "it couldn't have been worth it."

• • •

"THERE WAS NEVER any threat to The Netherlands," the U.S. president said to his Dutch counterpart. "The device was aimed at my country."

"I assume then it was safely diffused," the president of The Netherlands said.

"We neutralized it."

"Good."

"Ilic is currently in the air over Hungary," the U.S. president said. "We want to return him to the World Court to finish the trial."

"What are the other choices?"

"I have two fighters following your jet right now—" the president said quietly.

"No," the president of The Netherlands said. "We cannot condone assassination. I'll call and have our jet diverted back home. I'll clear it with the queen later."

"That's the best choice," the president agreed.


"THEY'RE TAKING HIM back," the U.S. president said.

"Good," the Serbian president agreed.

"You still have problems in your country," the U.S. president noted, "that need to be dealt with."

"Mr. Milorand has agreed to help with that," the Serbian president noted, "and the problems will be dealt with quickly, I can assure you."

"We have agents still inside your country," the U.S. president said. "Do I have your assurance that they will be given safe harbor?"

"I would like them removed," the Serbian president said, "as soon as possible."

"We'll have them extracted as soon as possible," the U.S. president agreed.

"You mentioned a possible candidate to take over leadership of the BIA."

"Yes," the U.S. president said.

"Have him contact the chief of the Belgrade Police; I'd like to talk to him."

"We will do that."

"Mr. President," the Serbian leader said, "I want to thank you and your men."

"Glad we could assist you," the U.S. president said. "I only hope this leads to stronger ties between out two nations."

The U.S. president disconnected and turned to his aide.

"General Benson next," he said quietly.


RADKO ILIC STARED down from the jet as it crossed the Danube River. He was so close to home now he could almost feel it. Over a mountain range and they would be over his country. Another pass over the Danube and they would reach Belgrade. The champagne, and the brandy that had followed, was making Ilic feel expansive.

"Perhaps we should have alerted the citizens to my return," he said, picturing in his mind a ticker-tape parade from the airport into Belgrade.

"Maybe, sir—" the lawyer started to say.

Just at that instant the rest-room door opened and two men climbed out. In the first man's hand was a Heckler-Koch 9-millimeter. The second held a pair of handcuffs.

"How'd you—" the lawyer started to say as the Falcon banked and started a turn to the north.

"Secret panel," the second man said, slapping the handcuffs around Ilic's wrists. Reaching over, he handcuffed the lawyer as well. "It leads back into the cargo compartment."

"Check for telephones or radios," the man holding the gun said.

The second man patted them both down and removed their telephones. Flipping the switches to off, he stowed them in a side compartment. The Falcon was leveling out now, and the turbines outside the window spooled up as the pilot increased speed.

"Where are you—" Ilic started to say.

"Back to jail," the man with the gun said, "where you belong."

The second man stared down at Ilic and his lawyer for a second, then turned to his partner. "You hungry?"

"Hungry over Hungary," the man with the gun said.

"Let me see if these pigs left us anything to eat."


MATHER WALKED OVER, with his assault rifle pointed skyward.

Zoran peered up from his scope. "He should be arriving shortly," he said, a little perturbed that Mather was not in place.

"We've been ordered to stand down," Mather said.

"What happened?"

"I don't have all the details," Mather said, "but the situation has apparently been diffused. You have been ordered to contact the chief of the Belgrade Police as soon as possible."

For the past few hours Zoran's emotions had run the gauntlet from fear to elation. Now that the situation was over, he was not quite sure how to handle it. "Belgrade Police?"

"Yes," Mather said. "He's going to hook you up with your president."

Somehow Taft had pulled it off, Zoran thought. "Taft?" he said.

"Taft was hurt," Mather said quietly. "They're not sure he'll make it."

# EPILOGUE

LARRY MARTINEZ STARED down at the hospital bed where Taft had lain for the past twelve days. It was just past 8:00 A.M. The summer sun outside the window was bright and clear. Inside the room, the light was a little more dim, with a sconce above Taft's head illuminating only his upper body. The sounds were muffled and the smells antiseptic. Martinez was sure that Taft was hating where he was.

The doctors at Walter Reed Army Medical Center had done what they could for Taft, but now, they said, it was up to him. Taft's heart had stopped again in the ambulance from the oil rig site to Faith Memorial Hospital in Norfolk, but they shocked him back into a regular rhythm. Had not Rogers and Schilling acted quickly he would have died, the paramedics told Martinez when he had arrived in Nebraska.

Martinez had taken charge once he reached Norfolk, coordinating with the doctors at Walter Reed by phone. The doctors in Nebraska had administered the new protein drugs that were being given to stroke victims to attempt to arrest any damage to Taft's brain, but he had been in a coma almost from the start, and the prognosis did not look good.

Martinez had been given leave from his duties—make that ordered by General Benson—to stay by Taft's side during the hours Martinez would normally be at work. Martinez, as he always did, treated his new assignment seriously. The doctors and nurses had told him there was some research indicating that coma victims might grow better if they were stimulated by someone talking to them—as if their conscious mind heard the words and tried to heal itself so it might respond. The theory had never really been proven, but Martinez was taking no chances.

Martinez had taken to filling Taft in on the mission's aftermath.

Today, like every day for the past dozen, he would start at the end of Taft's involvement and recap everything that had happened until this time.

At noon Martinez would turn on the television, and he and the comatose Taft would watch *Jeopardy*, with Martinez shouting his answers at the screen. Then he would go down and eat lunch, and when he returned he would describe his meal in detail, as he knew Taft's interest in food and dining. With any time he had remaining, Martinez would read from books or attempt to teach Taft's unconscious mind Spanish. Then he would go home for the night and pray for his partner's recovery.

"So," Martinez said, sliding into a chair next to Taft's bed, "here we go again."

The monitors were beeping in light tones as they monitored his partner's life signs, but Martinez had grown used to the effect and ignored the gentle rhythm.

"Once you were struck by the bolt of electricity and went down, the deputy you were working with, Rogers, and the air force pilot, Major Schilling, gave you a little CPR until the ambulance arrived," Martinez said. "I don't know if you saw that from where you were. The Norfolk police carted away the Serbs who were working with Ratzovik, and they are currently being held at the maximum-security prison in Colorado, awaiting trial under the National Security Terrorism Act. That probably won't start for a few months—but because of what happened, we're sure they will be quickly convicted and sentenced. Now, Mr. Ilic—" Martinez started to say as a doctor walked in the room.

"How's he doing?" the doctor asked.

"I don't know," Martinez said. "You're the doctor."

"Those tests we performed yesterday came back," the doctor said, ignoring the jibe and staring down at a chart. "His actual brain functions are strong, and his responses are growing better each day."

"What about his leg?" Martinez said.

"We repaired what ligaments we could," the doctor said, "but it was pretty torn up."

"When he comes out of this, will he limp?"

"*If* he comes out of this—probably not," the doctor noted. "But I doubt he'll ever play competitive tennis."

"There's no *if* about it," Martinez asked. "What about snow skiing? He loves to ski."

"Not as good as before," the doctor said, turning his head because of the noise from a commotion in the hall beyond the curtain.

The curtain was pulled back and a pair of men dressed in black suits with listening devices in their ears appeared. They stared at Martinez.

"You Martinez?"

"Yes."

"Secret Service," one of the men said. "The president is here."

The curtain was pulled back the rest of the way, and the president and a gaggle of aides and hangers-on filled the room. Martinez rose from his chair, and the president extended his hand. Martinez shook it.

"I'm here to present Mr. Taft with the National Intelligence Service Award."

Martinez nodded as the president turned around and retrieved the medal from an aide.

Turning back, he spoke. "In thanks from myself and the citizens of the United States for your sacrifice and bravery in time of need, I hereby award this medal of valor to John Taft, senior special agent, National Intelligence Agency."

The president bent over and pinned the medal on the pillowcase near Taft's head. "Mr. Taft, your nation thanks you."

Several flashbulbs went off for the photographic record; then the president turned to the crowd. "If you could please leave the room, I'd like to talk to Mr. Martinez in private."

The room cleared out, leaving only Taft, Martinez, the doctor, and the president.

"If you're through here," the president said to the doctor.

The doctor nodded and walked out, shutting the door behind him. Once the room was clear, the president spoke. "How's my man doing?"

"He seems to be getting better," Martinez said. "I spend all day talking to him to keep his mind going, and according to the doctors, his body is slowly healing."

"You men been partners a long time?" the president asked.

"Long, long time, Mr. President," Martinez said quietly.

"What do you talk to him about?"

"I go over the mission, mainly," Martinez said, "fill him in on the details and such."

"Is that what you were doing when I arrived?"

"Yes, sir," Martinez said. "I was just filling him in on Mr. Ilic."

"Mind if I have a go?"

"By all means."

"Once we knew you had stopped the electricity from doing any significant damage," the president said, "I got ahold of the president of The Netherlands and got them to agree to take Ilic back. The jet he was in was almost in Serbian airspace when they turned it around. From what I heard, Ilic was apoplectic when he realized he was being taken back to The Hague to finish his trial. I wish we both could have been there to see that. The man needs to pay for his crimes—and I hope that is what happens."

The president stared over at Martinez, who nodded for him to continue.

"You stopped the electrical charge just in time. We lost a few electrical panels at the Norfolk switching station, and there were some limited power outages over the next few days, but the systems have been repaired now. I've ordered a full-scale examination of the power grid with the idea to separate the various areas so they are not so interdependent. The work is already taking place. Since this ended I've received reports from our engineers and scientists about what might have happened had you not been successful. The economic losses could have ranged into the trillions of dollars. The possible loss of life from widespread power outages was estimated in the thousands to tens of thousands. You did a great thing."

The president looked over at Martinez.

"I haven't been able to learn much about the situation in Serbia right now," Martinez said. "That's more State Department business than intelligence. I think John would like to know about that."

An aide poked his head past the curtain. "Mr. President," he said, "we've got—"

"Tell them we'll be late," the president said, dismissing the man.

Martinez smiled.

"Presidential privilege," the president said easily. "The job doesn't pay much, but the benefits are good sometimes. Okay, John, here's the latest from Serbia. After we recovered the device and cleaned up as much of the evidence there as we could, the Tesla device was shipped back here, where our scientists are currently studying the design. As soon as Ilic was diverted back to The Netherlands, the Serbian president did a carefully orchestrated coup among his top military staff. These loyal to Mr. Ilic were retired and threatened with charges of treason if they continued their activities, and the chief of the Belgrade Police was elevated to the head of a National Police force loyal to whatever duly elected president is in power. The BIA was gutted from top to bottom, and Mr. Milorand was placed in charge. The agent who helped you in Serbia, Zoran Slavja, was made his assistant. The DCI spoke to him, and he asked to thank you for him and his family. He also told the DCI that his sister wishes to visit you as soon as possible."

Martinez glanced at the monitors and thought he saw a blip.

"Well that's about it," the president said. "I've got to go now, but you get better quickly. We need men like you serving the country."

The president rose, and Martinez followed. "Be right back," he said to Taft.

Once they were out in the hall, the president spoke. "How'd I do?"

"Thanks," Martinez said, shaking his hand again, "I think it helped."

Several aides started walking down the hall toward the president.

"I told General Benson," the president said, "and I'll tell you, too. Whatever you need that can help Mr. Taft or make his time with us more comfortable, all you need to do is ask—and I mean that. That man in there," the president said, pointing to the door, "saved this country. Whatever he needs, he has."

"You could pray for him," Martinez said.

"That, Mr. Martinez," the president said, turning to leave, "I'm already doing."

Martinez opened the door to the room and entered. "So where were we?" he said.

Taft's eyelids began to twitch.